BEYOND
WORD
PROCESSING

Using Your Personal Computer as a Knowledge Processor

BERNARD CONRAD COLE

McGRAW-HILL BOOK COMPANY

New York   St. Louis   San Francisco   Bogotá   Guatemala   Hamburg
Lisbon   Madrid   Mexico   Montreal   New Delhi   Panama   Paris
San Juan   São Paulo   Singapore   Tokyo   Toronto

The author of this book has made every effort to ensure that the program descriptions are accurate and complete. However, neither the publisher nor the author makes any warranty that the programs described in this book will enable the reader to achieve any particular result, and they assume no responsibility or liability of any kind for errors in the program descriptions or for the consequences of any such errors. To aid the reader in comparing programs, some of the screen displays appearing in this book have been slightly modified.

BEYOND WORD PROCESSING: Using Your Personal Computer as a Knowledge Processor

A BYTE Book

1 2 3 4 5 6 7 8 9 D O C D O C 8 7 6 5

ISBN 0-07-011698-9

Library of Congress Cataloging in Publication Data

Cole, Benard Conrad.
  Beyond word processing.
  Bibliography: p.
  Includes index.
  1. Data base management.   2. Microcomputers—Programming.   3. Text processing (Computer science)
4. Computer programs.   I. Title.
QA76.9.03C63 1985   001.64   84-21872
ISBN 0-07-011698-9

Editor: Karl Weber
Editing Supervisor: Margery Luhrs
Book Design by Patrice Fodero

Trademarks

Below is a list of trademarks used in this book, together with the firms in whose names the trademarks have been registered.

Apple Lisa Macintosh MacTerminal MacWrite ProDOS	Apple Computer, Inc.
BIBLIOTEK	Scientific Software Products, Inc.
CARDBOX	Caxton Software
CARDFILE NOTEBOOK SYNOPSIS	ProTem Software, Inc.
CITATION	Eagle Enterprises
CLIP	Thoughtware, Inc.
CP/M MP/M	Digital Research, Inc.
Datafax	Link Systems
DAYFLO	Dayflo, Inc.
Documate	Orthocode Corp.
DOCUMAX	Signum Microsystems
DocuMentor FirstDraft	PromptDoc, Inc.
DOCUPOWER!	San Francisco Computing!, Inc.
EAZYFILE KWICINDX	Miracle Computing
8085 8086 8088	Intel Corp.
ELECTRIC BLACKBOARD	Santa Cruz Software Services
EUREKA!	Mendocino Software Company, Inc.
Factfinder	Forethought, Inc.
FinalWord	Mark of the Unicorn, Inc.
Find It Quick	Instant Software
FRAMEWORK	Ashton-Tate
411 Freestyle SELECT	Select Information Systems
FYI 1500 FYI 3000 SUPERFILE	FYI, Inc.
Idea Processor	Ideaware, Inc.
KAMAS	Compusophic Systems, Inc.

KWICREF/1	Chen Information Systems, Inc.
LEADING EDGE	Leading Edge Corp.
MailMerge	MicroPro International Corp.
StarIndex	
WordStar	
Max Think	Max Think, Inc.
MEMOPLAN	Chang Labs
MicroLIB	Advanced Micro Techniques
MICROSHELL	New Generation Systems, Inc.
MICROSOFT WORD	Microsoft Corp.
MS-DOS	
MicroTools+	Carousel MicroTools, Inc.
MINDex SYSTEM-ONE	MINDex Infosystems, Inc.
MultiMate	Softword Systems, Inc.
NS16000	National Semiconductor Corp.
PC-DOS	International Business Machines Corp.
PCFILE	TexaSoft, Inc.
Perfect Writer	Perfect Software
PieWriter	Howard W. Sams and Company
PROLOG	Prosoft, Inc.
QUESTEXT	Information Reduction Research, Inc.
SAMNA+	Samna Corp.
Sci-Mate	Institute for Scientific Information
Search	Micro Alliance Corp.
Sequitur	Golemics, Inc.
SIMPLIFILE	Durant Software
Spotlight	Software Arts
STARMATE	Solution Technology, Inc.
ThinkTank	Living Videotext, Inc.
THOR	Fastware, Inc.
TR-DOS	Tandy Corp.
TRS-80	
UCSD P-SYSTEM	Regents of the University of California
UNICA	Knowology, Inc.
UNIX	American Telephone and Telegraph
VisiDex	Visicorp, Inc.
VisiWord	
WORD PERFECT	Satellite Software International
WORD VISION	Bruce and James Publishing
XyWrite II	Xyquest
Z80	Zilog Corp.
Z8000	
ZyINDEX	Zylab Corp.

TO PATRICIA ELIZABETH

Contents

Acknowledgments

This book would not have been possible without the help of a large number of companies, friends, and acquaintances. I express my appreciation to all of these companies and individuals for supplying programs for review and evaluation and for their patience in answering my questions. In particular, I wish to acknowledge the help of the following:

Ginny Goodwind and James Kimmel, FYI, Inc.

Steven Hartley, MINDex Infosystems

Bruce Haanstra, Mendocino Software

Digital Marketing

Win Hirsch, Link Systems

Merle Strauch and Lee Cook, Micro Alliance Corp.

Information Reduction Research

Institute for Scientific Information

Robert Nathaniel, Mark of the Unicorn

Judy McClaine and Valentina Kelly, MicroPro International

San Francisco Computing!, Inc.

I am also grateful to the staff and management at Cody's Bookstore and Dave's Magazine Store and Smoke Shop in Berkeley, California, for their well-stocked shelves of computer books and magazines and for going out of their way to obtain the material I needed to complete this book.

A special word of appreciation is due the staff and management of Larry Blake's Restaurant in Berkeley, at whose tables much of this book was written.

In addition, I would like to give a special thank-you to Peter Hollenbeck, Marv Downey, and Dave Haverty of The Computer Center, Inc. of Berkeley for their support over the years. Without their aid at critical times, it would have been much more difficult to complete this book.

Finally, a long overdue thanks to Larry Curran, whose early support and understanding at *Electronics* magazine are significant factors in whatever success I have had to date.

I hope to periodically update this book with continuing information about existing products and new chapters on new products. I would greatly appreciate any information from manufacturers concerning new developments in their products.

PREFACE

How to Use This Book

This is a book that has not so much been written as experienced. The technique of "knowledge processing" is something I use in my everyday work as a professional free-lance writer, and it's been a significant factor in the success I have had as a science and technology writer. It is based on years of reading, study, and evaluation of software, first for my personal use, and more recently in preparation for writing this book.

In my search for programs that would enhance the capabilities of my personal computer as a writing tool, I found that software user manuals often presented stumbling blocks. The problems I ran into were of three kinds: (1) user manuals that were too hard to read because they were badly written—written by computer professionals for computer professionals, (2) user manuals that were too hard to read because they were too "user friendly," and (3) user manuals that were too hard to read because they were too long and overly detailed.

In the first case, the writers of the manuals assumed too much reader knowledge and sophistication concerning computers. In the second, they assumed too little reader knowledge. In the third case, they assumed too much reader patience. In all cases, the kind of information needed to evaluate a particular program was scattered haphazardly throughout the documentation.

If most computer users are like me, they want some brief explanation of the purpose of a program and how it achieves that purpose before they jump into learning how to use it, no matter how "user friendly" it is. What I consider ideal is a brief, linear, step-by-step description that explains the operation of the program in enough detail to get started. Any further documentation should serve only as reference material. However, most programs have manuals that are anywhere from 150–500 pages long, requiring days and even weeks to read and understand. It is my belief that once you understand the logical flow of a program—how it "thinks"—and the sequence of steps necessary to get from here to there, any further documentation is unnecessary. For most programs, this can be done in 3000–5000 words. With such brief, "fast track" descriptions, most users can go directly to the programs and, with the aid of the menus and help messages, quickly become proficient.

It is with these thoughts in mind that I've written this book. It is designed to be used as:

- A comparison shopping guide to aid the user in choosing from among a bewildering array of programs.
- A travel guide, a companion document to the somewhat confusing user's manuals supplied with most programs.
- A "fast track" introduction for users who want to get up and run with a program as quickly as possible.

The primary sources of the information in this book are the various program manuals and my experience with each program. Each program description has a common structure, with sections that tell the user, in sequence:

1. About the main features of the program.
2. About the basic architecture and program modules.
3. How to create a knowledge base (kbase) using the program.
4. How to enter text into the newly created knowledge base.
5. How to convert external word-processing files into a format suitable for incorporation into the knowledge base.

6. How to set up the text and document files in the knowledge base for quick retrieval.

7. How to retrieve specific text and document files using a particular program's search procedures.

8. How to send knowledge base files to an external file or to a printer

As a result of this parallel construction, you can use the book as a shopping guide, comparing programs section by section, choosing the program most appropriate to your needs and, more important, most compatible with your work habits and thought processes.

After the program has been purchased, the step-by-step linear description in this book can be used as a travel guide or road map through the user manual. As with a road map, this book is designed to give you an idea of the main points of interest and how each relates to the others. Having reestablished a sense of direction, you can with confidence go back to the manual for detailed instructions.

I have attempted to provide some overview information that might be useful to the newcomer to personal computing (see Chapters 2 and 3, and the "Comments and Evaluation" sections of many of the chapters). However, the primary audience for this book is *not* the computer novice. Rather, the book is aimed at professionals who have used a computer in their work long enough to learn the basics, and long enough to know—or at least suspect—that they are not using the full potential of their machines as writing tools.

In this context, the kinds of readers who will find this book most useful will be:

- Professional writers who've been using a personal computer as a word processor and who want to make it a more effective writing tool.

- Professionals who write with a personal computer in their work, including physicians, academic professionals, teachers, lawyers, and journalists, to name a few.

- Users of personal computers in small- to medium-sized businesses who must track and retrieve a wide variety of documents and text-based material stored in magnetic form.

- College students who want to replace the laborious paper-based process of taking notes on lectures and reading with a computer-based method of organizing them for quick retrieval and learning.

It is my hope that all readers of this book will find using their personal computer as a knowledge processor as useful and rewarding as I have.

Bernard Conrad Cole

Part I

WHAT IS KNOWLEDGE PROCESSING?

CHAPTER 1

Writing Is More Than Word Processing

The computer stores seem to be filled with programs designed to simplify word processing and to correct spelling and grammar. And the bookstore shelves seem to be packed with books on using computers. So what more could a professional writer or a professional who writes need to increase his or her productivity?

Plenty more.

Specifically, what's needed is some way to process ideas, concepts, blocks of text, and even complete documents in the same way a database management program manipulates numeric and alphanumeric data: by collecting related and diverse pieces of information into a central pool, reordering that information in a variety of ways, and getting back that reordering in a form that can be used. The aim of this book, which is the result of a five-year learning experience, is to explain as simply as possible how to use your personal computer to perform what I call "knowledge processing."

This book comes out of my struggle over the past six years to find ever more efficient ways of using my computer as a writing tool. The discovery that I could use my computer as a knowledge processor has had an impact almost as revolutionary as my discovery that I could use the computer as a word processor.

In my first year as a free-lance science and technology writer specializing in computers and semiconductor electronics, I was lucky enough to increase my income by almost 40 percent. But using a standard electric typewriter, I still worked as many hours as I had in my previous job as bureau chief for McGraw-Hill's *Electronics* magazine. With my purchase of a personal computer and a word-processing program, I was able to reduce my writing time by 50 percent and my rewriting time by 75 percent.

Looking for more ways to improve my productivity, I investigated various other ways of manipulating text. One of the first things I did was to look into some of the hundreds of database management system (DBMS) programs supplied as part of the software package with most personal computers. However, despite all the advertising touting the advantages of DBMS programs as "computerized file cabinets," they are not well-adapted to the text- and document-processing needs of the professional writer.

On the face of it, a DBMS program *should* be helpful in this sort of task. In the most fundamental sense, a DBMS allows the user to collect related diverse pieces of data, reorder that information, and get back the result of that reordering in a form that is useful. But the most powerful feature of a DBMS is also its basic weakness; that is, it is a *data* retrieval and manipulation system, not a *document* or *text* retrieval and manipulation system.

While it is possible to configure a DBMS to store text-based information, this alternative has several limitations. First, a DBMS is highly structured in terms of the way data is entered, with many constraints on field length, record length, and file length. Second, while many DBMS programs can output information in a form compatible with most word processors, the reverse is not always true. Third, with such programs, particularly the general-purpose ones, a considerable amount of learning experience is required to understand the structure of the program and the methods of querying it well enough to be able use it to configure a database. It is as if you are required to learn a special word-processing language and then use it to construct your own word-processing program—all before you can actually get down to the business of writing with your computer. Similarly, although it is possible to reconfigure many DBMS programs to perform primitive knowledge-processing functions, the effort involved is in most cases not worth the effort.

Fortunately, however, software companies are now paying greater attention to the needs of writing professionals, and increasing numbers of programs oriented toward text and document manipulation are beginning to appear.

Using such programs as knowledge processors, I've been able to reduce my research time by almost 50 percent, analysis and collation by 50 percent, and the organization effort involved in writing by as much as 75 percent.

In fact, such programs have transformed my computer from a mere writing tool into an extension of my brain and my memory.

Why Is Knowledge Processing Necessary?

The answer to this question lies in the fact that writers manipulate more than words and facts; they manipulate ideas—that is, knowledge.

Let me put it in the form of a simple equation:

$$\text{Writing} = \tfrac{1}{5}R + \tfrac{1}{5}A + \tfrac{1}{5}O + \tfrac{1}{5}C + \tfrac{1}{5}T$$

where R is reasearch and study
A is analysis and evaluation
O is organization of information in the form of ideas, facts, and concepts—in short, knowledge
C is creativity
T is the actual typewriting process

Of course, there is nothing a computer can do about the C in the equation. That's up to the writer. But the computer can make it possible for the writer to focus most of his or her energies on the creative part of the equation.

All those word-processing, spelling, and grammar-checking programs—and the books explaining them—have gone a long way towards reducing the drudgery and tedium associated with the mechanical process of putting words on paper. But as you can see, these programs only deal with about 20 percent of the whole process.

In dealing with the remaining 60 percent of the equation represented by $R + A + O$, there was, until recently, little that was very helpful. What each of them and evaluating them in terms of their use as outline editors and category-oriented text-retrieval programs.

Finally, Part VI describes how writing professionals can make full use of the software already built into their operating systems and word-processing programs to perform many knowledge-processing functions.

Knowledge processing is one of the fastest-developing areas in personal computing, with as many programs introduced in the last year as in the previous three or four. Because of this, some programs have become available that I have not been able to analyze and evaluate completely. To keep this book as current as possible, I have included brief descriptions of these programs in Appendix A, along with a glossary of terms (Appendix D) and a comparison table (Appendix E) listing all of the pertinent features of each of the programs discussed in the main text.

CHAPTER 2

Data Processing versus Knowledge Processing

Until relatively recently, most applications of the personal computer—other than word processing—have involved its use as a processor and manager of data, defined here as alphabetical or numerical information organized in a discrete, structured format. Similarly, most software developments have involved enhancing the computer's ability to process, manipulate, store, organize, and retrieve data. A brief survey of the various personal computer magazines yields literally thousands of articles and advertisements for database and data-file management programs of all sorts.

By comparison, little attention has been given, until recently, to knowledge processing and management—the organization, manipulation, storage, and retrieval of information in text and document form. Indeed, the comparatively few programs available for use on personal computers capable of organizing text and documents are usually dismissed in most personal computer magazines as a subcategory under the general subject of database management.

In the world of mainframe computers and minicomputers, however, the problem of text and document management is generally recognized as being separate from, but of equal importance to, that of database and data-file management. The various programs and systems developed for this

purpose go by several different names: text-file management, text processing, document management, document storage and retrieval, text storage
and retrieval, and, more generally, information storage and retrieval. But
what they share is the same basic aim: the processing and management of
human knowledge in text and document form in the same way that database
management systems process and manipulate data.

Typical of such large text- and document-oriented systems are the large
commercial information retrieval systems, such as DIALOG, MEDLARS,
ORBIT, and BRS. The techniques and strategies used on these retrieve-
only systems, developed in the mid-1960s and early 1970s, were succeeded
in the mid-1970s by a wide range of storage and retrieval systems developed for use by organizations concerned about how to manage the flood
of electronically produced documents stored in their computer systems.
One prominent system is STAIRS (STorage And Information Retrieval
System), developed by International Business Machines (IBM) for use on
its mainframe computers. Other systems include BASIS, developed by the
Batelle Institute; TSI International's DOCUMASTER; SCRAPBOOK by
Triad Computing; and Infodata Systems' INQUIRE.

No matter what the size of the computer system upon which they are
used, there are several important differences between such text- and doc-
ument-management systems and the more numerous traditional database
and data-file management systems. These differences involve

- Their content and structure
- Their physical file organization
- Their logical organization
- How one queries for and retrieves the required information

A description of these differences and an overview of the workings of the
large-system text-management programs will help you understand what
your personal computer can do as a knowledge processor.

Database Fundamentals

In a database, information is highly formatted— separated into records,
fields, and files—and subject to numerous updates and changes. A *record* is
an organized collection of data, divided into elements called *fields*, all of
which are related in some way. A personnel record, for example, contains

information about an employee, such as his or her social security number, first name, last name, middle name, date of birth, next of kin, and address. Whereas different field and record types may vary in length, a specific type usually cannot exceed a certain size. For example, the field for your social security number in a personnel information database will accept no more than nine characters, which must be numeric in form.

Various fields in a record can be designated as *key fields*, which are used to (1) uniquely identify a record, (2) sort the records into ascending or descending order on the basis of the value of the key in each record, and (3) specify records to be updated or retrieved. Key fields that uniquely identify a record are called *primary keys* (for example, the social security number of a personnel record). Key fields that are not unique and may be contained in a number of different records are called *secondary keys* (for example, age in a personnel record). Based on these keys, a database or data-file management program can search, sort, and retrieve records or portions of records, then organize and present them for output to a display, printer, or file in tabular form or to another program as the basis of some numerical calculation.

The methods by which one can query a database using such programs are rather limited because of the need for precision and accuracy in calculations based on the result of a search. Usually only three search methods are used:

1. The simple query, in which the program searches for a particular keyfield and no other.

2. The range query, in which the program searches for all fields and/or records that fall within or outside a particular range.

3. The so-called *Boolean* searches, which use Boolean logic operators such as AND, OR, and NOT to expand or narrow the range of a search.

Linking key fields or keywords with AND narrows the range of a search, whereas linking them with an OR broadens a search. NOT is used to qualify AND and OR, excluding particular keywords.

Knowledge Base Fundamentals

A text-file– or document-oriented knowledge base (kbase) differs from a database in a number of fundamental ways.

First of all, text and document files are essentially unformatted. The fundamental unit of storage is not an alphabetical character or even a word. Most often, the lowest common elements containing useful information are sentences, paragraphs, or even complete documents. Second, the files' content is full of the fuzzy logic of human thought and language, with widely varying sentence lengths, differences in writing style, variable spelling of words meaning the same thing, words with many different meanings, acronyms, synonyms, antonyms, and other oddities. Third, text- and document-oriented knowledge bases are usually much larger than formatted databases. For example, a formatted database is considered fairly large if it contains 100,000 or so characters, which is about the size of a single document in a large document database. And finally, where numerical databases are characterized by a high degree of updating and change, a knowledge base consisting of text and documents is relatively static and unchanging.

Because of the above characteristics, only a few of the many file organization and storage techniques used in DBMS programs have been applied to the construction of text- and document-oriented knowledge-base management programs. These include the *serial*, the *ordered sequential*, the *indexed sequential*, the *inverted index*, and the *hierarchical* approaches. Let's briefly consider how each of these works.

The Serial Approach

Also called the linear list approach, this is the simplest approach to organizing textual material, and it does not require that the material in the file have any order whatsoever. Searches are done by comparing the search string to the text. This technique is somewhat comparable to the search/find/replace function of a word processor. Its main advantage is that it allows adding material to or deleting material from the text base without concern for its order. Its drawback is that the search process is time-consuming. This is because the computer must examine the entire text sequentially in order to determine which portions must be retrieved. Thus, although this approach requires very little memory space and does not require modification or updating when new material is added, it can be used only where the knowledge base includes a relatively small number of items.

The Ordered Sequential Approach

In this approach, use is made of the fact that certain portions of the records stored in a file are of special importance to the persons who want to retrieve them. In most documents, the most common method of searching is by author, title, or journal name. These keywords are then sorted into alphabetical order by, say, the author's last name. Adding a new document or block of text into such a file requires that it be reordered and that space be made available at the appropriate location in the sorted file. The time required to make a search using this method is still relatively great, and the size of the file must be kept quite small.

The Indexed Sequential Approach

A common way to speed up the search of a knowledge base is to develop an index file based on keywords identified in the text. Associated with each keyword in this index is a code that identifies or points to its specific location in the text file. In such an approach, the order of the keywords in the text provides the order of the keywords in the index.

With this method, the index file may contain more than one reference to a particular keyword, since each is associated with a unique location in the main text file—it is the index that is searched sequentially, not the main text file. Each time a particular keyword is located in the index file, its associated code points to its location in the text file.

Since the index is searched instead of the actual text file, search times are reduced drastically compared to the search times with the serial and ordered sequential approaches. However, the indexed sequential method has one major disadvantage: when new records are added to a knowledge base, both the file and the index must be updated.

The Inverted Index Approach

To overcome the disadvantages of the indexed sequential approach without losing its search speed advantages, most commercially available free-form text and document retrieval systems use the inverted index approach.

With this approach, the index file is also used to store a set of unique keywords, each of which has not one code but several, identifying the locations of the keywords in all the documents in the knowledge base. This index file is then divided into sets of items or documents with common keywords. Unlike the indexed sequential approach, where the entire index file must be searched to find all occurrences of a particular keyword, with the inverted index approach it is only necessary to search for a single occurence.

Since only small portions of the index need to be accessed, search times for large document bases are further reduced. Although this approach requires that the index file be updated each time new items are added to a knowledge base, it is not necessary to reorder either the text or the index files. The new information is simply placed at the end of the file.

The Hierarchical Approach

In this approach, text is stored in a tree structure, with pointers linking items at one level to items in the levels immediately above and below. To search for specific text blocks or documents in such a structure, the user starts at the root of the tree and is guided by pointers to other levels along the various branches. On the basis of information contained at each branching in the form of headings, you can make choices as to which branch to follow. Although it is usable by even the most unsophisticated and naive users, this approach limits the amount of text that can be viewed at one time. It also requires that you back up to the nearest node and choose a new search path if you've followed the wrong branch.

Entering Text into a Knowledge Base

To enter text into a knowlege base (kbase), two main approaches are used: (1) manipulating the text so that it fits into a particular format in terms of field, record, and file length, and (2) free-format input, whereby the user has complete freedom in terms of length and content.

In those systems using the first approach, the structuring of the text is kept as unobtrusive as possible through the use of line-by-line prompting or form-filling techniques.

In the line-by-line menu-driven technique, the program issues instructions for each of the fields required by the structure. To keep you from exceeding the limits of the field, such a program may use any of several different techniques: (1) it may automatically word-wrap the text to the next line, (2) it may not allow you to enter additional text, or (3) it may warn you to enter additional text in the next record or screen.

In form-filing systems, the user is presented with a form on the screen that can be filled out and stored in the base in a single operation.

In the free-form approach to text or document input, although the user is not constrained by limits on length or content, it is necessary to add control characters or markers (delimiters) to indicate where one document or block of text begins and where another begins.

Querying a Knowledge Base

Where the text- and document-processing programs developed for use on large computer systems really shine is in the sophistication of their search and retrieval query procedures, a necessity because of the richness and complexity of human language. In addition to procedures roughly equivalent to those developed on traditional DBMS programs, such systems allow a user to:

- Find any document or block of text containing two keywords in the same sentence.
- Find any document or block of text containing one keyword immediately followed by another keyword.
- Find any document or block of text containing one keyword followed, after an arbitrary number of words, by a second keyword.
- Find any document or block of text containing two keywords within a specific number of words.
- Find any document or block of text containing two keywords within a specific number of words of one another.
- Find any document or block of text containing at least one occurrence of a specific number of keywords.
- Match a character string, followed by two or more arbitrary numbers, followed by a second string.

As we'll see in the next chapter, many of the knowledge-processing options available for use on personal computers are less sophisticated than those available on larger systems. However, this is rapidly changing as the central processing units used in personal computers become more powerful, and much of the software now used on larger systems migrates downward to smaller systems.

CHAPTER 3

Choosing the Right Knowledge-Processing Program

At present, there are several hundred online text- and document-oriented information retrieval services and a like number of commercially available text storage and retrieval systems developed for mainframes and minicomputers. Comparatively, the development of similar programs for personal computers has proceeded much more slowly.

The World of Knowledge Processing

No more than a dozen full-fledged, free-form text- and document-oriented knowledge-processing systems (including the ones described in Part II and Appendix A) are now in general use on personal computers. The count rises to about 75 or so if the more limited electronic index card, bibliography, and hierarchical programs (including those described in Parts IV and V) are included. Let's survey the characteristics of these differing types of knowledge-processing programs.

Record capacity ranges from about 500–2000 characters for most of the electronic index cards to 512,000 characters for SUPERFILE (Part II). File capacity in most cases is limited by disk capacity. The one exception is SUPERFILE, a multidisk system that is virtually unlimited in terms of the number of files that can be sorted under a single knowledge base.

The keyword-oriented electronic index card programs use sequential, ordered sequential, and indexed sequential file architectures and require text to be entered with some thought given to field and record size. To hide their data-file-like structures, these programs input text using line-by-line prompting or form filling. Keywords are specified by their location in the text file.

Most of the free-form keyword-oriented knowledge processors discussed in Parts II and III, however, use the inverted index approach and place no limits on length or content. Special delimiters are used in most cases to indicate the beginning and end of a specific document or block of text. In some cases, such as with SUPERFILE and MINDex SYSTEM-ONE, the user is required to manually place these markers at the beginning and end of the text.

In most of the other free-form programs described in Part II, the user can either enter the markers manually using a word processor and then load the text into the knowledge base or use the programs' internal text editors. Keywords are specified either by location (SUPERFILE), by markers and delimiters (NOTEBOOK), by manual placement in an associated keyword file (MINDex SYSTEM-ONE), automatically (SUPERFILE and NOTE-BOOK), or via all four techniques (Datafax).

Keyword capacity ranges from one to five per record for most of the electronic index card programs and up to 250 per entry with SUPERFILE. The length of the keywords that can be stored with each record ranges from about 20 to 255 characters. Keyword search-string length ranges from 20 to 64 characters. For those programs that allow you to search a kbase with AND, OR, and NOT operators to link keywords, multikeyword capacity ranges from 1 or 2 keywords for most of the index card programs to up to 64 per search.

Search and retrieval speeds depend on file size and keyword length and complexity. For a simple, two- or three-keyword search string, this is typically 300–400 retrievals per second for an electronic index card program, as compared to 50–100 retrievals per second for a more complex free-form knowledge-processing program.

In regard to search strategy and query method, the keyword-based electronic index card programs are the most limited, allowing retrieval of information (1) by matching the search string with specified keywords, (2) over an alphabetical range, or (3) by using a limited range of Boolean AND, OR, and NOT operators. The free-format knowledge processors allow queries of much greater complexity, including not only AND, OR, and

NOT but various multiple keyword combinations as well. However, the range and power of the available search combinations are still much less than the range and power of programs developed for use on large computer systems.

The tree-structured programs discussed in Part V combine search-by-category methods with simple search-string matching to locate the desired text. In exchange for this simplicity of operation, these tree-structured programs give up storage capacity, ranging from 25 to 50 lines of text per category and subcategory in the case of the electronic index cards to 99 lines of text in the case of QUESTEXT. The complexity of the tree structures range from a 99-branch, 99-subcategory, 99-heading capability for QUESTEXT to a single-branch, 100-level capability for ThinkTank.

Choosing the Right Program

Which knowledge-processing program is best for you depends on (1) the hardware and software requirements of your particular system, (2) cost, (3) ease of use, (4) what you want to use it for, and, finally and most important, (5) your compatibility with a particular program and the way it "thinks."

Such factors as speed of search and retrieval should not be a major factor in your choice. Although there are differences, the speed of search and retrieval of most programs is much beyond what the individual user really needs. For example, most of these programs can search for and find particular entries in hundredths or thousandths of a second. They are also capable of displaying several hundred entries per minute on your CRT. Such speed is useless in most cases because of the human factor; that is, you cannot read, much less comprehend and analyze, that many entries in a minute. To simply scan each of the retrieved entries takes me at least three or four seconds at a minimum, and typically much more. To review the content of 100 single-line entries takes me at least three or four minutes. And to look over the content of 100 or so screen-sized blocks of text normally requires 10 to 15 minutes. Therefore, we'll ignore speed and focus instead on the five main criteria listed above.

Hardware/Software Requirements

The first consideration in choosing a knowledge- processing program should be compatibility with your operating system. Operating under

CP/M are SUPERFILE, NOTEBOOK, QUESTEXT, CITATION, SYSTEM-ONE, CARDFILE, and CARDBOX. Designed for use under the UCSD P-SYSTEM on both Apple IIs and IBM PCs are MINDex SYSTEM-ONE, Datafax, and ThinkTank. Operational under MS-DOS/PC-DOS are NOTEBOOK, CARDFILE, QUESTEXT, SUPERFILE, PCFILE, Datafax, and EAZYFILE. Designed for use on the Apple II computer under DOS are VisiDex and BIBLIOTEK.

Other factors are also important, such as disk capacity, number of disk drives, and whether the program spans multiple disks or is confined to a single disk. To determine the particular requirements of each program, refer to Appendix E or consult the System Overview section included at the beginning of each chapter in Part II.

Cost

If cost is a major consideration for you, it would be wise to investigate ways to get the most out of the programs you already have. For this, refer to Part IV.

Ease of Use

If ease of use is your chief criterion, you should choose one of the tree-structured programs. This should also be your choice if you are looking for a program that will help you organize your thoughts and your material in a logical, categorical manner. Of these programs, the easiest to use is EAZYFILE. The most powerful in terms of numbers of levels, categories, and branches in QUESTEXT.

Among the keyword-oriented programs, the index card programs, because of their limited search capabilities, are the easiest to use. Of the more complex free-form programs, Datafax is the easiest to use because of its tree-like command structure and the automated manner in which it stores text and performs searches.

Knowledge-Processing Functions

It is important for you to determine which of the knowledge-processing functions described in Chapter 1 are important to you and to choose a program accordingly. In the pages that follow, we'll briefly survey the various categories of knowledge-processing programs, highlighting the particular functions that are best—and worst—at performing.

General-Purpose, Free-Form Knowledge Base Programs

Most flexible in terms of the number of knowledge-processing functions that they can perform are the free-form programs surveyed in Part II. They can perform almost all the functions discussed in Chapter 1 except for outline editing. This kind of program can be used:

1. As a simple index card program to aid in the organization of your paper files.

2. As a research aid in compiling and organizing large numbers of bibliographic citations.

3. As an automated means of sorting and storing the results of online database research.

4. As a method for analyzing and comparing facts and ideas and as a way to look for patterns and structure in the information you have collected.

5. As a fast and efficient way of "cutting and pasting" together an article or book by letting the program do the searching of the knowledge base.

6. As a means of organizing your disk-based files of articles and background material for instant access.

7. As a method of building up specialized knowledge bases that can be used as information resources and as extensions of your own memory.

Most flexible of the programs in this category are SUPERFILE and SYSTEM-ONE. They are particularly effective in the analysis and evaluation of the facts that have been collected and stored in a knowledge base. They are also good cut-and-paste tools. In addition, because they allow construction of knowledge bases that can span multiple disks, they are the programs of choice in systems incorporating floppy-disk rather than hard-disk drives.

NOTEBOOK is most useful for the first three functions listed above, especially for structuring information in bibliographic form, which may require more space than is allowed by the index card and bibliography programs. Datafax is also good for relatively structured applications. But whereas the format you set up initially with NOTEBOOK is the one you are stuck with, Datafax allows you to change its structure midstream, with only slight modifications to the keyword index, unless you entirely rebuild your kbase. Sci-Mate is perhaps the most structured of the free-form programs. Its strong point is its compatibility with the format used by many online databases and the ease with which the information obtained can be altered to fit the user's personal needs.

Tree-Structured Programs

In recent months, the popular-computing press has ballyhooed the emergence of a new type of programming aid for the writing professional: the so-called idea processors, also variously known as thought processors, outline processors, and outline editors.

A lot of nonsense has been written on this subject, for such programs are no more than an old structure—the hierarchical or tree structure—in new clothing. What such programs have in common is that, because of their tree structure, they force the user into organizing his or her ideas and thoughts into categories and subcategories. All tree-structured programs are useful in two basic areas: outlining and templating.

Outlining

An important aspect of the writing process is outlining and organization. The various hierarchical programs make outlining easy because they take care of the mechanics of categorization and subcategorization and allow concentration on the ideas. Moreover, they make it possible to easily produce an elegantly organized outline from a disorganized set of thoughts.

Templating

Another useful function of such programs is the creation of templates. A template is a detailed report outline that can be changed and filled out very quickly to produce a final report. Thus, when it is necessary to produce a number of documents that repeat the same basic structure, such a program can be used to store the general structure in its higher levels. Individual reports can then quickly be produced by filling in the specific details at lower levels.

Where hierarchical programs differ is in the additional functions they offer. For example, there is ThinkTank. Although it is basically an outline editor, it also functions as a primitive index card program. EAZYFILE, on the other hand, has been designed to serve as a tree-structured index card program, but it can also function as an outline editor.

Of all the programs in this book, FirstDraft is the one that can most truly be called an outline editor, with most of its functions focused on this goal.

QUESTEXT, in addition to performing the functions of outline generation and templating, can serve as a full-function knowledge base. Whereas a program such as ThinkTank can store the equivalent of two or three paragraphs under each category, QUESTEXT can store up to three or four pages under each.

THOR (see Appendix A) is basically a fairly sophisticated word-processing program that allows the user to store files in a hierarchically related form.

Finally, there is FRAMEWORK (see Appendix A), which uses the outline structure as the "framework" for an integrated software package that combines a word processor, a database manager, a spreadsheet, and graphics capability.

Index Card/Bibliographic Programs

One of the most ubiquitous forms of text storage and retrieval is the electronic index card/bibliographic citation program. Unlike the free-form text/document storage and retrieval knowledge-processing programs described in Parts II and III, most index card programs are basically customized versions—prefabs—of traditional DBMS programs, configured to allow entry of text files and to hide as much of the data-oriented structure from the user as possible.

Although such programs are relatively structured, confining you to a limited number of characters per line and lines per "card" and limiting you to a small number of ways to organize, search, and sort the text, they have some advantages, depending on the application.

First, precisely because of their relatively structured and limited format, search and retrieval speed is usually faster than with the free-form knowledge-processing programs. This is not the result of any inherent structural advantages. Rather, index card programs force you to confine your text to short items of roughly identical length and roughly the same number of keywords, whereas free-form programs allow records and files of any length to be stored and literally hundreds of keywords to be designated. While it is possible to achieve similar speeds with a free-form knowledge-processing program by constructing a text format roughly equivalent to that of an index card, sticking to that format requires considerable discipline and attention on your part.

Second, updating and changing the textual information is much easier and quicker than with a general-purpose free-form knowledge-processing program. Again, this is a result of the highly structured format of an electronic index card program. Just as your operating system stores data files in 1K or 2K blocks, regardless of how much information is contained in each block, so too an index card program stores text information on "cards" of specific lengths, no matter how much text is written on each one. In a free-form program, the amount of storage space required is variable, depending on the length of the text file.

In a kbase of textual material formed by using a free-form program, an index is created that indicates the location in memory where each entry begins and ends. If you add or delete material from an entry, you change its size and the location in memory where it ends, and where the next entry begins, requiring you to recollate and re-index the entire file.

In an index card program, the fixed size of each entry allows you to modify the text, adding or deleting material on each "card," without having to re-index. In most cases, if you try to go beyond the fixed limits of each card, the program will stop you and ask you to create another card.

Given these characteristics, for what purposes would you choose an electronic index card program over a more general-purpose free-format knowledge-processing program?

Generally, index card programs are best where rapid retrieval of short text entries is important, or where the information contained on each card will change frequently.

Many business applications, such as tickler files and customer and product information files, fall into this category. As a writer, I find the index card format especially useful in the beginning stages of research, when I am not only looking for specific information, but also for what *type* of information I will need or what is available. At this stage, I usually change the content of my card files several times before I've pinned down the direction I want for my research. I've also found the index card format useful in the beginning stages of building a tickler file of prospective sources.

The speed of retrieval is important in what are called "real-time" applications, in which an immediate response is necessary. Because an index card program can search through its kbase of brief text entries in milliseconds, an electronic index card could be used by, say, a telephone operator whose job it is to respond to customer inquiries with specific information useful in solving a problem.

A regular index card could serve the same purpose, of course. But an electronic index card allows you to cross-index in a wider variety of ways. Furthermore, you must physically reproduce and update a number of different files even when just one entry is added to the standard set of index cards; however, in its electronic form you need only create and add one index card and the program can do the rest.

Determining Your Compatibility

Just as important as determining whether a particular program is compatible with your system is determining whether it is compatible with you and the way you think.

More than almost any other type of software, each knowledge-processing program surveyed in this book reflects the thought processes of the persons who developed it. Even very similar programs incorporate very different ways of performing essentially identical functions. Thus, it is very important for you to analyze closely how various programs "think"— the logic of their operation. But even with the help of the user's manuals, this is difficult to do, for each manual has its own peculiar organization, which is often not reflective of the organization of the program at all.

To help you analyze how each program functions in the creation and operation of a knowledge base, the chapters in this book have been constructed, as far as is possible, in a parallel fashion. This book should make it possible for you to determine, by comparing each of the basic functions of knowledge processors side by side, which program you are most comfortable with and which best suits your needs.

Building a Knowledge Base

Regardless of which program you choose, the process of building a knowledge base will be much easier if you follow a few simple rules:

1. When starting a new knowledge base, scan through some of the text files that will go into it and put together as complete a list of keywords as possible. Refer to it when building your raw text files to make sure keywords are being used consistently.

2. Keep notes on the items contained in each file, the specific file-names and contents, and the date each file was last updated.

3. Once you've indexed a particular knowledge base, keep up-to-date printouts of the current keyword vocabulary available when typing or entering new text items. This will ensure that you don't re-invent or misspell keywords.

4. Create a small, temporary working knowledge base with newly typed text and use it to locate and correct errors, especially in the keywords. Add items to the main knowledge base only after they've been thoroughly corrected.

5. Modify as many text entries as possible in each category before creating or updating your knowledge base.

Part II

GENERAL-PURPOSE, FREE-FORM KNOWLEDGE PROCESSORS

CHAPTER 4

SUPERFILE 1500

The Archetypal
Knowledge Processor

Developed by FYI, Inc. and distributed by Software Marketing Associates, FYI SUPERFILE 1200 is in many respects the archetype of a free-form, general-purpose knowledge-processing program designed specifically for the storage and retrieval of documents and text stored in computerized form.

As discussed in Chapter 2, a database management program usually involves setting up a group of fields of specific lengths defined according to the particular type of alphanumeric data to be stored and manipulated: names, addresses, product numbers, phone numbers, and so on. Each of these fields must be predefined and prelocated within each record. And when a user enters information, it must be done according to these predefined rules.

SUPERFILE, on the other hand, takes existing text files and makes an index of selected keys and sets no requirements as to format or length. Entries can be anywhere from a paragraph to hundreds of pages long.

Once you've selected the words that describe the essential meaning of your document—the *keywords*—and have directed the program to compile an index, searching for and retrieving this textual information is easy.

When you enter a sequence of keywords describing the type of document or section of text you are looking for, SUPERFILE first tells you on which disk the entry is located and waits for you to slip it into the drive. Once the correct disk is in the drive, SUPERFILE then calls up the original document or series of documents and sends them to the output you designate: the CRT screen, the printer, or a separate file. And since SUPERFILE searches an index rather than the actual text in the knowledge base, the search time is extremely short no matter how long the document—it searches about 100 entries per second, with 10 keywords per entry.

SUPERFILE Overview

Written in machine language and a company proprietary high-level language called CONVERS (a dialect of FORTH), SUPERFILE can run on any 8-bit personal computer built around an 8080, 8085, or Z80 microprocessor and operating under either the CP/M-80 or the MP/M-80 operating system; it can also run on a 16-bit system built around either the 8086 or 8088 and operating under either CP/M-86, MP/M-86, or MS-DOS.

The maximum number of keywords that can be stored in your knowledge base dictionary is determined by the amount of random-access memory you have, since the dictionary is loaded into memory during searches. Each keyword or phrase, which can be from 1 to 64 characters in length, requires 4 bytes in addition to the actual characters. So a 64K byte computer allows a capacity of 3000 keywords per knowledge base if you use just alphabetical keywords. SUPERFILE also allows you to use integers from 0 to 31,999 as keywords. Up to 250 keywords can be entered with each item, linked by AND, OR, and NOT.

It is disk storage capacity, however, that determines the maximum number of items that can be indexed into a knowledge base. Each indexed item takes 10 bytes for pointers plus 2 bytes per keyword. A single-density 8-inch disk with 243 kilobytes (243K) storing only the dictionary and index would have a capacity of 6000–8000 indexed items, with the items averaging 8 keywords. Records and file sizes can be of any length up to 512,000 characters, and the number of files per knowledge base is limited to 99.

Only the compact index (.NDX) and dictionary (.DIC) files are required to fit on a single disk. The text files in your knowledge base can be stored on any convenient number of other disks, floppy or hard.

The mechanism by which SUPERFILE operates is simple. When scanning a new raw-text file for indexation and inclusion in your knowledge base, the program searches for the beginning of the entry. Next, the program scans the keyword area of the entry, picking out each keyword or phrase and comparing it to those already in the dictionary. If a match is obtained, a 2-byte code previously assigned to this word is used. If no match occurs, the new word or phrase is assigned the next available code and stored in the dictionary file. When the end of the keyword area is reached, the codes are sorted and placed in an index file buffer. When the buffer is nearly full it is written to the index file.

When starting a search, the keyword codes are sorted and stored in groups representing each AND clause in the search sequence. The index file is read in and the codes for each item are compared to the search criteria. When a match is obtained, the pointers are stored and used later to direct retrieval.

Creating a Knowledge Base with SUPERFILE

Creating a knowledge base from the text files contained on your disks is a six-step process:

1. Determining the type of information to be contained in the knowledge base.
2. Formatting the text items for entry into the knowledge base.
3. Creating and selecting the keywords associated with each entry.
4. Setting up the knowledge base files containing the items to be indexed.
5. Naming the raw text disks.
6. Transforming your text files into a properly indexed knowledge base.

With SUPERFILE, only the last step is automatic. Proper implementation of the first five steps is your responsibility. So for this program to be of maximum use and to operate at full efficiency, you must devote some thought to developing and managing the information in each knowledge base you create with SUPERFILE.

Determining Knowledge Base Content

Depending on your needs, some of the knowledge bases constructed from your text files will have a short life span, whereas others will be useful for many years. For example, if SUPERFILE is being used to create a "writing base" to aid in the long and often tiresome cut-and-paste process involved in organizing your notes into an article or report (see Chapter 10), the knowledge base will be of short duration. If it's being used to organize your text files into a general knowledge base for easy and instant retrieval (see Chapter 9), it'll probably be of longer duration.

As a result, it is important to determine what you expect your knowledge base to do. If, for example, you are developing a knowledge base that will consist of bibliographic information for scientific or academic use, the entries should contain a complete literature citation, an abstract or discussion, and appropriate keywords.

With SUPERFILE, it's possible to create quite large knowledge bases into which you can dump all sorts of textual information. However, the information will probably be more useful if you create several separate and narrowly focused knowledge bases that are organized according to function (such as interviews, correspondence, personnel information, and product information) or type (microprocessors, astronomy, genetic engineering, and so on).

Determining how many knowledge bases to create and what to put in each depends on what types of information you want to search simultaneously. Do you want to search personnel and correspondence files together? If so, they should go into the same knowledge base. If not, they should go into separate ones.

Formatting Your Text Entries

With SUPERFILE, formatting is simple, especially when compared to most database management programs and to some of the other knowledge-base programs discussed later in this book. There are only four things that need to be added to the text:

1. A heading marker at the beginning of the entry: *C
2. A keyword start marker, heading the keyword list: *K
3. A list of keywords, each separated by a right slant: /
4. An end-of-entry marker at the conclusion: *E

There are also two optional markers that can be added:

1.   A short-form marker—a single asterisk, *
2.   A number that is placed at the beginning of the entry, above the *C

The short-form marker, *, follows the *C and a brief portion of text and separates them from the main text in the entry. The short form is particularly useful in knowledge bases containing abstracts or other text citations, since it can be used for obtaining a bibliography. It can also be used with customer and client information to obtain a mailing list. Furthermore, it is useful in speeding up the retrieval and selection process, since the whole entry need not be displayed, just the short form describing the pertinent information in the entry.

The number placed at the beginning of each entry will allow numerical sorting of the entries with a sort-and-merge utility supplied with SUPER-FILE. Explained in more detail later in this chapter, this utility is useful in organizing bibliographies, employee/customer/student lists, product descriptions, and so on. If this option is used, no blank lines are allowed within a particular entry. One blank line, however, must separate entries. Note that (1) the C, K, and E must be capital letters and (2) *C, *, *K, and *E must not be used in the text or in the keywords of an entry.

Screen 1 shows a simple example showing the location of the markers within an entry and how the keywords should be arranged.

Selecting the Keywords

In SUPERFILE—and in all the programs discussed in this book—*keywords* are words and phrases used to find and recall entries from a particular knowledge base. They describe an item in a cross-referenced manner so that you will be able to find what you want even when you don't remember the exact details. Keywords describe groups and classes of information. A proper selection of keywords will allow you to find only those items meeting specific search criteria.

Keywords for each entry should range from the general to the specific. With general keywords, it is possible to retrieve all of a group or category of entries. Specific keywords allow you to narrow the focus of the search.

For example, suppose you are writing a treatise on the sociological and philosophical significance of those parables of our time, TV sitcoms. The

```
*C
May 1, 1983
John Doe
1492 Christopher Avenue
Columbus, Ohio 11492
*
Dear John:
   I am sorry I have to write this. It is as
painful for me to send it as it is for you to
receive it. I am breaking off our engagement and
am marrying someone else. I will return your
ring later. I must first earn enough money to
pay off the money I borrowed against it in order
to visit my new fiance.
                                    Sincerely,
                                    Marsha

*K
DOE/OHIO/COLUMBUS/ENGAGEMENT/LOAN/MARRIAGE/VISIT
*E
```

Screen 1

knowledge base of source material relating to this subject might contain such diverse items as abstracts of the episodes of various series, interviews with writers and directors about the hidden truths just below the surface of this apparent tripe, and analyses by the major theologians, philosophers, and deep thinkers on the meaning of it all. The keyword listing describing one such entry might look like this:

1985/EPISODE/FRIENDSHIP/ADVERSITY/LAVERNE&SHIRLEY/
SQUIGGY

In this example, 1985 and EPISODE are general terms that might apply to numerous entries in a knowledge base also containing abstracts of episodes from *Happy Days*, *Three's Company*, *Taxi*, and others. The keywords

FRIENDSHIP, ADVERSITY, LAVERNE&SHIRLEY are even more specific, allowing a search to be much more narrowly focused.

Very specific keywords should be used when an entry has a particularly unique content. In the above example, SQUIGGY is the keyword that identifies the unique aspect of this particular entry. For some types of knowledge bases, such as product information, one or more unique keywords are necessary for each entry. In general, though, use of specific keywords should be minimized to avoid quickly filling the dictionary/index disk to its full capacity. Rather than relying on highly specific keywords to narrow the scope of a search, remember that with most knowledge and database programs the AND, OR, and NOT functions, linking keywords in the correct combination, allow you to narrow the scope of a search considerably.

Keyword spelling can cause problems, especially after you get hundreds or thousands of entries into a knowledge base. Avoid plurals whenever possible and try to be consistent in your spelling of keywords in each entry.

Most important, don't try to enter items into a knowledge base and assign keywords without thinking. Take care in the creation of the keyword list, for unless you have control over the keywords, you may retrieve the wrong information or even lose information—the fact you need will be in the knowledge base somewhere, but you won't be able to remember the keywords you need to retrieve it.

Setting Up Your Knowledge Base Files

To make SUPERFILE work most efficiently the files containing the items need to be reconfigured with filenames and types or extensions that are compatible with SUPERFILE and of a size that balances search speed, ease of location, and efficient use of disk storage space.

Filename and Type

When a knowledge base is indexed under SUPERFILE, all the filename types or extensions are converted to Dnn, where nn is any number from 00 to 99. This designation is used to identify specific files and the items contained in a knowledge base when the dictionary and index are formed. Thus, if you have filename extensions beginning with a D (such as the .DOC protocol within WordStar), you should change them to some other set of characters. An easy file type to remember is .TXT. Thus a file that is designated FILENAME.DOC should be changed to FILENAME.TXT.

The program asks you for the names and types of files to be indexed. Under SUPERFILE you have two options: (1) to enter the exact filenames and types and (2) to use the program's ambiguous filename capability. With the first approach, no more than ten filenames can be entered at a time. With the second approach, it is possible to enter more with a single ambiguous filename. It is possible to enter ten different ambiguous filenames, such as *.TXT and *.LTR, and SUPERFILE will index all of the files with the types that you've designated.

For example, suppose you have three disk files of articles written for a variety of magazines and you want to use them to start, say, an "archival knowledge base"; let's say these files have been designated MAGART1.TXT, MAGART2.TXT, and MAGART3.TXT. Rather than entering each filename and type when information is requested, you simply enter the following: *.TXT.

If you don't specify a file type, most operating systems, including CP/M and PC/MS-DOS, will consider the type to be blank and the ambiguous filename *. will index all files with a blank filename.

File Size

The natural process when building a knowledge base, especially one consisting of files that already exist, is to make each file an entry; that is, to simply add the appropriate markers to the text in the file and index it into the knowledge base. However, although it is easier to find a particular entry with each item entered as a separate file, it is probably more efficient to combine several entries into a single file. There are four reasons for this. First, most operating systems, including CP/M and MS-DOS, allocate space in 1K or 2K blocks, leaving unused space with small files. Second, using larger files keeps down the number of disk directory entries, an important consideration in systems using hard-disk storage with capacities in the megabyte range. Third, larger files are easier to index into a knowledge base, since only one filename has to be entered. The fourth reason for combining smaller files into larger ones has to do with the particular numbering system SUPERFILE uses internally, in which the filename extension for the raw text files is converted to a .Dnn format. This means that the upper limit for the number of files in a particular database is 99. However, there is no limit on the number of entries in each file or on the size of the file.

Although this restriction may not be a problem for large text files, such as a file of magazine articles, it's probably not practical for knowledge bases consisting of numerous short entries, such as a bibliography or a research note-card file. Nor is it practical where you've built up a large backlog of written material, such as letters or various types of articles, and want to index them into a knowledge base for easy retrieval.

Naming the Raw Text Disks

When you create or add to a knowledge base, SUPERFILE will ask you for the name of the raw text disk. During the search mode, the program will tell you to insert the disk with this name each time you want to retrieve text on that disk.

To avoid confusion, you should give some thought to developing a consistent system for naming your disks. Until you become reasonably familiar with SUPERFILE and have completely worked out what you want to put in your knowledge base files, your best bet is to use the *name and number* system suggested by FYI, Inc.

This system uses a combination of a name and a number for each disk. The name should have some obvious and direct relationship to the information on the disk, and the number should be unique to that disk. For example, a situation comedy knowledge base would have names such as the following:

PARABLE KBASE DISK NO. 1

PARABLE KBASE DISK NO. 2

PARABLE KBASE DISK NO. 3

Other disk name identifiers might be the year written or the type of entry. Regardless of the system used, it is important to be consistent in disk naming, or you will not be able to find the correct disk when it is needed.

Indexing Your Knowledge Base

With the above preliminaries out of the way, the process of creating a knowledge base, updating it, and searching and retrieving text is a relatively automatic, menu-prompted process.

When SUPERFILE creates a knowledge base, it creates two new disk files. The dictionary file (FILENAME.DIC) contains all of the keywords, and the index file (FILENAME.NDX) contains the disk and file locations of all of the entries.

Each separate knowledge base consists of one disk containing the customized SUPERFILE program (SF.COM), the customized utility program (SUP.COM), the dictionary and index files, and as many disks as necessary for the raw text. The process of creating a knowledge base is initiated by simply entering the command SF into the keyboard. From the Sign-on Menu that appears on the screen, you can select one of four options:

```
(0) Exit to operating system
(1) Change logged disk
(2) Create new database
(3) Access database
```

When option 2 is selected, the program asks for the following via a series of self-prompting menus:

1. The name of the disk file that will be used for the new database

2. Which disk the dictionary and index files should be stored on

3. The title of the new knowledge base

4. The current date

5. Any comment, up to 64 characters, to accompany the knowledge base

6. The name of the disk containing the text files and which drive the disk will normally be placed in

7. The exact filenames on the raw text disk that you want to include in the new knowledge base

SUPERFILE then tells you that it is working on each of the files and displays the number of entries added, the number of keywords, the number of entries, and the remaining memory available. At the end of this process the new knowledge base has been created, and you can do a search.

Updating a Knowledge Base

It is often necessary to update a knowledge base to (1) correct errors or add new information to previous entries, or (2) to add new entries.

Although this process is not as automatic with SUPERFILE as with some of the other knowledge-processing programs surveyed in this book, updating with SUPERFILE is certainly no more complex than performing a copy operation with a word processor.

Adding New Entries

To update a knowledge base, first use your word processor to format the new entries to be added by following the first five steps in the list above. Second, delete the old dictionary and index files. Third, change the extension types of the files you want to add to a particular knowledge base from their current designations to .TXT; this can be done with the RENAME command or a similar subroutine available in the SUPERFILE utility program. Finally, load SUPERFILE and select Sign-on Menu option 3 (Access database). What appears is the Main Menu with the following options:

```
(0)  Exit from program
(1)  Search database
(2)  Display dictionary
(3)  Add more date
(4)  Re-index this database
```

In response to questions presented to you by the program, supply the present date, comments, the name of the raw text disk, and the names of the new files.

Modifying Knowledge Base Files

After modifying the .Dnn files in your knowledge base to your satisfaction, all that is necessary is to load SUPERFILE and select Main Menu option 4 (Re-index this database). The program looks for all .Dnn files on each disk in a particular knowledge base, directing that the appropriate disk be inserted at the proper time. During re-indexing, the program looks at all the files and indexes all it finds. If some of the .Dnn files have been eliminated, the program looks for the following .Dnn files and renumbers them.

Searching a SUPERFILE
Knowledge Base

The one common feature of most general-purpose, free-form knowledge base management programs surveyed in this book is the ability to retrieve virtually any item stored in a disk file with the correct combination of keywords linked by **AND, OR,** and **NOT.** With SUPERFILE, in particular, up to 64 keywords can be linked using AND alone, 32 with OR alone, and anywhere from 32 to 64 using both, depending on the ratio. /NOT occupies the space of one keyword.

The function of AND in linking keywords is to increase the selectivity of a search. When keywords are linked with AND, a knowledge processor such as SUPERFILE retrieves only those entries that have all the keywords combined with AND. For example, the search string "UNREQUITED and EPISODES and LAVERNE&SHIRLEY" retrieves only entries with all three of these keywords from the Parable knowledge base; in effect, it searches for all episodes of that sitcom concerned with the theme of unrequited love.

Linking keywords with OR results in widening the scope of a search. Thus the search string "UNREQUITED or REQUITED or LOVE" will retrieve entries that have any one of these keywords.

/NOT excludes entries. The search string "UNREQUITED and EPISODES and /NOT LAVERNE&SHIRLEY" will retrieve entries that have the first two keywords, but not those with the third.

With SUPERFILE, once in the /NOT mode, it is possible to link keywords with AND and OR. The search string "EPISODES and BLINDDATE and /NOT SQUIGGY and LAVERNE" retrieves all entries concerned with blind dates, but not those that involve Squiggy and Laverne. On the other hand, the search string "EPISODES and BLINDDATE and /NOT LAVERNE or SHIRLEY" retrieves all entries concerning blind dates except those involving either Laverne or Shirley.

SUPERFILE has a number of other search commands that are useful and can be entered with only a right slash (/) and the first letter of the command:

/All (/A) sets up a search that retrieves all entries. By using /NOT, specific keywords can be excluded, allowing the search to be focused as narrowly as possible.

/Comment (/C) allows the user to insert comments that will be displayed in the search label.

/Standard (/S) allows the user to call up a search string that has been saved in a disk file.

Beginning Your Search

Before beginning a search, check over the list of keys by displaying the dictionary (Main Menu option 2). This choice, displayed on the screen, allows you to look at (1) the full dictionary, (2) a selected range, or (3) a partial match. Once you have put together a keyword search sequence, you should select Main Menu option 1 (Search database), which will direct you to enter your keywords in combinations of AND, OR, and /NOT.

Retrieving Text from Your Knowledge Base

A few seconds after you enter your search sequence (long enough for the program to search through its index and dictionary files), SUPERFILE will respond, telling you the number of entries it has found that match the search sequence you have entered. It will then present a number of menus, asking you the following:

1. Full entry or short entry?
2. Continuous output or display with optional output?
3. Send output to screen, printer, or separate file?

Once you have chosen the way in which you want to retrieve the text entries from your knowledge base, you simply insert raw text disks as instructed by the program.

The choices you make among the various alternatives presented depends on a number of factors, including your experience with SUPERFILE and the stage you have reached in your research. No matter what your experience with SUPERFILE, scanning through the matched entries with the short form is recommended if you are still in the initial stages of your research and do not have a well-defined search sequence worked out. With the short form, several hundred selections can be veiwed within a few minutes, allowing you to quickly view the contents of your knowledge base, analyze trends, and develop a search strategy.

SUPERFILE normally sends the results of all searches, short or long form, to the screen as one continuous output. For the beginner, the best strategy is to scan the entries in the short form and then switch to the long form and direct the program to "DISPLAY WITH OPTIONAL OUTPUT." Then, as you see an entry you want to incorporate into your final document, you can direct it to either the printer or another file. The program will ask you for a new filename for each entry you select. The whole process usually takes about 20–30 seconds. For a search sequence that results in the retreival of about 100 entries, from which you select 60, with each about 500 words long, the total elapsed time will be about 15 minutes. Another 5 minutes or so are then required to combine all of these files into a single longer file.

As you gain confidence and experience with the construction of search strings, you can use a faster way of retrieving text by directing the program to send the results to an external file in the continuous mode. Depending on the length of the search sequence, the length of each keyword, and the length of each entry, the time required to save the results to a single long file is about 5 minutes.

Sorting Your Files

The utility program package supplied with SUPERFILE (SUP.COM) provides a number of powerful capabilities that can be used with SUPERFILE entries before and after they've been indexed into a knowledge base. The most useful include sort/merge and file split.

The sort is a character sort based on the first part of each entry. If numbers (zip codes, parts numbers, or bibliography numbers, for example) are at the beginning of the entry, this feature will sort/merge them in numerical order. If the entries contain names, SUPERFILE will sort/merge alphabetically. After a sort/merge, the output can be sent to one large file or split into multiple files with the file split option. This option will allow alternation among several open files and will append entries to those files without writing over the information in the files.

Comments and Evaluation

In comparison with most of the knowledge-processing programs in this book, SUPERFILE contains a minimal number of features. Indeed, its very simplicity of structure and syntax is one of its strengths, enabling it to be adapted to almost any text/document storage, retrieval, and manipulation chore the user requires.

The flexibility and simplicity of SUPERFILE do exact a price, however. And that price is that many operations that are automatic and structured with other programs are left up to the user to perform. Specifically, you are required to—or given the freedom to, depending on your point of view—file, index, and cross-reference documents in your knowledge base as you create them with the word processor.

For those who are uncomfortable with too much structure and organization and require more room for doing things their own way, SUPERFILE is the answer. One additional point to consider is that SUPERFILE allows knowledge bases to span multiple disks—a feature that is absent from almost all other knowledge base programs now available.

CHAPTER 5

MINDex SYSTEM-ONE

The Mind Expander

SYSTEM-ONE from MINDex Infosystems is a Pascal-based text storage and retrieval system currently available for computers running under UCSD P-SYSTEM versions II.0 and IV.0 and Apple Pascal 1.1 It will also soon be available under CP/M and MP/M.

A key feature of this knowledge-processing program is the ability to search for and retrieve text files through use of an "inquiry by example" technique. Making use of a user-generated, thesaurus-like keyword listing of synonyms (words of different spelling but similar meaning) this program is different from the other programs in this book in that it does not require the use of formal Boolean logic (AND, OR, NOT, and so on). Further, SYSTEM-ONE provides an ordered list of retrieved records by closest calculated match, a feature absent from strictly Boolean-based knowledge-processing programs.

It works with relatively free-format text records created and updated using the P-SYSTEM text editor. Under any other operating system, being forced to use the operating system editor is a tedious and onerous chore. But the P-SYSTEM editor has many of the features of standard word-processing programs and is a pleasure to use. Under CP/M, a standard word-processing program can be used to create the appropriate text files.

Text records may be of any length, spanning multiple files and disk volumes, using a simple sequential file-naming convention.

SYSTEM-ONE Overview

SYSTEM-ONE requires a minimum of two disk drives. One contains the SYSTEM-ONE code file as well as various access support files that are generated automatically and maintained by the system. The other drive is used to handle the required text files. Although the code file is only 38K bytes long, it is best to use a system with more than 52K bytes, since dynamic memory allocation is used during execution. The more memory is available, the faster SYSTEM-ONE can scan the text files in your knowledge base.

To use SYSTEM-ONE, you must supply four different types of text files: the *abstract file,* containing your knowledge base with the text grouped into records; the *thesaurus file,* containing the keywords, grouped into records of words with similar meaning or with some common link, that you want to use for indexing and retrieval; and the *temporary inquiry* and *archive inquiry files,* which are used to store your most frequently used inquiries. The first two files are generated using an external text editor. Temporary inquiry files are created interactively under the umbrella of the program, whereas archive inquiry files are created by combining the smaller temporary files into a single larger one, using an external text editor. The basic difference between the two is that a temporary inquiry file contains a single inquiry record, whereas the archive inquiry file consists of many such records.

Upon system initialization, the MINDex system seeks out the thesaurus file. If it's not present, an error message is displayed, and control is returned to the operating system. If the thesaurus file has not been processed previously, it is scanned and converted into two SYSTEM-ONE function support files, a dictionary and an inverted thesaurus. After the thesaurus file has been processed, SYSTEM-ONE seeks out the associated abstract file, scanning and then compressing it into a more manageable form.

During scanning, each abstract record is converted into a compressed numeric representation of its contents relative to the concepts contained in the thesaurus file. Direct-access links are established between the abstract file and the thesaurus file, which make it possible to retrieve or display specific files and records within files on command. Before compression, the abstracts can be modified using the system text editor. After compression and modification, the supporting retrieval and access information for specific records or a related set of records is modified using an update function.

Search and retrieval are accomplished by comparing a compressed inquiry to the compressed abstracts, which results in a list of abstract numbers in order of calculated match. Selected records from this list, a subrange, or the entire list may then be viewed under operator control. During this retrieval process, temporary inquiry files are created interactively. As many of these temporary inquiry files as you want may be created, tested, and refined. If you use them regularly, they can be added to the main inquiry archive file. Once the thesaurus and abstract files have been processed, the inquiry archive file is similarly scanned and compressed.

Although the text records and files can be of any length, the MINDex SYSTEM-ONE limits the number of thesaurus records for a particular abstract text file to 500 and the size of a keyword to no more than 20 characters. Furthermore, because of the numbering method used, the number of files in a specific knowledge base cannot exceed 99 (01 . . . 99). A number of other parameters, such as the maximum number of abstract records in any particular file, the maximum number of inquiry records in the inquiry archive file, and the maximum number of unique keywords in the thesaurus file, are definable by the user. However, for most efficient operation of the system you should stick with the release values: 1000, 100, and 1000, respectively.

Creating a Knowledge Base with SYSTEM-ONE

Of the programs surveyed in this book, SYSTEM-ONE is second only to SUPERFILE in the ease with which your standard text files can be converted into a knowledge base of records that can be retrieved on demand. Basically, creating such a knowledge base with SYSTEM-ONE involves:

1. Converting your text files into abstract files
2. Selecting keywords and setting up a thesaurus file
3. Renaming your files to fit SYSTEM-ONE style
4. Scanning in the abstract and thesaurus files
5. Setting up SYSTEM-ONE for search and retrieval

Converting Text Files into Abstract Files

The only alterations that must be made to text files in your system involve the addition of one or more of three reserved characters used to trigger special functions and features: the tilda (˜) and the left and right braces ([ ]). Although the program adds them automatically, it is recommended that you add the special record numbers yourself: A1, A2, . . . for abstract records; T1, T2, . . . for thesaurus files; and I1, I2, . . . for inquiry records.

The most important of these characters is the tilda, which is used as the MINDex standard record mark. It triggers the SYSTEM-ONE text scanner, indicating the beginning of a text record. The left and right braces are MINDex standard word group–delimiting characters. Activated or deactivated via the Setup function (to be discussed lated), delimited word groups are treated differently according to the type of file and the action being performed on the file. Within a thesaurus file, delimited word groups are treated as comments rather than descriptors. In the abstract and inquiry files, by activating or deactivating this function, you can direct SYSTEM-ONE to scan either the delimited word groups or the whole text for descriptors, thus considerably speeding up the search process.

For example, suppose you are a writer for the daytime soap opera *As Your Stomach Turns,* the continuing saga of John and Marsha and their extended family of sexual athletes and emotional cripples. Considering the intricate plot twists and turns, you might find it useful to build a knowledge base—called Soap—that chronicles, week to week, in summary form, the numerous liaisons that occur. Part of the file for one week's set of episodes, with the SYSTEM-ONE delimiter characters and special record numbers added, would look something like this:

```
~ A1 plagued with doubts about [John] and his
  [infidelities], [Marsha] goes home to sort out
  her emotions. Before she has time to think things
  through, [Bob] stops by, offering her a shoulder
  to cry on.
~ A2 [Donald], meanwhile, is puzzled by the behavior
  of his fiancee, [Joan], who had initially agreed
  to marry him once his [annulment] was final. She
  has now, without any explanation, rejected him.
~ A3 Meanwhile, over at the university, [Sandra] is
  in no mood to listen to [Tom] and his apologies
```

```
when he comes over to talk to her at the student
union.
```

Selecting Keywords for Your Thesaurus

One of the drawbacks of knowledge base programs (such as SUPER-FILE) built around the use of AND/OR Boolean logic is that you have no direct control over the amount of text retrieved and no real assurance as to how closely what is retrieved fits your requirements.

SYSTEM-ONE attempts to overcome this limitation by using a thesaurus (or synonym dictionary) approach to keyword selection. In SYSTEM-ONE, thesaurus records are constructed containing one or more keywords, all of which are conceptually related and which in total describe a central idea or concept contained in a related abstract file.

Each collection of keywords is formally referred to as a descriptor. As with the abstract records, tilda characters are used to indicate the beginning of a thesaurus record containing such a set of keywords.

The thesaurus is the conceptual frame of reference within which the program indexes the content of its associated abstract text record or file. It acts as a filter through which SYSTEM-ONE views the text records contained in the abstract.

The particular power of this approach is that it allows you to link together not only words that are explicitly related, such as synonyms, but words that have numerous implicit and highly idiosyncratic relationships. In many respects, this approach very closely approximates the fuzzy logic of human thought, resulting in the retrieval of text that may better fit your requirements than text obtained through searches based on Boolean logic. To SYSTEM-ONE, a keyword can be any contiguous sequence of up to 20 characters, beginning with any letter or digit and including characters that may be embedded within the sequence, such as "−," "/," "=," "_," and "&."

In the Soap knowledge base, one such thesaurus record of related keywords might include many of the different synonyms for the various emotions and groups of related individuals, as follows:

```
~ T1 love desire want long fancy crave yearn hunger
  lust
~ T2 gratify satisfy slake appease quench gladden
  please
```

```
~ T3 enthrall delight enchant bewitch enrapture
  fascinate
~ T4 annoy hate irritate enrage gall aggravate irk
  vex
~ T5 John Marsha Jenny Sandra Joan
~ T6 Marsha John Donald Bob Tom
```

In SYSTEM-ONE, such thesaurus records serve two functions. Their first and primary function is to serve as the link between the abstract records and the internal dictionary and inverted index used by the I(nquire) and R(elative retrieval) functions to locate specific text. Their second function is to serve as a resource you can browse through using the D(isplay) function while trying to develop a list of keywords you may want to include in an I(nquire) operation.

Naming Your SYSTEM-ONE Files

To distinguish among the three types of text files—abstract, thesaurus, and inquiry—SYSTEM-ONE uses a file-naming convention in which each trio of files constituting a specific knowlege base must start with a name of up to six characters. This is followed by a two-digit sequential number and the character string:

.A.TXT for abstract text

.T.TXT for thesaurus text

.I.TXT for inquiry text

For example, in the knowledge base consisting of text files tracking the adventures of John and Mary week by week—Soap — the filename of the first abstract file would be SOAP01.A.TXT, and that of the first thesaurus text would be SOAP01.T.TXT. Any additional abstract and thesaurus files would be named in a similar manner, except that you would increment the two-digit number: 02, 03, . . . , 99.

A similar set of files is developed during the search process using the I(nquire) function. For example, the first inquiry file generated for the Soap knowledge base would be SOAP01.I.TXT.

Scanning in Files and Records

When booted up, SYSTEM-ONE first displays the MINDex logo and a request for the knowledge base to be loaded. Once you've entered the knowledge base name and inserted the disk with the appropriate abstract and thesaurus files (and, if they exist, the temporary and archive files), SYSTEM-ONE scans the entries, calculating vector values for any new thesaurus descriptors and their associated abstract records.

Records contained in these text files are then numbered sequentially and automatically by SYSTEM-ONE, independent of which file each is in. For example, suppose SOAP01.A.TXT has 50 records in it and SOAP02.A.TXT has 75. When these records are scanned into your Soap knowledge base, the records in the first abstract file are numbered A1 to A50 and those in the second are numbered A51 to A75. Thesaurus records and inquiry records are similarly numbered.

Once your knowledge base (in this case, Soap) has been scanned and loaded into your computer, the main SYSTEM-ONE prompt line appears at the top of your CRT screen offering the main commands, beginning with the MINDex version and the name of the knowledge base, as follows:

```
[SOAP]: H(elp) D(isplay) I(nquire) U(pdate) S(etup)
E(xit)?:
```

These commands are executed when you enter the first letter of the selected function from this list in the space at the end of the prompt line following the question mark and the colon.

Searching a SYSTEM-ONE Knowledge Base

This program provides three mechanisms by which you can search a SYSTEM-ONE knowledge base:

1. The D(isplay) command
2. The I(nquire) command
3. The R(elative retrieval) command

Using the D(isplay) Function

When the D(isplay) option is selected from the main system prompt, a new prompt line listing the various options available for display will appear on the screen:

```
T(hesaurus) A(bstract) I(nquire) R(elative) S(ystem)
Q(uit)?:
```

The D(isplay) level commands allow you to view the text records from any of the text files as well as some of the internal access support files.

Selecting the appropriate option from this submenu allows you to view records from any text file—thesaurus, abstract, or inquiry—one at a time or sequentially, over a range of records or through all of them. The options available to you are the same regardless of whether you choose to display a thesaurus, abstract, or inquiry file.

Display of the various access support files via the S(ystem files) command allows you to sequentially display their contents. This is used for diagnostic purposes to determine proper system functioning, and some understanding of the files' structure is required to decipher their contents. Most users of SYSTEM-ONE, however, need not concern themselves with this particular use of the D(isplay) option, as it is not necessary to take full advantage of this program as a knowledge processor.

In implementing a search strategy based on the use of the I(nquire) function, the D(isplay) T(hesaurus) option is the most useful, since it can be used to develop a list of keywords. When you choose this option from the Display prompt line, the following list of choices is presented:

```
G(iven word) A(ll recs) R(ange) O(ne rec) S(etup)
Q(uit)?:
```

If the thesaurus files in your knowledge base are relatively small, the best way to develop an effective keyword list is simply to scan through the various records using All, Range, or One commands from the Display Menu. If these files are fairly extensive, the best procedure is to use the G(iven word) command, which results in the following display:

```
DISPLAY CONCEPTS FOR WHAT WORD? (Hit Return to
Quit):
```

Suppose you want to search for all the episodes of *As Your Stomach Turns* in which Tom appears. If you enter the keyword "Tom" after the colon, another display will appear with the identifying numbers of the records containing that particular keyword and related characters, along with a choice of display options similar to the following:

```
DISPLAY CONCEPTS BELOW FOR "Tom": A(ll) O(ne)
S(etup) Q(uit)?:
[17] [32] [51] [57] [64] [70] [74]
```

These numbers tell you that in thesaurus records 17, 32, 51, 57, 64, 70, and 74 there are references to Tom and other related characters and concepts.

If you select the O(ne) command, SYSTEM-ONE will then ask you which concept number should be displayed. If you select the number 32, MINDex will respond with a selection of keywords from that particular descriptor/record, such as:

```
CONCEPTS NUMBER? (Hit 0 or space bar to Quit): 32

    [T32]
    Tom
                Marsha
                Joan
```

If that is not what you are looking for, or if you need additional keywords to fill out the search sequence you are going to use with the I(nquire) function, back up to the DISPLAY CONCEPTS prompt line with the Q(uit) function and make another selection, continuing until you find what you want.

Once you have developed a backlog of inquiry records, a more efficient way of finding an effective search string is the D(isplay) I(nquire) option, which operates in a manner similar to that of the D(isplay) T(hesaurus) command.

In either case, after you have found an appropriate set of keywords—in this case, those that accurately describe a particular set of dramatic circumstances in the Soap knowledge base—you are ready to proceed to the next step: using the I(nquire) command to locate the appropriate text records in the Soap knowledge base. This is done by using the Q(uit) key, pressing it repeatedly until you back up to the main prompt line.

Searching with the I(nquire) Function

The I(nquire) function allows you to retrieve abstract records based on an example record from the inquiry archive file or from temporary inquiry files created at the keyboard.

During the retrieval process, if an abstract of interest is found, it can be sent out to a temporary inquiry file, which may contain only one such record. However, many separate temporary inquiry files can be made and used to retrieve relevant abstracts. If a particular temporary inquiry is regularly used, it is merged with the inquiry archive file, which can contain up to 100 such records per knowledge base.

Upon choosing the I(nquire) option from the main prompt, the following display appears:

```
A(rchive) T(emporary) L(ist) P(reserve) S(etup)
Q(uit)?:
```

If you select the T(emporary) command, SYSTEM-ONE will direct you to enter a temporary inquiry filename no more than six characters long, according to the protocol described earlier. If this is the first inquiry file, the name you should enter is SOAP01. The program then automatically enters the record marker and number and asks you for the inquiry record.

Suppose, after surveying the various thesaurus records for references to Tom and his interaction with other characters, you have determined that you want to locate all abstract references to Tom, Marsha, John, and Joan at an office party. Once you enter your inquiry record "TOM MARSHA JOAN JOHN OFFICE PARTY" and save it to a temporary file, the program scans it, begins a search of the knowledge base, and lists in a column each word in your inquiry while searching for it.

If you wanted to search on the basis of a previously generated search string, you would select the A(rchive) option and enter the record number found by browsing through the inquiry files with the D(isplay) command, upon which the program would execute the retrieval process.

In either case, at the end of the retrieval process, the abstract record numbers that may fit this inquiry are presented in the LIST display:

```
LIST: A(ll) R(ange) O(ne) S(etup) Q(uit)?:
The absolute weight of inquiry 1 is 2.
```

```
Following are 4 of top matching abstracts by
[Number/Weight ]

[16/5 ]  [25/3 ]  [14/2 ]  [2/1 ]
```

The list of abstract number/relative weight values is presented in order from the highest weight to the lowest and either from left to right or from top to bottom. The first abstract number is 16, which was found to have five occurrences of words contained in the search string.

After you enter the appropriate command following the LIST prompt line colon, SYSTEM-ONE will display the appropriate abstract records one at a time, over a range, or all at the same time, in sequence. If, for example, you selected the O(ne) command and entered the abstract number 2, the program would display something like this:

```
A2/1


  At the Christmas office party, Tom, the president
of the firm, opened the door to the executive
conference room and found Marsha, John, and Joan and
asked, "Can I join you?"
```

Using the R(elative Retrieval) Function

A third way to search for and retrieve abstract records of interest to you is by using the R(elative retrieval) function, accessible from both the Display and Inquiry modes. It is especially useful in searching very large knowledge bases, when it is often necessary to go through the inquiry process many times, refining the search string to find more information about the subject you want. R(elative retrieval) allows you to progressively refine or broaden your inquiry without typing in new search strings again and again.

To do this, the R(elative retrieval) option allows you to use an abstract that contains the kind of information you're looking for in your knowledge base as a template, using it as if it were an inquiry record to retrieve other closely related abstracts.

This process can be repeated. If, in the list of abstracts retrieved from your Soap knowledge base using record 14 as the template, you find that record 28 is more suitable, this may be specified in the next iteration.

There are two ways to retrieve text from a SYSTEM-ONE knowledge base for use with your word processor: (1) via the P(reserve) option on the Inquiry Menu and (2) by modifying the program's default settings using the S(etup) commands available on almost all of the menus.

Retrieving Text with the P(reserve) Command

During the normal process of search and retrieval using the I(nquire) options, abstracts that are displayed on the screen go into a temporary disk file. This allows you to scroll back and forth through the various selections looking for those which meet your requirements. However, if you leave the program or execute another sequence, this file will be erased or replaced with another list. The P(reserve) command allows you to save each such listing under a disk filename that you specify.

Retrieving Text with the S(etup) Command

The problem with the method described above is that the order in which these records are arranged reflects keyword frequency rather than the document in which they are to be used.

To get around this problem, note the abstract records you want, note their associated numbers, and reorganize them in an order appropriate to the document you are writing. Then go to the S(etup) option, accessible via several different menus in the program, and change the default output device from CONSOLE to either PRINTER or an external disk file of your choice. Finally, select the O(ne record) option from the Abstract Display Menu and enter the record numbers in the appropriate order.

In addition to changing the output device, the S(etup) feature also allows you to change many of the dynamic parameters of the system, as well as those that are fixed at specific release values by the manufacturer but are redefinable by the user.

The S(etup) option on the main prompt, if chosen, will lead you to the Main Setup Menu, which allows you to change both types of parameters. The selection of S(etup) options at all other levels leads to the Temp Setup Menu, which allows you to change the parameters for a specific operation; these parameters will revert to the default values when you exit the program.

Dynamic parameters include a variety of options that may need to be changed during normal system operation, depending on the function being performed. For example, output is typically displayed on the console screen, but through the S(etup) option you can direct it to a printer, another disk file, or other text-oriented devices. If you are still in an exploratory mode, searching for appropriate abstract files, you should probably maintain the system in the CONSOLE output mode. If you've narrowed down your search, selected the specific records you want, or refined your inquiry search criteria, you can direct output via the S(etup) command to another file or directly to the printer. Another dynamic parameter is the form length parameter. If you are sending the output to the console, this should be either 16 or 24 lines. If the output is to the printer, it should be 66. Other alterations that can be made include turning various formatting options on or off, suppression or activation of the printing and indexing of delimited word groups, and inclusion or exclusion of retrieval statistics.

Comments and Evaluation

The techniques used by SYSTEM-ONE for constructing a knowledge base and searching it are much more sophisticated and complex than the corresponding techniques of most of the other programs in this book. In the hands of an experienced user, they are also very powerful. Although SYSTEM-ONE is difficult to learn to use with any degree of facility, the effort will prove to be worth it, for these techniques will give you a much greater degree of control over your knowledge base, especially as it grows in size. This is because SYSTEM-ONE, in a manner of speaking, learns as you learn. First, the effectiveness of your thesaurus records grows over time as you increase the number and type of synonyms in any particular entry. Second, as the size of your inquiry record files increases, so does the precision of your searches.

More than almost any other program in this book, SYSTEM-ONE allows you to build knowledge bases that can, in a very real sense, become extensions of your brain, reflective more of the fuzzy logic of human thought than of the AND/OR, on/off logic of your computer.

Virtually any kind of knowledge base of text files can be maintained on SYSTEM-ONE: bibliographies, card catalogs, card files, research notes and abstracts, and complete articles. Some care should be taken, however, in determining how the files and the various records contained in each are configured. In particular, you should give some thought to the number of records contained in each file. If you're setting up a bibliography or card catalog, each full entry should begin with the tilda record marker (~). The number of such records per file is up to you, as long as it falls below the upper limit of 500 per file. If you're compiling a card file of research notes, each subject should constitute a separate record consisting of one or more paragraphs. For simplicity in collecting and categorizing your notes, each record entry should be contained in its own file.

Where you're building up a knowledge base of articles or reports that you've written on a particular subject, each article should have its own file. Within each article file, the number of records depends on how you are going to use the knowledge base. If you simply want a sophisticated document retrieval system with a high degree of indexing and cross-indexing of subject and keyword, the entire file should be classified as a single record with a single tilda marker at the beginning.

If you want to be able to access various parts of each article, it is necessary to add more record markers. The most straightforward way to format the content is to make each paragraph into a record. A more logical organization is to make each heading and/or subheading a separate record. Not only does this require less effort in formatting each article file, it allows you to make your keyword selection much more focused and specific.

CHAPTER 6

NOTEBOOK

The Text-Oriented Database Program

Protem's NOTEBOOK is exactly what its marketers, Digital Marketing, describe it as: a traditional database management system that has been adapted for storing, sorting, and retrieving text. Like full-function DBMS programs, it uses the field, record, and file format; unlike them, NOTE-BOOK does not burden the user with the details of setting up a system for storing text information. The number of records that can be stored is limited only by disk capacity.

NOTEBOOK Overview

Within the above limits, NOTEBOOK is capable of handling and managing blocks of text with some flexibility. The size of each knowledge base depends only on disk capacity—160K bytes on a 5.25-inch SSDD floppy diskette and 800K bytes on an SSQD 8-inch floppy disk. Each record can have up to 20 fields. The size of each record and field is dependent on the type of microprocessor used—8- or 16-bit. In 16-bit personal computers using the CP/M-86 and MS-DOS (PC-DOS), each record can hold up to 32,000 characters (about 500 lines of text or 20 double-spaced pages), with a maximum of 4000 characters per field (about 70 lines or 3 pages). The

CP/M-80 version is much more limited, however, with each record holding up to 4000 characters and each field a maximum of 500 characters (9 lines). Line length is 55 to 60 characters in all versions. NOTEBOOK requires 128K bytes of RAM on a 16-bit system and 64K bytes on an 8-bit system.

In NOTEBOOK, the records in a particular knowledge base consist of a set of fields that describe one category or item of information. Each field is associated with a particular heading, which is the name assigned to the field. Each heading can have a maximum of 18 characters and each knowledge base can have a maximum of 20 headings.

The user looks at a knowledge base in NOTEBOOK through various "views," or different sets or collections of records. The complete knowledge base is the widest view. You can create other views that display only those records that meet criteria that you specify or in which the records have been sorted in a particular order. With this program you can have as many different views of the same knowledge base as you want.

NOTEBOOK creates four main files for every knowledge base. These are:

FILENAME.DAT   The file containing the actual text

FILENAME.IDX   The index to the .DAT file

FILENAME.DEF   The headings

FILENAME.MSC   Miscellaneous information

The disk containing the knowledge base also contains a FILENAME.VW for each view created and a FILENAME.RPT for each report format created. When you have modified a file in your knowledge base, previous versions are saved as backup files, as indicated by the following filename types or extents:

.BDT   Data backup file

.BIX   Index backup file

.BDF   Heading backup file

.BMS   Miscellaneous backup file

.BVW   View backup file

.BRP   Report backup file

When you build a knowledge base file with NOTEBOOK, you need only enter the name for the knowledge base you want. The extents are added automatically by the program.

Various NOTEBOOK operations are invoked by means of function menus displayed at the bottom of the screen at various times. These functions include:

sA(ve)	Saves all additions and modifications to the knowledge base.
B(egin)	Takes you to the first record of the knowledge base.
C(ompact)	Compacts the knowledge base, removing any files marked for deletion and reclaiming empty space on the disk. It is also used to repair a damaged knowledge base.
E(nd)	Takes you to the last record of the knowledge base.
H(eading)	Invokes a screen and menu for editing the headings of a knowledge base.
P(rint)	Invokes the print menu from which you can edit the format of reports and print them or write them to a disk file.
Q(uit)	Saves all additions and modifications to the knowledge base, exits NOTEBOOK, and returns to the operating system.
foR(eign)	Permits you to read in other knowledge bases and files from outside NOTEBOOK.
S(elect)	Creates a new view containing a subset of the entire knowledge base.
sO(rt)	Sorts any view of the knowledge base on the first 20 characters of any field.
U(ndo)	Returns to the edit screen. If you have just worked on a current record, these changes will be deleted and the record restored to the previous text.

V(iew)   Displays a version of the knowledge base that you
                   have previously selected or sorted, or displays the
                   entire base.

?(help)   Displays a short explanation of each of the
                   functions.

Each function is invoked by the simple procedure of pressing the capital letter immediately preceding the right-facing parenthesis: (

Creating a Knowledge Base with NOTEBOOK

When you log on to NOTEBOOK, the program asks for the name of
the knowledge base to be created or accessed. After you enter the name
you've selected, one of two things occurs:

1. If a knowledge base by that name does not exist, NOTEBOOK
    goes to a heading screen, where you enter brief headings describ-
    ing each of the categories under which information will be stored
    in each record.
2. If the knowledge base already exists, NOTEBOOK goes directly
    to the edit screen and displays the first record.

Creating Category Headings

Creating the categories (up to 20) by which you want to describe the
text information stored in a particular knowledge base is a very straightforward procedure. Once in the Heading Screen mode, you simply type in
the headings that describe each category, one per line, in 18 characters or
less.

One record within such a knowledge base would look like this on the
screen:

```
[headings ]     [fields ]

Author          Cole, Bernard Conrad
Title           Beyond Word Processing
Subject         Text-oriented "knowledge management"
```

All other records would have the same headings, but the fields would contain different information.

A bibliographic knowledge base might have category headings such as author, title, publication, subject, and descriptors. The subject field would be used to describe the subject of the book or article, in whatever detail was required, in up to 9 lines in 8-bit systems and in up to 70 lines in 16-bit systems. The descriptor field contains words that would be helpful in retrieving records.

A much more complex knowledge base might be devoted to a particular subject, such as a compendium of the TV adventures of the United Federation Starship *Enterprise*. It might have the following headings:

```
(1) Episode
(2) Foe Type
(3) Planet of Origin
(4) Name of Foe
(5) History of Foe
(6) Location of Action
(7) Federation StarDate
(8) Text
(9) Descriptors
```

As shown, the subject field is an 18-character description of what is discussed in a particular entry. Under Episode you would enter the name of the TV episode, such as "The Corbamite Maneuver." The Foe Type would be one of the many enemy races surrounding the Federation, including the Klingons, Romulans, Metrons, Talosians, Andorians, and Skarr. The Foe Type field would include the specific member of the enemy race that Captain Kirk is opposing. Information under each category can fill anywhere from 9 to 70 lines, depending on which version of the program you are using.

You can add new headings to your knowledge base at any time, but only sequentially, at the end of the list; that is, you can't reorder the headings and insert a new heading between two existing ones. However, the particular order of the headings is unimportant and has no effect on the efficiency of searches using the S(elect) and F(ind) functions.

Entering Text into Your Knowledge Base

Text is entered into the knowledge base only while NOTEBOOK is in the Edit Screen mode, when it is possible to enter, add, delete, or modify information in the knowledge base, using control functions similar to those used in most word-processing programs. A sample entry in the StarTrek knowledge base while in the Edit Screen mode would look something like this:

```
(1) Episode              The Corbamite Maneuver
(2) Foe Type             Romulans
(3) Planet of Origin     Unknown
(4) Name of Foe          Unknown
(5) History of Foe       Extremely militaristic,
                         they are similar to
                         Vulcans in physiology
                         but are allies of the
                         Klingons. They never
                         take captives and
                         destroy themselves when
                         captured.
(6) Location of Action   Altair Sector, near
                         Boundary
(7) Federation StarDate  2453
(8) Text                 When cornered by Romu-
                         lans in a space web,
                         Kirk told Romulans that
                         Enterprise was made of
                         ""Corbamite,'' which
                         reflects energy back
                         upon attacking ship. It
                         worked.
(9) Descriptors          Romulans, Corbamite,
                         Altair
```

At the bottom of the display is a Help Menu displaying the various edit functions as well as status information concerning the knowledge base, including:

1. The name of the knowledge base (StarTrek). If the user is viewing a subset or selection of the knowledge base, the name of the particular view will precede the name of the knowledge base.

2. The record displayed/total number of records in the view. In this case, 1 record of a knowledge base containing 25 records is being viewed.

3. The space remaining in the current field (%FF) and the space remaining in the current record (%RR).

4. Whether the Insert mode is on or off.

If a record is too large to be displayed all at once, you can move up and down through the entry a field or a line at a time via a set of scroll commands.

Once you've finished the editing of a record, there are several ways to move to another entry. To go to the next record, you simply move the cursor to the bottom of the screen and then down one more line. To move back to the previous record, move the cursor one line beyond the top of the screen. If you are in the middle of the knowledge base and want to create a new record, go to the Function Menu and invoke the E(nd) command, which will take you to the end of the knowledge base. Invoking the sA(ve) command saves all additions and modifications made to the knowledge base while in the Edit Screen mode.

If at any time you want to enter another category into the knowledge base, simply go back to the heading screen by pressing the Escape key on your computer and then the H(eading) command.

Entering External Files

Information created by other data and knowledge base programs and word-processing programs can be entered into a NOTEBOOK knowledge base by invoking the foR(eign) command from the Function Menu. NOTEBOOK asks whether the data is in the B(asic) or N(otebook) format and then asks for the name of the file in which it is located. Once given the appropriate information, NOTEBOOK reads it into the knowledge base, adding in the new records.

To format each external file for entry into NOTEBOOK, each record must begin with a line consisting of only a percent sign followed by the word "start" (% Start:) and end with a line consisting of "%End," with both followed by a carriage return. Each field must be prefaced by a "%Heading:", which is identical to a NOTEBOOK knowledge base heading except that it must begin with a "%" and end with a ":". The line length of such entries cannot exceed 50 characters.

Searching a NOTEBOOK Knowledge Base

Searches of a NOTEBOOK knowledge base are done using the F(ind), S(elect), and V(iew) commands.

With F(ind), NOTEBOOK performs a straightforward character string search. With S(elect), NOTEBOOK allows you to perform categorical searches that allow selection of records that fit certain primary and/ or secondary conditions. V(iew) permits you to move from one view to another.

Views are different sets or collections of records in a NOTEBOOK knowledge base. The S(elect) and sO(rt) functions create views that contain specified information or are sorted in a particular order. A view is not a copy of the knowledge base. Rather, it is an alternative display of the knowledge base. A knowledge base can be displayed from as many points of view as you wish using this function.

F(inding) a Record

With this command you can quickly locate a record where a particular field begins with a word or phrase of up to 20 characters. It is most useful when you wish to find a particular record for editing purposes and do not want to page through the knowledge base one record at a time.

When you first "boot up," NOTEBOOK displays the headings in the knowledge base and asks on which heading/field the F(ind) function will be performed. For example, a display of the F(ind) command for the StarTrek knowledge base when you want to find all information concerning encounters of the Starship *Enterprise* with the Romulans might look like this:

```
FIND the next record where a field begins with a
word you specify:

(1) Episode
(2) Foe Type
(3) Planet of Origin
```

```
(4) Name of Foe
(5) History of Foe
(6) Location of Action
(7) Federation StarDate
(8) Text
(9) Descriptors
```

```
Enter number of heading to FIND on: 2
Enter the character string: Romulans
Search forward or backward (F or B): F
```

F(ind) is designed to locate a record based on whatever character string is entered into the chosen field, even if the entire field is not entered. For example, if asked to find "Romu," NOTEBOOK will find the first entry that begins with these characters.

Creating a View

With the S(elect) command, you can create a view containing all records having certain characteristics in common. NOTEBOOK will select from whichever view you are in when the S(elect) function is invoked. To select from a different view, it is first necessary to use V(iew) to change the view, then S(elect). The Default view for any new knowledge base is the overall view of all the categories and fields. NOTEBOOK first displays a menu from which a field can be chosen to select on. The menu for the StarTrek knowledge base would look like this:

```
(1) Episode
(2) Foe Type
(3) Planet of Origin
(4) Name of Foe
(5) History of Foe
(6) Location of Action
(7) Federation StarDate
(8) Text
(9) Descriptors
```

```
Enter the number of the field to select on:
```

If you wanted to create a view containing all records referring to action by the *Enterprise* during a particular period, you would enter the field num-

ber 7. The program would ask you for the relationship between the field
you had chosen and the characters to be matched, and then for the characters themselves. You'd choose "is equal to" and "StarYear 2453," as
shown below:

```
Select all pages where subject has specified
characteristic:

(1) is equal to
(2) is not equal to
(3) is less than
(4) is less than or equal to
(5) is greater than
(6) is greater than or equal to
(7) contains
(8) does not contain

Enter number of desired relationships: 1
Enter text to be matched: StarYear 2453
```

NOTEBOOK Knowledge Base Selection Criteria

With the S(elect) and sO(rt) functions, you can search for pages on the
basis of any of several relationships defined by a number of primary and
secondary selection criteria. Primary conditions include:

Equal to: This means that the text entered in the menu exactly matches
the text of the field in a record, except that the search is indifferent to
upper or lower case.

Not equal to: This means that the text does not match the text entered.

Greater than/Less than: With these criteria, the text entered is compared with the text in the field, character by character, until two characters are found that do not match.

In comparing words, NOTEBOOK considers a word to be "less than"
another one if it precedes it in alphabetical order. For example, the word
"Romulan" is less than the phrase "Skarr" because R precedes S in the
alphabet. Two words such as "collect" and "collate" would be compared
by NOTEBOOK until the fifth character, when it would determine that

"collate" is less than "collect." Under S(elect), NOTEBOOK is indifferent to case, so that r has the same value as R. Under sO(rt), however, the upper-case alphabet is of lesser value than the lower-case alphabet.

Secondary Selection Criteria

After the first set of conditions has been selected for matching, NOTE-BOOK asks whether another condition is to be added to the selection and displays the following choices:

NO second condition

AND with second condition

OR with second condition

If AND or OR is chosen, the menu with the seven selection criteria is displayed again. As discussed in earlier chapters, ANDing narrows the search and increases the selectivity, whereas ORing widens the search. If the second condition is ANDed with the primary condition, only those records that meet both conditions are displayed. If the two conditions are ORed, any view meeting either condition is displayed.

Saving Selection Views

After both primary and secondary selection conditions have been set, NOTEBOOK asks you to enter the name of the view to be created. The name may have up to eight alphanumeric characters to which NOTE-BOOK adds the filetype extension .VW. NOTEBOOK then makes the selection and indicates how many records the new view contains, saving it for later searches.

Narrowing the Search Further

NOTEBOOK allows you to repeat the selection process as many times as needed to narrow down the choice of records in a view. You can save the new selection under the same name as the earlier one, thus replacing it. Or it can be saved as a view with a different name, allowing both to be available for future use. When you are finished selecting, NOTEBOOK displays the first page in the newest view.

Via the sO(rt) command from the Function Menu, it is possible to sort any view of a knowledge base in ascending or descending order on the first 20 characters of any field.

NOTEBOOK sorts the view you were in at the time the function was invoked. If you want to sort on a different view, all you need to do is to change the view and then S(elect).

The sorting sequence is the same as that used by the select function, except that the former is case-sensitive; that is, all upper-case letters have less value than all lower-case letters. This allows ascending sorts (from smaller to greater) or descending (from greater to smaller).

Retrieving Text from a NOTEBOOK Knowledge Base

NOTEBOOK allows preparation of reports from a particular knowledge base customized to a user's specific requirements. Invoked via the P(rint) command in the Function Menu, NOTEBOOK displays a screen containing a Print Functions Menu and a Page Layout Menu. The first allows you to direct the reports you have created with the V(iew) command to be sent either to a printer or to a separate disk file. Although NOTEBOOK provides a predefined report format, it is also possible to customize the report to your needs via the second menu.

Comments and Evaluation

Unlike SUPERFILE and SYSTEM-ONE, which allow creation of a knowledge base that can span many disks, the extent of a specific file covering a single knowledge base in NOTEBOOK is limited to a single disk. It is possible to have multiple disks devoted to a single subject or knowledge base, but the user will have to use some other program, such as a disk catalog utility, to keep track of what is on specific disks. Overall, however, this program is best suited to systems with hard disks containing many megabytes of memory space.

Although it incorporates a full-screen editor that uses WordStar-type commands, NOTEBOOK does not include the line wrap-around feature associated with most word-processing programs. This makes it awkward to enter text files of any substantial length. Since NOTEBOOK does accept external text, the best procedure is to write the text for entry into your knowledge base using a word processor with wrap-around, keeping in mind the record limits of the particular version of NOTEBOOK employed.

In general, NOTEBOOK is for use by those who like the structured format of a database program or electronic index card system, but who require greater file, record, and field capacity than is offered by these traditional alternatives. The text files should also be ones that are relatively structured, such as form letters, bibliographies, abstracts, personnel files, product descriptions, change orders, contact reports, and client and customer files. If, however, your text files are varied in length and run into the tens or hundreds of kilobytes (10–100 pages), open-format text search programs such as SUPERFILE and SYSTEM-ONE are better alternatives.

CHAPTER 7

Datafax

The Electronic File Folder

If any knowledge-processing program covered in this book can be characterized as a true electronic filing system, it is Datafax from Link Systems. Analogous in operation and terminology to a manual filing system, Datafax even allows storage of pages of text in "folders." Each page contains 24 lines of text (a full screen), with each line 40 or 80 characters long. Each folder can hold up to 255 such pages and can be cross-referenced by keywords up to 60 different ways. Each knowledge base, or volume, can store up to 3000 folders. Unlike SUPERFILE and SYSTEM-ONE, in which a knowledge base can span multiple disks, each diskette in Datafax represents one and only one knowledge base.

Datafax Overview

Written in Pascal and designed to operate under UCSD P-SYSTEM, Datafax is currently configured to operate on the Apple II/IIplus/IIe, with 64K bytes of RAM; the Apple III, with 128K bytes, and the IBM PC, with 128K bytes and either two floppy-disk drives or one floppy- and one hard-disk drive. Datafax requires that six files be resident on your system diskette. These files are SYSTEM.INTERP, SYSTEM.PASCAL, SYSTEM.MISCINFO, SYSTEM.START-UP, SYSTEM.LIBRARY, and

73

DATAFAX.INFO. The first three are required for operation of the P-SYSTEM; the second three are for operation of Datafax. The seventh file, DATAFAX.DATA, is created by you and contains the text to be stored in the knowledge base; it is usually stored on a separate diskette in a second drive.

Datafax is operated via a hierarchically structured, menu-driven command tree with several levels:

1. Module selection
2. System commands
3. Search criteria
4. Folder operation
5. Text editing

Each level in the command structure is nested within the one just previous to it and is accessible by one or more of the commands at the higher level.

At the first level of the command structure are the module selections. The various commands at this level allow you to execute operations that affect entire diskettes of programs or data. These commands, displayed in a menu, include:

S(etup) a new database

O(pen) an existing database

B(ackup) a diskette

F(ormat) or erase a diskette

C(onfigure) a system

T(ranslate) text files

S(etup), B(ackup), F(ormat), C(onfigure), and T(ranslate) are self-contained modules and do not lead to lower command levels. These are used to set up your system, files, and diskettes prior to actually entering text into a knowledge base constructed with Datafax. These various commands allow you, respectively, to define the physical constraints of your knowledge base, copy the contents of a knowledge base from one diskette to another, format or erase a diskette for operation under the P-SYSTEM, adapt the Datafax program to the various pieces of hardware in your com-

puter, and translate text files created by word processors operating under
PC-DOS/MS-DOS or CP/M into the P-SYSTEM format and back.

O(pen), on the other hand, leads to the second level of the Datafax
command structure, the system command level. At this level, you are
directed to open one of the following functions listed in a command line
at the top of the display:

```
N(ew), E(xamine), S(can), P(rint), D(elete),
U(nload), L(oad), K(eys), A(utokey), F(ile), and
Q(uit)
```

The last five system commands, Load, Keys, Autokey, File, and Quit,
are self-contained, and do not lead to lower command levels. Examine,
Scan, Print, Delete, and Unload, on the other hand, lead to the third and
fourth levels (search criteria and folder operation).

At the third level, you specify the search criteria you want to use in the
retrieval of specific folders or sets of folders through the use of keywords.
Search criteria available at this level include:

```
Keyword, And, Or, Range, Sort, All, Last, and
Wildcard
```

The commands available at the fourth level:

```
E(dit), D(elete), P(rint), C(opy), and N(ext)
```

allow you to modify or alter the condition of a particular folder or folders.
The lowest level in the Datafax command tree is the Editor mode. This
level is accessed in one of two ways: (1) via the New command at the system command level, if you are entering text in a new folder, or (2) via the
Edit command at the folder level if you're modifying text in an existing
folder. With the Datafax Editor you can enter and delete text in various
folders or in their associated keywords lists.

No matter where you are in Datafax, it is possible to back out of a
particular command at any level and climb the command tree to previous
levels by pressing the Escape key in response to a prompt or question. The
same key can be used to cancel almost every command you select, returning
you to higher levels along the same path used to get to a lower level in the
first place.

Creating a Knowledge Base with Datafax

Creating a knowledge base (kbase) with Datafax is a five-step process: (1) defining your kbase structure, (2) opening a kbase file, (3) entering text into a folder, (4) selecting keywords that uniquely identify the function of the folder, and (5) selecting keywords from the text, both general and specific, that can be used to retrieve pertinent information from any part of the kbase regardless of the folder in which it is contained.

Setting Up Your Knowledge Base

To make searches as fast as possible, Datafax requires that each kbase diskette be configured according to a specific format. This is done via the S(etup) command from the Module Selection Menu, which asks you the unit or drive number on which your kbase will be stored and the size of the kbase in blocks. In Datafax, a block is 521 bytes in length. The largest kbase that can be created on a standard single-sided disk drive under the UCSD P-SYSTEM is 199,680 bytes (390 $\times$ 512). So if you're using a single-sided diskette, you should enter 390 blocks as the size of your kbase. For a double-sided diskette, the largest kbase is 790 blocks. For hard disks, even higher capacities are possible. However, regardless of media, the upper limit on any particular Datafax kbase is 2047 blocks (about 1 megabyte).

Opening a File

If the S(etup) operation is successful, Datafax will redisplay the Module Selection Menu. In order to access this or any other existing Datafax kbase, the program needs to know where to find it and verify its existence. This is done by selecting the O(pen) command from the Module Selection Menu. In response, Datafax requests that you enter the drive or unit number on which the diskette containing the kbase will reside. Once this has been done, Datafax will attempt to open a file on the kbase previously created using the S(etup) command. If this is successful, the CRT will clear and the second-level system commands will be displayed at the top of the screen.

Entering Text into a Folder

To enter new information into a Datafax kbase, all that is necessary is to select the N(ew) option from the system command line. A new line then appears at the top of the screen telling you that Datafax is now in the Editor mode.

The Datafax Editor incorporates many of the features of a standard stand-alone word-processing program. Cursor commands using control characters allow you to move the cursor around the screen. Editing commands, also using control characters, allow you to insert and delete characters and lines. Other commands allow you to insert, copy, and delete screens/pages and generally modify and alter the contents of a folder, as well as move back and forth through the screens/pages in a folder. In addition to these commands, there are commands to reprint a screen that is being displayed.

Entering External Text Files

To get the fullest use possible out of any knowledge-processing program, there must be some means of converting your existing text files into a compatible format. With Datafax, this is done by using the T(ranslate) module from the first level of commands to convert your DOS-compatible word-processing files into P-SYSTEM–compatible files and then use the L(oad) command available on the second level to enter the text into a specific Datafax kbase.

Before translation, each text file must be formatted to conform with certain rules. Each file must begin with a delimiter character, one that is not used for any other purpose in the file. Usually this is either the asterisk or the reverse oblique stroke(/). On the line following the delimiter, one keyword *must* appear that is no more than 28 characters long. Other keywords can be listed, each on its own line. The keyword or keywords are then followed by another delimiter. After the second delimiter, there can be up to 6120 lines of text, with each line up to 80 characters long. If a file is longer than the 6120-line Datafax folder limit, it can be structured into two separate folders as shown in Screen 1.

Modifying a Folder

To modify an existing folder in your kbase, the same page editor is used. But to gain access to a particular folder, it is necessary to use the

```
/
KEYWORD ONE
KEYWORD TWO
/
TEXTTEXTTEXTTEXTTEXTTEXTTEXTTEXTTEXTTEXTTEXT
TEXTTEXTTEXTTEXTTEXTTEXTTEXTTEXTTEXTTEXTTEXT
TEXTTEXTTEXTTEXTTEXTTEXTTEXTTEXTTEXTTEXTTEXT
TEXTTEXTTEXTTEXTTEXTTEXTTEXTTEXTTEXTTEXTTEXT
/
KEYWORD ONE
KEYWORD TWO
/
TEXTTEXTTEXTTEXTTEXTTEXTTEXTTEXTTEXTTEXTTEXT
TEXTTEXTTEXTTEXTTEXTTEXTTEXTTEXTTEXTTEXTTEXT
TEXTTEXTTEXTTEXTTEXTTEXTTEXTTEXTTEXTTEXTTEXT
TEXTTEXTTEXTTEXTTEXTTEXTTEXTTEXTTEXTTEXTTEXT
/
```

Screen 1

Examine or Scan command from the System Command Menu to search for
the appropriate folder. Once in the folder level, Datafax will display the
following functions at the bottom of the screen:

`E(dit), D(elete), P(rint), C(opy), N(ext)`

Selecting the Edit function opens the folder that has been selected and acti-
vates the Datafax page editor.

Entering Keywords into Your Knowledge Base

Once text has been entered into Datafax, it may be saved to disk, no
matter whether it is one word, one line, or a full screen/page of text. Datafax will not save the text unless at least one keyword has been entered that
can be associated with that particular screen/page. Datafax allows you to
enter keywords into your kbase in one of three ways.

The first and most direct way is to enter keywords while you are using
the page editor. Whenever you come across a word that you feel should
be saved as a keyword, simply place the cursor over that word and execute
the Mark key function (Control X).

The second way is to invoke the Key Function Menu, which gives you the option of entering or deleting keywords that are not necessarily mentioned in the text. You are then given the following choices:

```
Keys: A(dd), R(emove), F(orward), B(ack):
```

In addition, the page display is replaced by a list of keywords associated with the folder.

The Add key function allows you to add keywords that do not appear in the page text of a folder or that include characters that are not legally part of a word, as with two-word keywords. When this function has been invoked, Datafax asks for the keyword you want to add. You can then enter any keyword you want, providing it does not exceed 28 characters in length. If there are more than 20 keywords associated with a folder, a specific word may not be on the display. The Forward and Back key functions allow you to move back and forth alphabetically in the keyword listing. When the Remove key function is invoked, different actions are taken depending on whether there is only one keyword associated with a folder or two or more keywords. When there is just one, the keyword is removed automatically. When there are more than one, Datafax asks you to select the keyword to be removed.

The third way to enter keywords is via the Autokeys command, which is executed via the second- or system-command–level menu. When it is selected, Datafax displays an Autokeys Menu:

```
Autokeys: C(lear), A(dd), R(emove), F(orward),
B(ack):
```

This menu allows you to establish a set of keywords that are to be applied automatically to any new folders entered into the kbase. The Add key function allows you to enter any valid keyword up to 28 characters long, the Clear key function removes all keywords in the Autokey list, and the Remove key function permits the removal of a single Autokey from the list without clearing the entire list.

Using Keywords to Structure a Knowledge Base

The efficiency with which you can search a kbase using Datafax depends largely on how well you structure it beforehand. If you want to take full advantage of this program's sophisticated command structure, it is extremely important that you give a great deal of thought to the keywords you assign the various folders and pages.

The method I find most comfortable is to separate the keywords I use into four broad types: (1) functional keywords that are unique to a folder, are independent of the content, and specify the general category of information contained; (2) keywords that reflect the information contained in the text, but that are general enough to apply across all folders; (3) keywords that reflect the textual information, but that are general enough to apply across all pages only in a specific folder type; and (4) keywords that are specific to the information contained on a specific page or set of pages in a folder. In addition, depending on the general category, it is possible for each page within a folder to have a specific structure.

In a Datafax kbase, these functional keys would be inserted using the Add key command from the Key Function Menu. The second category of keywords, applicable across all folders, is inserted using the Add key command from the Autokey Menu. The latter two categories are added using the Mark key function while entering text into the kbase with the page editor.

For example, suppose you are a serious *Dr. Who* fan interested in all aspects of this worldwide science fiction subculture. The set of keywords you would use in the Dr. Who knowledge base would describe particular types of entries and separate the textual information into several broad categories:

EPISODES	Contains abstracts of each *Dr. Who* episode.
WHICHWHO	Contains information on the various actors who have played Dr. Who during the show's long history.
WITHWHO	Contains information on the various Dr. Who companions and the actors and actresses playing them.
WHOTHEORY	Contains information on the theory of time travel.
WHOTECH	Contains information on the future technology used by Dr. Who.

ENEMIES   Contains information on Dr. Who's
                           enemies and the actors and actresses who
                           play them.

Other categorical keywords with which you could structure the information in the Dr. Who kbase might include Writers, Directors, Designers,
Producers, and Script Editors.

The pages in each of these broad categories would each have a different
structure. The pages in the Episodes folder, for example, would have a
traditional bibliographic structure with episode title, author, director,
actors, and date, followed by a brief abstract of the episode.

General keywords that would be applicable across all entries would
include TARDIS, DR. WHO, and TIME LORDS. Keywords applicable
to particular folders would depend on the category type. For the ENE-
MIES folder, this would include such keywords as THE MASTER, DAL-
EKS, CYBERMEN, and so on. Keywords that are specific to a page or set
of pages depend on the particular episode, character, actor, or other functional subcategory you are writing about.

Searching a Datafax Knowledge Base

Of all the free-form knowledge-processing programs discussed in this
book, Datafax probably has the widest array of search alternatives. They
include:

Single Word–Single Key: The simplest of all search criteria under Datafax, this is a simple matching operation, comparing the search string to
all the keywords entered in a keyword table created by Datafax. It is
the fastest of all of the search alternatives. For a kbase with about 1000
different keywords, Datafax only requires four read operations to find
the folders you want. For example, entering the keyword DALEK
would retrieve all entries, regardless of category type, that relate to
DALEK.

Multiple Word–Single Key: This method allows you to search for mul-
tiword key phrases entered into the kbase using the Key function
command.

Boolean Searches: These use the AND/OR functions to link two or more keywords. For example, in the Dr. Who kbase, "EPISODES and THE MASTER and DALEKS" would select only those entries under the EPISODES category that contain mention of both of these arch-enemies of Dr. Who. On the other hand, "EPISODES and THE MASTER or DALEKS" would broaden the search, directing selection of all episodes with not only both together, but each individually.

In addition to these search options, Datafax offers the following:

Wildcard: As a result of entering a keyword followed by an equals sign (such as DALEKS =), all folders containing a keyword starting with the indicated characters are retrieved.

Range: This option retrieves all folders containing a keyword within a specified range, such as all those beginning with the letters A through D.

Last: Used in place of a keyword, Last allows you to call up the search sequence for the previous search conducted. In this way you can repeat your last search or widen or narrow its scope without having to retype the keywords.

All: This option causes all the folders in the kbase to be selected. Unlike the other searches, this one actually proceeds through the text pages of the kbase rather than following a keyword path. It is particularly useful in recovering a kbase that has been partially destroyed, since it will retrieve any valid text page it finds.

Sort: This option allows you to order a group of folders over a range of keywords.

Once you have defined your search criteria, you can then search through your kbase, using Scan to quickly skim through the folders that have been located and then using Examine to perform a more relaxed survey.

Scanning Your Selections

After you have entered your search sequence in response to the Scan command prompt, Datafax searches through the kbase. Once it has found one or more folders that satisfy the criteria, the program displays the first line of each folder that meets the selection criteria, with up to 24 lines per screen/page, along with the following subcommand menu:

```
Scan: E(dit), D(elete), P(rint), C(opy), M(ore)
```

Selecting the Edit command opens the folder whose first line is being displayed. Delete allows you to delete folders. Print allows you to print the contents of a folder. Copy causes a new folder to be created with text identical to the folder being copied. If More is selected, Scan will display the next set of up to 21 folder lines. If any of the other subcommands are selected, Datafax will ask which folder you want. At this point you should respond with one of the menu letters on the screen in front of each folder line, which range from A through U.

Examining Your Selections

Although the Examine command is quite similar to Scan, there are substantial differences in the ways the two are used. The Examine command is used to browse through the folders in a knowledge base, editing, deleting, copying, or printing each folder. Once the search set has been established and one or more folders have been located, Examine displays the first page of the first folder found, along with the following subcommand menu:

```
[1 of nn folders] E(dit), D(elete), P(rint), C(opy),
N(ext)
```

The numbers in brackets in the prompt line indicate which folder is being viewed out of the total number of folders in the search set. The commands operate in much the same way, except that More is replaced by Next, which will cause the display of the first page of the next folder.

Retrieving Text with Datafax

The contents of your kbase are of little use, except as a reference library, unless you can retrieve text and send it to a selected output, such as a printer, the display, or another file. Datafax provides a number of different ways to do this.

One alternative is to use the Print command at the folder level to print out the folder that is currently being displayed on the screen. This alternative has a number of limitations. First of all, if you have a number of folders you want to print out, it is necessary to move sequentially through your kbase at the folder level, printing out the selected folders. Second, more often than not the results of a search are not useful in and of themselves and need to be incorporated into an external file for generation of a final report with a word processor. The Print command at the folder level does not allow you to send folders to an external file. Third, what you see is what you get; that is, the printout is an exact duplicate of the contents of the folder. There is no way to reformat the contents. Fourth, this alternative requires that the program diskette be online during execution.

To get around these limitations, Datafax also provides a more sophisticated Print command available at the second, or system, level of the command tree. Selection of this command produces the following query:

Print: M(odify options), S(elect folders)

If you choose to modify the printing options, Datafax will present you with the following choices with preset default values, all of which you can modify:

```
A) Print keys                   No
B) First line of folder         1
C) Last line of folder          All
D) Number of pages per folder   All
E) Print folder separators      Yes
F) Print page separators        Yes
G) Blank lines between pages     0
H) Blank lines between folders   0
I) Form feed between folders    No
J) Print file                   Printer:
```

In addition to allowing you to format the Datafax folders for output to a printer, this option allows you to not only direct the folder to a separate external file but select which portions of a folder to send to an output device.

As used by a writer, a kbase is an information resource to be used in the writing of a specific document. Selecting the J option allows you to redirect the output to a file of your choosing.

Selecting Folders

Choosing the S(elect folders) option results in a prompt line that requests that you enter the keyword criteria for the folders you want to print out or send to an external file. The method by which the keywords are selected is identical to the method used with the Examine and Scan commands. Indeed, before using this option, good search strategy dictates that you use Examine and Scan to find the folder you want and use the same keyword sequence to select the appropriate folders for printout.

If a set of folders meeting the criteria is found, Datafax will report the number of folders found and ask if you wish to review the folders before printing. This review option allows you to view the first page of each folder prior to printout. This option, in effect, allows you to determine the final selection criterion by accepting or rejecting any given folder.

Selecting Pages and Lines

Seldom is it necessary or useful to print the entire contents of a folder. Often all you want is a few lines, a few paragraphs, or a few pages. The normal default value for this option is All. Entering any number up to 254 (the upper page limit for each folder) directs Datafax to print out each folder up to the page number specified. More flexible are options B and C, which direct Datafax to output that portion of a folder between any two lines. The highest meaningful last line number (C) is 6120 (255 pages × 24 lines). The first line number can be any number up to 6119.

Translating Files

Unless you're using a UCSD P-SYSTEM compatible text editor or word processor, the external files you've created will not be in a form useful to you. The T(ranslate) module available on the first level of the Datafax command tree allows you to take a Datafax-generated external file and convert it into a format compatible with any DOS (IBM, MS, or Apple) program, which includes most commonly used word processors.

Comments and Evaluation

Datafax in many ways represents the middle ground between the relatively open programs, such as SUPERFILE and SYSTEM-ONE, which are designed to organize files generated by a word processor into a kbase, and the relatively structured, closed format required by NOTEBOOK.

Like NOTEBOOK, Datafax is a closed system, incorporating a text editor to enter information into a kbase. Where it differs is in the sophistication of the Editor, which approaches stand-alone programs in its ease of use, and in the fact that it places few limits on the structure or length of the text entries.

Although it is possible to convert external files into the Datafax format, this is not a program to be used to convert your existing text files into a kbase. For that, programs such as SUPERFILE and SYSTEM-ONE are more suitable. For most of the other knowledge-processing functions outlined in Chapter 1 (except for outline editing and processing), this program is more than adequate.

Where Datafax outshines the other free-form knowledge-processing programs in this section is in the sophistication of its keyword selection structure and in the variety of keyword search methods available. Its one limitation in this area is the lack of a NOT function, which function makes it possible to exclude particular pages or folders. On balance, however, this is not a major limitation.

CHAPTER 8

Sci-Mate

The Researcher's Assistant

Sci-Mate is a general-purpose knowledge-processing program with a card-file format specifically designed to aid the professional researcher. Designed by a major vendor of online database services, the Institute for Scientific Information (ISI), it is a powerful text and document storage and retrieval system in the hands of writing professionals who make extensive use of online databases for their research.

Sci-Mate is divided into two major components. One is the *Universal Online Searcher* (UOS), which incorporates several standardized bibliographic/abstract template interfaces to simplify and automate the process of accessing, searching, and downloading research information from an online database to personal computers. The second component is the *Personal Data Manager* (PDM), which makes it possible to create electronic index files for the storage of bibliographic information and abstracts generated by the program's built-in text editor, external files created by your word processor, and information downloaded from online databases with the Searcher.

What makes Sci-Mate unique among the general-purpose, free-form knowledge-processing programs surveyed in this section is that although it is designed with a card-file format, it does not limit the amount of text you can enter. When you come to the end of a card, the program automatically stores the first card and displays another blank card. This continues for as long as you want. And when you retrieve one card, the others are called up also.

UOS is designed to operate both as a companion program to the PDM module and on a stand-alone basis. It provides an easy, standard search interface to many of the large online databases that serve the research community, capturing records and transferring them to personal files in a PDM knowledge base work file. As opposed to dialing up each online host computer separately, the UOS provides one simple way of connecting to all the various systems. The program provides three ways of searching commercial databases.

Sci-Mate Search Mode: In this mode, the program presents you with menus and prompts for all your search requests and then automatically translates your responses into the language of the system you are searching. This interface allows you to use powerful search techniques without training in the search languages. It does require, however, that you have an understanding of the basic content, scope, and structure of the database you are searching. It is designed to allow you to access any of ISI's databases, including ISI/BIOMED, ISI/COMPUMATH, ISI/GEOSCITECH, SCISEARCH, and SOCIAL SCISEARCH, which together provide coverage of over 16,000 professional journals.

Native Search Mode: In this mode, you communicate directly with the search system of the database, using the language of the search system, without Sci-Mate aid or intervention. It requires that you have training and/or documentation from the online service you choose as well as database knowledge. It is designed for use with four of the largest database services—DIALOG, NLM, BRS, and ORBIT—which together provide access to over 250 unique databases.

Passive Terminal Mode: This mode turns your personal computer into a terminal with access to any online system for which you have the password. Once you are connected, it is equivalent to the Native Search mode. It is to be used for online services other than ISI, BRS, DIALOG, NLM, and ORBIT—for instance, the Dow Jones News Retrieval Service, The Source, CompuServe, and the NIH/EPA databases.

In the first two modes, Sci-Mate automatically connects and disconnects you from the host system. In the Passive mode, however, none of the interconnection is automated or prompted. You must dial the appropriate data communications phone numbers, respond to network and online service requests, provide passwords on request, and log-off. In all three modes, you can transfer the record from an online database search to a work file with the PDM software.

Sci-Mate Overview

Sci-Mate is designed to operate under either the 8-bit CP/M 2.2 or the 16-bit CP/M-86 operating systems and is also available in customized versions for the Apple IIplus, Apple IIe, IBM PC, Kaypro 4 and 10, TRS-80 II/II12, Vector 3 and 4, and any Z80-based computer. A minimum of two disk drives is needed, but a hard disk is recommended.

In addition to the UOS and PDM programs and two other programs (TEMPLATE.DAT and TNAMEFIL.DAT) that are used to control the templating of user files, a complete Sci-Mate system consists of the following types of files:

User Files: There are up to 64 per knowledge base, each of which stores text information of a particular type or in a particular format.

Index Files: There are up to 64 per knowledge base, which contain the keywords and pointers to the record locations in the user files.

Report Files: Short files of which there can be almost any number, and which contain the format instructions for the various types of columnar reports you may wish to generate from information in the user file records for printout.

Strategy Files: Short files of which there can also be almost any number, and which contain saved search strategies used in scanning your own files and online databases.

Template Files: There are two per knowledge base, which contain the blank forms for up to 50 different types of card-file templates, six of which are supplied with the program.

Work Files: There are two per knowledge base, which are used as temporary storage areas for records from online databases, records from word-processing and database management programs, records transmitted from other computer users, and records from other knowledge base–processing programs.

Help Files: Supplied with the distribution but are not needed online for the operation of the program, and which can be deleted or stored on a backup disk once you have learned to operate the system.

On a personal computer with two floppy-disk drives, it is a good idea to store as many of the system programs as possible on your system drive, which is normally drive A. However, they can be assigned as a group to any drive. The only system programs and files you need on the system drive are the customized portions of both UOS and PDM (CUS-TOM.CUS, CUSACC.CUS, and STATUS.DAT) and the customized version of the utility programs—in total no more than 80–90K bytes or so. This will leave you with more than enough room on the system drive disk for storage of temporary files created by the system during normal operation as well as the template and strategy files. If you have limited disk capacity, you should separate the UOS and the PDM, place them on separate system disks, and transfer downloaded files from one to the other using one of your operating system utilities. This leaves as much room as possible on the actual text storage diskette for Sci-Mate records.

The number of records you can store in a user file depends on the capacity of your disks, the number of user files per disk, and the size of your Sci-Mate records, which can vary from 102 to 1894 bytes or characters of text. If your floppy disks have a capacity of about 130–190K bytes, you can store between 690 and 1013 short records and 60 to 98 long records. For an average 400K disk, the number of records ranges from 2130 short to 206 long. On a standard 5-megabyte (5M) hard disk, the number of records ranges from 26,667 short to 2581 long. The maximum number of Sci-Mate records per user file, however, can never exceed 32,768. The user file space available per diskette can also vary according to the amount of space you wish to allocate to work-file space. Usually, I try to set aside about one-quarter of my disk capacity as work-file space.

Creating a Knowledge Base with Sci-Mate

In a knowledge base created with Sci-Mate's PDM program, you can store up to 64 user files for keeping different types of information. Each user file consists of records, and each record is divided into fields of information. When a record is created or transferred into a user file, it is provided with fields according to the template used to prepare them. Records that describe one type of textual information are structured with the same template, such as a Reprint template for a collection of reprint articles. The information contained in the knowledge base can then be printed out or displayed either in the record format or in the form of lists of selected information from the records stored in any user file.

A Sci-Mate PDM knowledge base is operated through a series of four or five standard menus. Once you've inserted the Sci-Mate system and data disks in their appropriate drives and have called up the program by entering the command "SCIMATE," you are presented with the main port of entry into the system, the Main Sci-Mate Menu, which presents you with the following options:

```
(1) Enter the Universal Online Searcher
(2) Enter the Personal Data Manager
(3) Enter or change today's date
(4) Receive instructions on the use of Sci-Mate
(5) Leave the Sci-Mate system
```

Creating a User File

Sci-Mate knowledge bases are created and accessed via the PDM program, which is accessed by selecting option 2 from the Main Sci-Mate Menu.

When you enter PDM for the first time, your knowledge base will be blank until you create some user files. The program will ask you if you want to create one. If you do, it will prompt you to enter a name for the new file, which can be up to eight characters in length. Once you have done this, the Main PDM Menu will appear on the screen:

```
(1) Search the user file
(2) Enter a new record
(3) Display/copy work-file records
(4) Select/create another user file
(5) Create and update templates
(6) Generate document request status report
(7) Generate columnar report
(8) Return to Sci-Mate Menu
```

Once you've opened up your knowledge base, this menu will appear immediately after you enter the SCIMATE command. Thereafter you can create additional user files by selecting option 4 from the PDM Menu.

Creating Record Templates

Once you've created a user file, you need to give it some structure. This is done by creating some record templates for it by selecting PDM Menu option 5. This causes the program to display the Main Template Menu, which will give you a choice of the following:

```
(1)  Display an existing template
(2)  Change an existing template
(3)  Add a template to the file
(4)  Delete a template from the file
(5)  Copy an existing template
(6)  Return to the Sci-Mate Menu
```

The first step in creating a template is to review the templates supplied with the program by selecting option 1 from the Template Menu; the program will respond by displaying the names of the templates already in the system and asking which one you want to see. Depending on which template you choose, the program will display the appropriate filled-in template definition form.

After surveying the various templates already in existence, you can create a new template in one of three ways with this program: copying an existing template (Template Menu option 5), changing an existing template (option 2), or adding a new template to the file (option 3). In each case, a template definition form is displayed—blank or filled in, as is appropriate—by the program, asking you whether you want to

1. Add more fields
2. Insert a field
3. Change a field
4. Delete a field
5. Add the template to the file

In the case of a new template, you are asked to enter the template name and its source. Once the form has been changed, copied, or created, you select Definition Form option 5, which adds the new template to the existing ones. In the case of copying or changing, you are also asked to change the template name and source before adding it to the template file.

With Sci-Mate, you can have up to 50 different types of templates per knowledge base, 48 of which you can create. The program is delivered with 6 templates already created (numbers 1 through 6). The first two are related to ISI's UOS program and cannot be deleted. Template 1, called ISI, is designed for use with UOS and is used for formatting records from all ISI databases. Template 2 is called Report Flags and is used to name flags for status reports on records in your files. Templates 3 through 6 are included as examples.

All templates to be used in your Sci-Mate are configured by filling in a template definition form. If you are building a knowledge base of information about microprocessors based on template 3, the template definition form would look something like this:

```
Display Template 7       Name: Micro       Source: BC
_____

Field      Name        Code     Field     Name      Code
- - -       - -         - -       - -       - -       - -

1          TITLE        TI       11
2          AUTHOR       AU       12
3          JOURNAL      JR       13
4          DATE         DT       14
5          KEYWORDS     KY       15
6          ABSTRACT     AB       16
7                                17
8                                18
9                                19
10                               20
```

A blank card based on template 7 would look something like this:

```
NEW RECORD AN-11:

TITLE:
AUTHOR:
```

```
JOURNAL:
DATE:
KEYWORDS:
ABSTRACT:
```

As shown, each template consists of the following elements:

1. The name of the template (MICRO), which can be up to 20 characters long and describes the type of template.

2. The template number (7), which must be provided when the program asks you to identify a template.

3. The source code, an optional one- or two-character code used to indicate the source of the template (BC)—this can be the initials of the person creating it or, say, the online database from which the information to be stored is derived.

4. The field names, up to eight characters long, one for each of the up to 20 fields in each template.

5. The field code numbers, one- or two- character codes used in creating templates for offloading from specific online databases.

Entering Text into a Sci-Mate Knowledge Base

Now that you've given your PDM files a structure, you are ready to type in records to create the actual text files. This is done by selecting option 2 from the Main PDM Menu (enter a new record). The first screen that appears will ask you to specify the source of the data and the template number you want to use as a structure for your text entries. If you wish to enter an unformatted record, just hit Return. In either case, a blank template will appear on the screen displaying an accession number (AN-11 in the above screen, for example) assigned by the program to the record to be entered. After each record you enter, you must type Control S to save the record in the file. To stop entering files and return to the Main Sci-Mate Menu, wait for the next blank record to appear and hit Escape.

Despite its card-file–like format, Sci-Mate does not limit the amount of text you can enter into a file, although it does place limits on the amount that can be entered onto one record—1894 characters. If your record is particularly long—say, a lengthy abstract or a long record from an external file—Sci-Mate can link records and make them appear as if they were one record. It does this by assigning two or more accession numbers to the material to be entered and creating two or more records that it links together automatically. When you search a file, the record in which a "hit" occurs is displayed, with a note at the top if there is a preceding link and a note at the bottom if there is a following link. The only time you are aware that the program has split a very long "record" into two records is when you are approaching the end of the 1894-character limit. At that time, it displays a message telling you that there is a space for 100 more characters and that if you want to continue the record you must press Control N. If you continue to add more text to the record, Sci-Mate will count down the characters left. If you don't hit the Control N before the end, Sci-Mate will lock the system, after which no more characters can be entered. If you want to enter more text, type a Control N at some convenient breaking point before the end of the countdown, saving the record and bringing a new blank record to the screen. The new record will have the same field names as the previous record.

Copying In Word Processor Text Files

Copying external text files generated by a word processor into a Sci-Mate file is a relatively straight-forward process. First, you must create a word processor template according to the rules outlined earlier for other templates. Second, you must reformat the text files with your word processor using the Sci-Mate delimiters and record headers and assigning appropriate field names at the beginning of each file.

The record header consists of three parts, with the first part required and the others optional: (1) four asterisks, marking the beginning of every record—if they are not included, Sci-Mate will not recognize a new record, but will view it as a part of the previous record; (2) the two-character source code; and (3) the template name. The possible record headers are:

```
****
****source
****template name
****source/template name
```

It is necessary to assign a field code to mark the beginning of each field in a record to be formatted and incorporated into a Sci-Mate file. In the word processor record, a field code consists of two capital letters followed by a space; it is entered as part of the text. Such field codes begin the first line of every field. Any text line not beginning with a field code starts with three spaces. An example of one such record is as follows:

```
AU author name
TI title of article
JR title of magazine or journal
DT date of article in journal
KY keywords that describe content
AB first line of abstract field
   second line of abstract field
   nth line of abstract field
```

If you enter a record longer than 1894 characters, the program will automatically convert the oversized record into multiple linked records.

Once properly formatted, the text file is saved and renamed WORK-TEXT.DAT. You then enter PDM and select option 3 (display/copy work-file records) from the Main PDM Menu. The program then processes WORKTEXT.DAT, creating a formatted file named WORK-SCIM.DAT, after which it erases the original WORKTEXT.DAT. After the text file has been processed, the Workfile Menu appears:

```
(1) Copy the work file to the user file
(2) Display the work file
(3) Sort the work file
(4) Erase the work file
(5) Create a text file
(6) Return to main Sci-Mate Menu
```

From this menu, you select option 1 to copy the work file into the user file.

Copying In Online Files

The procedure you use to copy in records from an external online database depends on whether or not you have the UOS package. If you don't, it is necessary to reformat the records according to the procedures outlined for word processor text files. If you have the UOS and records captured from an online database using one of its search interfaces, the process is somewhat more automated. If you have been searching an ISI online database, Sci-Mate will automatically format ISI records or records with field labels according to templates created and stored in the PDM. If you've been searching other than an ISI database, you must either create a record template that matches the database format or reformat the database records into a form that matches one of the templates already stored in the PDM knowledge base before you copy the records into a user file.

Searching a Sci-Mate Knowledge Base

To search a file in your Sci-Mate knowledge base, select option 1 from the Main PDM Menu (search the user file). The resulting display presents you with three search options:

```
(1) Search by accession number
(2) Search text: find total hits before display
(3) Search text: display hits as retrieved
```

Searching by Accession Number

The most direct way of searching through a Sci-Mate knowledge base is by accession number, the unique ID assigned to each record when it is entered into a file. It is most useful for updating and editing an entire file of records.

Once you've chosen an accession number search, the next screen prompts you to enter the number of the record you want to retrieve. It will respond with a display of that record.

Although the content is identical to that seen when entering text, the accession search record display has different header information at the top of the screen. Specifically, it tells you that you have done an accession number search in the current user file for a specific Sci-Mate record number. It also tells you when the record number was entered into the file, the source, and the template type by the number that was used as the record format. Also at the top of the screen is a set of commands that allow you to modify, manipulate, and move back and forth through various records in a file. These include:

N(ext)	Enters the number for the next record you want to locate and display.
P(rint)	Prints the displayed record.
E(dit)	Calls up the text editor to allow you to modify the displayed record.
D(elete file)	Permanently deletes the displayed record from the user file.
S(top)	Returns you to the Main Search Menu.
Control N	Displays the next screen on a multiscreen record.
Control B	Goes back and displays previous screen of a multiscreen record.

Searching by Keyword

To search the file on the basis of the content of the text, you can use either of the two other options in the Search Menu. The basic difference between the two is that option 2 allows you to decide on the basis of the number of hits whether you want to continue searching using your present search sequence.

When you choose to search by keyword by selecting either option 2 or option 3 from the Search Menu, the program will ask you to enter your search statement. Sci-Mate will then look for all records to which the search statement applies. After its search of the file is completed, the program will display the number of records searched and the number of records retrieved in the Search Menu, giving you these choices:

```
(1) Display and edit hits
(2) Sort hits
(3) Copy hits to work file
(4) Generate a columnar report for the hits
(5) Begin a new search
(6) Return to the main Search Menu
```

Sci-Mate saves the retrieved records, or hits, in a subfile from which you can display, sort, copy, or generate a report from your most recent search until you enter a new search statement.

If you select option 1, the first record will appear on the screen with a set of commands identical in most respects to the set for the search by accession number, with the following differences:

N(ext)	Displays the next hit.
B(ack)	Displays the previous hit.
deL(ete hit)	Deletes the displayed record from the hit list, but not from the user file.

The search statements can perform any combination of the following tasks:

- Display every record—achieved by entering a null entry (just hit Return).
- Find any single word or phrase up to 255 characters long.
- Find any partial word.
- Find any number of words or phrases, full or partial, linked by AND, as long as the total search string does not exceed 255 characters.
- Find up to four words or phrases linked by OR, as long as the total does not exceed 255 characters.
- Find upper- or lower-case characters.

In searching for partial words, it is necessary to use a truncation symbol (#) at the end of any character string. A # symbol preceding a string allows a blank space or any number of characters in front of the string to be retrieved in addition to the partial word or phrase sequence. When embedded within a string, it can replace any character in the string.

Sorting Records

By selecting option 2 from the Search Menu, you can sort the set of retrieved records by any of the fields you have defined in the record template, including author name, source, and title, to name a few. When you select this option, the program will display a list of the templates that can be used for sorting the hits.

After selecting from this list the template used to format the records you now want sorted, Sci-Mate will ask you if you want a template override, which is meant for files containing records created by more than one template. Choosing this option means that all records in the user file will be sorted according to the fields in the template specified. Care must be taken with this override, since Sci-Mate actually sorts according to field position rather than by name. Thus, if you select a template to search according to author, and this is in position 2, all records will be sorted by position 2, even though in some templates the author field may have been in, say, position 3. If you choose not to override the template, only those records formatted with the selected template will be sorted on the selected field or fields.

In either case, once you've selected a template number, Sci-Mate displays a list of the field names for that template and asks you to specify two fields to sort by—primary and secondary. Sci-Mate first sorts all records on the basis of the contents of the primary sort field. If two or more records have matching data in this field, such as two articles by the same author, a secondary sort field is used to determine the order of these matching records.

Once the sort is completed, the Search Menu will appear and you will be able to select options to display and/or print the sorted records.

Retrieving Text from a Sci-Mate Knowledge Base

With Sci-Mate there are three ways to retrieve text from a knowledge base of text. You can use (1) the P(rint) command at the top of each record display, (2) option 3 from the Search Menu, or (3) option 5 from the Workfile Menu.

With the P(rint) command, it is only possible to print one record at a time when you are in the user file; in other words, you must first display a record and then enter to print it. With a large set of records, this is an arduous process.

Via option 3 from the Search Menu, you can copy the entire set of records that meet the requirements to the work file. Once in the work file, you can, by selecting Workfile Menu option 2, display the records one at a time or display and print all of the records.

Creating a Text File

The same set of records can also be incorporated into a text file compatible with a word processor by using option 5 from the Workfile Menu.

Sci-Mate records are stored differently in the user than in the work files. In the former, they are stored as individual records and, if templated, with field separators. In the work file, they are stored as a continuous stream of ASCII characters, where records are delimited either by a special character string consisting of four asterisks ****, or by a convention established by the host—usually a blank line followed by a record number.

The work file can be converted to standard text either by using a word processor to remove the various special delimiting characters or by using option 5 from the Workfile Menu. Sci-Mate removes all of the special characters automatically and then places the records into a file called "filename.EXT," where the filename is the one you have given the file and .EXT is the extension. This file is accessible as an ASCII file and can be used by any word-processing program that accepts such files.

Comments and Evaluation

The "fast track" description of Sci-Mate included here is only a brief and partial description of all of the options available with this program.

Compared to the other general-purpose, free-form knowledge-processing programs discussed in this section, Sci-Mate offers you the widest range of alternatives for generating, manipulating, and accessing both your own text files and files generated by online databases.

In exchange for this abundance of riches, Sci-Mate requires a somewhat more complex operating procedure, as the numerous menus indicate. However, the effort required is well worth it, especially if you make extensive use of online databases as part of your writing research.

Part III

GETTING DEEPER INTO KNOWLEDGE PROCESSING

CHAPTER 9

The Many Uses of a Knowledge-Processing Program

Whereas word-processing programs such as WordStar have turned the personal computer into a truly effective writing tool, the new knowledge base–processing programs such as SUPERFILE can do much more.

In my case, with more or less instant access to the knowledge base I've built up over the years in the form of documents, notes, and other text files, my personal computer has become an extension of my mind and memory. The resulting synergism has increased my productivity and creativity in a way word processing never did.

As discussed in Chapter 1, writing is more than word processing. In addition to the mechanics of writing and rewriting, the total writing process involves (1) research, (2) analysis and evaluation, and (3) organization of ideas, facts, and concepts and opinions (in short, knowledge) in a clear and organized manner. A kbase-processing program such as SUPERFILE can help you accomplish these tasks when used in the following ways:

- As a simple cross-referenced card file to aid in the organization of your paper files.
- As a means of organizing your disk-based files of articles and background material into an archival kbase for instant access.

- As an automated means of storing and then sorting the large numbers of references and citations that result from searching a computerized database such as DIALOG or BRS.

- As a quick and easy means of analyzing and comparing facts and ideas and looking for hidden patterns in the literature you've collected.

- As a fast and efficient method of "cutting and pasting" an article or document by letting the program search for, retrieve, and organize textual information.

In addition to their use as creativity- and productivity-enhancing tools at all stages of the writing process, general-purpose, free-form kbase-processing programs can serve a number of useful purposes in a variety of professional and business environments, primarily in their role as document-retrieval tools. Knowledge-processing programs can organize (1) tickler and calendar files, (2) correspondence, (3) client and customer information, (4) contracts, (5) product and parts information, and (6) contact reports, to name a few.

Organizing Your Paper Files

One of the easiest ways to get started using any kbase processor, and a way that will have an immediate benefit to the writing professional, is to start building a kbase of book and magazine references, citations, and abstracts. You can use as a starting point that jumble of clippings, scribbled notes on napkins, pages torn out of newspapers, and collection of magazines that most writers call their filing system.

In my case, the closest I've come to organizing the numerous bits and pieces into any coherent filing system is to maintain a general "In" box or file, into which I deposit various items as I come across them, regardless of the topic. Each month, or as soon as the box or file is full, I go through it and sort them as to subject, putting each pile into an appropriate drawer or box. When the drawer or box is full, that's a sign to me that the subject has reached a "critical mass," and is ready for review. I look through it, organizing the various items into separate stacks, according to subheading, which I then deposit into separate file folders. Then comes the process of analysis and collation. Once some pattern or trend begins to emerge, I then develop an outline for a magazine article or book. Let's look at how this kind of filing system can be operated using a knowledge-processing program.

Using SUPERFILE

With a kbase program such as SUPERFILE, the same basic procedures are maintained. But I've added another step. Periodically, as I sort the bits and pieces of information contained in my In box into their separate file drawers, I use my word-processing program to enter brief descriptions into a text file, using the *C, *, *K, and *E markers.

After I've gone through the information collected and created a disk file for all the references with my word processor, I then use SUPERFILE to add the new references to the kbase I've created.

For example, suppose that in the process of doing the research for an article, I collected quite a bit of information on artificial intelligence (AI) research and expert systems. A typical entry in this AI kbase using SUPERFILE would look like Screen 1.

Using SYSTEM-ONE

A similar format would be used with SYSTEM-ONE, with a tilda (˜) marker indicating the beginning of the entry and a space and another tilda indicating the beginning of the next. Instead of creating a keyword listing to be stored with the reference, each of the keywords would be added to the record in a thesaurus file containing words of similar meaning.

Using Datafax

To set up a similar kbase with Datafax, you would first open a file in the program, name it, and then access the internal editor. Using this editor, you would then enter the same information. For this entry to become "permanent" in the system, you must enter at least one keyword associated with this particular entry as well as at least one more than defines its type or *folder*. As described in Chapter 7, this can be done in one of three ways: (1) by using the Mark key function to designate a word you are entering with the editor as a keyword to be associated with that page; (2) by invoking the Key Function Menu, where you may enter a keyword (usually one that describes the type of information entered) that may not appear on the

```
*C
Wos, Larry, and Ross A. Overbeek. "AURA: A
Program that Automates Reasoning." Logos
Magazine, Argonne National Laboratory, Jan.,
1983. Pages 8 to 12.
*
This article describes computer programs that
automate reasoning and how they may make it
possible for man to carry out far more complex
reasoning tasks. A particular focus is AURA, a
program developed at Argonne and Northern
Illinois University that has helped solve open
equations in abstract algebra and formal logic.
It also describes future versions of AURA which
may someday become standard tools to aid
decision makers in all walks of life.
*K
WOS/OVERBEEK/1983/AURA/LOGOS/ARGONNE/NORTHERN
ILLINOIS/AUTOMATED REASONING/EXPERT SYSTEM/
CIRCUIT DESIGN/CHEMISTRY/ABSTRACT ALGEBRA/
REACTOR CONTROL *E
```

Screen 1

page itself, or (3) by using the Autokey to direct the program to enter a set of general keywords automatically into any entry.

Using NOTEBOOK

Of all the kbase-processing programs, NOTEBOOK is most specifically designed for this kind of application. It is highly structured and requires that you define the types of information you want to enter by field. The bibliography citation would look like Screen 2 when formatted according to NOTEBOOK requirements.

```
Author:      Wos, Larry, and Ross A. Overbeek
Title:       AURA: A Program that Automates
             Reasoning
Magazine:    Logos Magazine
Publisher:   Argonne National Laboratory
Issue Date:  Jan., 1983
Abstract:    This article describes computer
             programs that automate reasoning and
             how they may make it possible for
             man to carry out far more complex
             reasoning tasks. A particular focus
             is AURA, a program developed at
             Argonne and Northern Illinois
             University that has helped solve
             open equations in abstract algebra
             and formal logic. It also describes
             future versions of AURA which may
             someday become standard tools to aid
             decision makers in all walks of
             life.
Keywords:    Wos Overbeek 1983 Aura Logos Argonne
             Northern Illinois Automated
             Reasoning Expert System Circuit
             Design Chemistry Abstract Algebra
             Reactor Control
```

Screen 2

Using Sci-Mate

Sci-Mate also requires that you set up a card format for each type of entry. For this particular application, the format is exactly the same as that used with NOTEBOOK. However, the method of setting this format up is somewhat more circuitous, requiring that you fill in a template definition form that asks you to (1) give a name to the particular card type and kbase in which it will be stored, and (2) give a name and code number to each of the fields on the card.

Search Strategies

Except with SYSTEM-ONE, the strategy is to search the kbase using either Boolean AND and OR operators or simple character matching. In SUPERFILE, to find all references to the subject of how expert systems might be used to control nuclear reactors, all that's necessary is to enter the keywords:

REACTOR CONTROL or EXPERT SYSTEM or AUTOMATED REASONING

The citation shown above would be retrieved, as would all others with those particular keywords. If you were doing a search for all information on expert systems or automated reasoning and already had the *Logos* article, you could enter the keywords:

EXPERT SYSTEM and AUTOMATED REASONING and /NOT WOS and OVERBEEK

SUPERFILE would retrieve all references to expert systems and automated reasoning in the kbase except that particular reference.

And if for some reason you require an alphabetized listing of what's contained in your bibliographic kbase, you can use the sort and merge functions available with all of these programs. In the example shown above, this would result in an alphabetic sort by author.

As described in Part II, the search strategy used with a SYSTEM-ONE kbase is considerably different. Rather than using AND/OR logic, this program uses an "inquire-by-example" approach. Here you would first search the thesaurus by entering a keyword and using the D(isplay) function to find associated keywords. After building up an appropriate search string of keywords, you would search the abstract files with the I(nquire) function.

Building a Disk Directory

If you've been using your personal computer for any length of time as a word processor, you've probably built up a considerable kbase of interview notes, research notes, rough drafts, and final drafts stored in magnetic form on memory disks.

Over the period of a few years, a reasonably productive writer will have generated at least several thousand double-spaced pages of copy, requiring up to several megabytes of storage space. These computer-generated documents are usually stored on anywhere from 20 to 100 diskettes, depending on whether they are single- or double-density and whether they are 5.25 or 8 inches in size. Moreover, all these documents are filed under eight-character filenames, which become more cryptic with time.

As this base of textual material grows, you'll find it much more difficult to use it as a resource in current writing projects. For example, as a freelance writer I have written several thousand different documents—ghostwritten and bylined magazine articles and brochures and manuals on various microprocessors introduced since the early 1970s. I've found that, in writing about a particular aspect of microprocessor operation—say, how a particular processor handles data transfers over an internal bus structure—it is useful to compare its operation with that of other CPUs, both similar and dissimilar, selecting whatever may help me describe the operation of the particular CPU I'm writing about. In terms of time, this usually involves a trade-off between hunting through my disk files for the appropriate document and looking up the material in my original paper files.

There are disk directory programs that semi-automate this process. But all they tell you is where a particular file is located and on which disk, not what is in it. And unless you've been reasonably well organized about keeping a catalog someplace listing the subject of each article and the filename under which it is stored, making efficient use of the considerable store of knowledge you've built up will be difficult.

With a kbase-processing program such as SUPERFILE, it's possible to determine within seconds on which disk the documents covering a particular subject are located. Within a minute or so—the time it takes to insert the appropriate disk and initiate a search using the short-form option—you'll be able to see a brief description of each article, its associated keywords, its length in pages, and the amount of disk space it occupies.

To be usable by SUPERFILE, each document in your archive files should look like Screen 3.

Between the *C and * markers is the short-form description of what is in the file. Between the * and the *K markers is the text of the article, and between the *K and the *E are the keywords relating to the text file, which is stored under the filename IA16BITS.TXT.

Suppose you wanted to find detailed discussions focused only on Intel's

```
*C
12 PAGES
18 KBYTES
This article describes the new generation of
16-, 32-, and 64-bit microprocessors using CMOS
and NMOS process technology.
Includes a discussion of CPUs from Intel,
National Semiconductor, Bell Labs, Zilog, Texas
Instruments, and Motorola.
*
INTERFACE AGE
NEW MICROPROCESSOR CPU DESIGN ADVANCES AND THEIR
IMPACT ON PERSONAL COMPUTERS
By Bernard Conrad Cole
    When Gordon Moore and Robert Noyce of Intel
Corporation predicted at the beginning of the
1970s that by the end of the 1980s it would be
possible to put the equivalent of an IBM370
mainframe onto no more than a few silicon chips,
a lot of people laughed. The rest said it would
take longer . . .
*K INTERFACE AGE/MICROPROCESSOR/16 BIT/32 BIT/
INTEL/MOTOROLA/NSC/ZILOG/TI/BELL/Z8000/IAPX432/
NS16000/68000 *E
```

Screen 3

microprocessors or the iAPX32. You would enter the following combination:

INTEL and MICROPROCESSOR or IAPX32

SUPERFILE would then display either short- or long-form entries of all documents, including a discussion of Intel microprocessors or the iAPX32. Once you find the appropriate article and verify that it has the information you need, you can send it to a separate file where it can then be edited for inclusion in the article on which you're working.

Saving Online Database Research

Of all the general-purpose, free-form programs described in Part II, Sci-Mate is the most useful not only in searching online databases, but in storing the results of such searches, sorting them, and incorporating the information into a personal kbase.

Although the other programs are less powerful in this respect, the sort/merge capability all incorporate is useful in sorting the results into a form compatible with any particular kbase configuration.

Incorporating such files is most easily done with SUPERFILE and SYSTEM-ONE, using your word processor to edit the results, adding delimiters and keywords, and scanning the results into the kbase. Such files can be incorporated with NOTEBOOK and Datafax, but only with some difficulty. This is because such files must not only have the appropriate markers, but exceed the record size requirements of the particular program.

Building Tickler and Calendar Files

Another way to get acclimated to the operation of a knowledge-processing program, and at the same time derive some benefit, is to build a tickler or calendar file. I've found such an application useful in a number of ways in my work as a professional writer, in which I normally deal with as many as 20–30 business contacts in any one week. Specifically, I've used it to remind me of:

- Appointments with clients
- Deadlines for stories
- Calls to potential clients at a future date
- Deadline dates of special magazine issues
- The status of article drafts—when and to whom they have been sent

Indeed, any memo that needs attention sometime in the future can be written with your word-processing program, given the appropriate markers and keywords to let you retrieve the entry when something must be done, and added to your calendar-file database using SUPERFILE.

You could use every month, or even every day, as a keyword in this calendar file. Each client, interviewee, magazine, or article notation could have keywords for the dates when something must be done. For example, suppose you're doing research on a possible article on expert systems for a magazine based on a brief conversation with an editor who was unwilling to make a firm commitment until he had had a chance to think about it for a month or so. The tickler file entry for this future action item might look like Screen 4.

Using MAY and 1985 as keywords, SUPERFILE will list all of the action items for the month of May. Adding the keyword WEEK ONE, it will list all of those items that need action during the first week of the month. Adding OUTLINE lists all article outlines promised to various editors and when they are due during that month.

```
*C
Itor/Edward
Computer Users Magazine
198 Technology Drive
Silicon Valley, CA 95051
*
Talked to Ed Itor on April 1, 1985, about an
article on expert systems and how they will
affect the lives of the average personal
computer user. He expressed interest, but wanted
to discuss it with his editorial staff. Wants a
detailed outline in about four weeks and a
telephone conference about a week later. Should
set aside time first part of May to develop
outline.
*K
ITOR/COMPUTER USERS MAG./MAY/1985/WEEK ONE/
OUTLINE/EXPERT SYSTEM *E
```

Screen 4

Managing Your Business or Profession

Despite all the advertising touting the advantages of database management systems (DEMs) as "computerized file cabinets," they only address a small portion of the problems facing the average business professional who is trying to make efficient use of his personal computer. Equally important in any business is an efficient means of storing, retrieving, and manipulating text in documentary form, including change orders, client and customer information, contact reports, contracts, correspondence, personnel information, product information, property management information, and vendor information.

The chief advantage of kbase-processing programs is their compatibility, in most cases, with standard word-processing files. With SUPERFILE, for example, the word-processing file *is* the kbase file. All that is necessary is to add the appropriate SUPERFILE markers—*C, *, *K, and *E—and a few descriptive keywords, and a word processor file will be ready for addition to SUPERFILE's index and dictionary. Once that is done it is possible for the businessperson to manipulate the documents in his or her computer files with the same flexibility with which he or she manipulates data using a DBMS.

Outgoing Correspondence

One of the most underutilized kbases in any business is its incoming and outgoing correspondence files. Not that every effort isn't made to make use of them—in fact, books have been written on how to organize such files. It is just that the volume of letters in even a moderate-size business doesn't allow a businessperson to make use of them to the fullest extent.

Standard filing systems are usually organized in one of five ways: alphabetical, numerical, chronological, geographic, or by subject. Most businesses have a card file that cross-indexes according to one additional filing method. But paper files cannot be arranged so that any given entry can be retrieved by all five methods.

What is particularly frustrating is having shifted to a computer or word-processing system in the hopes that it would eliminate much of this hassle, at least with outgoing correspondence. But whereas the word processor will certainly simplify the writing of correspondence and reduce the amount of space required to store it, it will not simplify the filing task. If this has been your problem, you are probably still stuck with that card file, which, rather than telling you which cabinet a particular letter is in, now tells you which disk it is on and what filename it is stored under.

A free-form kbase program such as SUPERFILE allows you to take full advantage of those computerized correspondence files. With SUPER-FILE, you can cross-index entries in your files in as many ways as you want. In fact, you can easily cross-index outgoing correspondence at the same time you write it using your word-processing program. With SUPERFILE, of course, you don't want the *C, *, *K, and *E markers to appear on the printout. But most word-processing programs have a means of preventing this. In WordStar, for example, the ".." symbol is used to prevent the printing of the rest of a line; that is, none of the lines preceded by that symbol will be printed in the letter. However, the entire entry will be kept as a SUPERFILE entry. Screen 5 shows an example of how an outgoing letter would be formatted.

```
*C
September 14, 1985
Ms. Susan Morehead
Standard Products
3456 San Pablo Ave.
Oakland, CA 94701
*
Dear Ms. Morehead:

    Thanks for your letter of September 12. I'm
always glad to hear that our products are saving
customers time and money.
    I'll be in contact with you as soon as I've
some information on the new products and the
enhancements to our Model 45, in which you've
expressed some interest.

Sincerely,

Roberta Jones
Vice President of Customer Relations

*K STANDARD PRODUCTS/CA/SEPTEMBER/1985/ROBERTA/
JONES/CUSTOMER RELATIONS/REPAIRS/MODEL 45/
CORRESPONDENCE/SUSAN/MOREHEAD/REPLY *E
```

Screen 5

Each time a letter is typed on your word processor it can also "automatically" become a SUPERFILE entry for your Correspondence kbase. Properly cross-referenced in the keyword list, this will allow retrieval of specific pieces of outgoing correspondence and all other correspondence associated with them.

If, for example, you wanted to see copies of all the letters Roberta Jones wrote to Susan Morehead, you'd enter the following keywords:

```
ROBERTA and JONES and SUSAN and MOREHEAD and
CORRESPONDENCE
```

If you wanted to see all the letters that Jones wrote in September, 1985, you would enter the keywords:

```
ROBERTA and JONES and SEPTEMBER and 1985
```

Incoming Correspondence

Unless you've got one of those new optical character-reader or automatic-document-entry machines, you won't be able to eliminate incoming correspondence files. You will, however, be able to replace your file with a much more flexible cross-referencing system using SUPERFILE. Suppose you've received the letter shown on page 118. Your first step in creating an Incoming Correspondence kbase is to circle the words in the letter to be used as keywords. Next determine where you're going to file it; in this case, the letter would be filed in the Standard Products folder in file cabinet 4, drawer 3, folder location S-5. Using this information, the Incoming Correspondence entry for SUPERFILE would look like this:

```
*C
Item: letter from Susan Morehead, Standard Prod.,
      CA, to Roberta Jones
Date: September 12, 1985
Content: Thanks for fast repair of the Model 45.
         Describes problem with the transformer at
         1000 hours.
File Location: Cabinet 4
               Drawer 3
               Folder S-5

*K STANDARD PRODUCTS/CA/SEPTEMBER/1985/ROBERTA/
JONES/CUSTOMER RELATIONS/REPAIRS/MODEL 45/
PROMPTNESS/PROBLEM/TRANSFORMER/SUSAN/MOREHEAD/
CORRESPONDENCE *E
```

Standard Products
3456 San Pablo Ave.
Oakland, CA 94701

September 12, 1985

Roberta Jones
Vice President of Customer Relations
Redifix Machinery Co.
Highland Lakes, CT 12345

Dear Ms. Jones:

Thank you for your recent assistance in expediting the repairs on our Model 45. Your prompt response saved us considerable downtime and prevented some substantial costs on our part.

We do have another problem with the Model 45, however. The transformer works loose after 1000 hours of operation. It's not crucial at this point, but some changes need to be made in the design. I'd appreciate your looking into the matter and contacting me at your earliest convenience.

Cordially,

Susan Morehead

Susan Morehead
Vice President

If you wanted to see all the letters Jones has received about the promptness of repairs, you would enter the keywords:

ROBERTA and JONES and REPAIRS and CORRESPONDENCE

SUPERFILE would then bring up the entry as shown above, plus all others with the same keywords.

If you want to see all correspondence in 1985 related to repairs for everything except the Model 45, you would enter the following keywords:

CORRESPONDENCE and 1985 and REPAIRS and /NOT MODEL 45

SUPERFILE would then retrieve all entries with the three keywords CORRESPONDENCE, 1985, and REPAIRS, except for those with the keyword MODEL 45.

Personnel Files

Kbase programs such as SUPERFILE are also useful in the management of personnel records. It is often difficult to pull the right information from the files when planning a special project, filling a vacancy, or considering promotions.

It is usually not necessary to keep all of an employee's records in a kbase record. Instead, each file needs only enough information to identify employees with specific characteristics. A reference to the paper file can be made should you need additional information. A personnel file might look like Screen 6. With personnel entries like this, if you wanted to identify all employees who are ready for promotion from IC Assembler Class 3 to Class 2, you'd enter the keywords:

IC ASSEMBLER-3 and PROMOTION

With these keywords, SUPERFILE would retrieve the information on all employees currently in IC Assembler Class 3 and judged ready for promotion.

If you were looking for an employee to promote into a production

```
*C
Johnson/Samuel J.
3476 Semiconductor Drive
San Jose, CA 95051
*
Social Security: 123-45-6789
Employee Number: T2345
Date Employed: April 1, 1979
Job Category on Employment: IC Assembler, Class
                            5
Promotion History: IC Assembler, Class 4, Nov.
                   15, 1979
                   IC Assembler, Class 3, May
                   23, 1980
Disciplinary Action: excessive tardiness
Employee Review Record: six months: satisfactory
                        1980: probationary
                        1981: excellent
Promotion status: ready for promotion
Special characteristics: Works well with others,
is a leader, and is presently taking college
business courses. Complete file is in Cabinet 6,
Drawer 2, Folder J-5.
*K
IC ASSEMBLER/123-45-6789/T2345/ASSEMBLER-3/
EMPLOYMENT ANNIVERSARY APRIL 1/1979/PROMOTION/
LEADER/CONTINUING EDUCATION/DISCIPLINARY ACTION
*E
```

Screen 6

management position, but couldn't consider anyone who had had disciplinary action, you'd enter the keywords:

PROMOTION or LEADER /NOT DISCIPLINARY ACTION

The SUPERFILE program would then retrieve all information from your knowledge base on all employees who had never been disciplined and whom you'd judged to be leaders or who were suitable for promotion on the basis of advancing educational and/or skill levels.

Product Descriptions

Most products have a number of different documents associated with them, such as technical documents, spec sheets, application notes, brochures, and news releases.

There are a number of ways you can use SUPERFILE to handle product information. First, you can enter brief descriptions of the technical documents and cross-reference each one to a specific location in your paper files. The item summarizing the technical description of the tie bar assembly for the Model 45 Widget Machine is shown in Screen 7.

If you've been using your personal computer for word processing, you've got a second option: enter the complete document and then use

```
*C
Technical Description of transformer for Model
45 Widget Machine. Engineering Division, Redifix
Machinery Co., August, 1978.
*
Document contains engineering specifications and
drawings for transformer for Model 45. Document
was included in contracts to all suppliers of
transformer. Assembly is part number TB1234-6.
Document is located in Cabinet 16, Drawer 3.
*K
ENGINEERING SPECS/MODEL 45/PART NUMBER TB1234-6/
ENGINEERING DIVISION/AUGUST/1978/CONTRACT
SPECIFICATIONS *E
```

Screen 7

SUPERFILE to help you create specialized product descriptions. The entry would be essentially the same as the earlier description for cross-referencing above, except that the text between the * and the *K is replaced by the actual file that is on the computer.

Imagine that the Model 45 has a number of different options and can be customized to meet the particular needs of a customer. Each time you send out a price quote on the machine, you have to re-do the description in accordance with the various options. Using SUPERFILE, you can enter a description of each option into the kbase, retrieve only the options you want, and put together a customized description without retyping.

Contact Reports

Many businesses and agencies must keep reports on people who have been contacted for various reasons. With SUPERFILE you can cross-reference these reports and/or keep them as entries in a Contact Report kbase. A contact report might have the structure shown in Screen 8.

Organized in this way and cross-referenced, items in the Contact Report kbase can be manipulated in a number of different ways.

If you wanted to see all the contact reports on population studies related to the Midwest, you would enter the keywords:

MARKET STUDIES and MIDWEST and CONTACT REPORT

SUPERFILE would retrieve all entries with these keywords, including the one given above.

If you wanted to see all contact reports from Software Corp. dealing with the Midwest except those having to do with population studies, you would enter the following keywords:

SOFTWARE CORP. and MIDWEST and /NOT MARKET STUDIES

SUPERFILE would retrieve all reports from Software Corp. that relate to the Midwest except this one, which has to do with market studies.

If you wanted to remind yourself of all the follow-ups you're supposed to make in December 1985, you would enter the keywords:

TICKLE and DECEMBER and 1985

```
*C
Person contacted: Dennis Lessing
Address: Software Corp.
        1200 Industrial Parkway
        Midtown, OH 21546
        Tele: 123-456-7890
Contacted by: Martha Williams
Date: November 7, 1985
*

Mr. Moore said that the studies of potential
market in the Midwest are in their final stages
and should be available for use by early
December. We should contact him then.
*K
CONTACT REPORT/DENNIS LESSING/SOFTWARE/MARTHA
WILLIAMS/MARKET STUDIES/MIDWEST/TICKLE/DECEMBER/
1985/OCTOBER *E
```

Screen 8

SUPERFILE would retrieve this report and all others indexed as needing follow-up in December 1985.

Client and Customer Files

Every salesperson knows that personal attention to clients and customers means increased sales. But remembering all the details of all the transactions for each customer is a difficult, if not impossible, task. So it comes as no surprise that on the desk of every top salesperson is some sort of client and customer file, either on cards or on single sheets. After a while, though, such a system becomes bulky and unwieldy. It is also an awkward way to find the specific piece of information you need.

With SUPERFILE you can use keywords to retrieve information about your customers, what they bought, and when they'll need upgrades and a host of other information that'll increase sales. Use of AND, OR, and /NOT effectively allows you to retrieve exactly the information you need about your customers and clients. And by using the short form, retrieval, and SUPERFILE's Sort and Merge utility, you can even create name and address lists from your customer/client list.

One such listing, for John Doe of Doe Buoy Manufacturing, would look like the one in Screen 9.

Suppose, for example, you received a call from John Doe. You haven't heard from him since he first purchased your product and don't remember much about him. If you were on your toes and had put the disk with your

```
*C
Doe/John
Doe Buoy Manufacturing
1315 West 7th Street
Walla Walla, WA 24534
*
John bought the Model 45 in April 1984. He
bought the basic model and planned to add some
options in December 1985. He uses it in the
manufacture of monitoring buoys for NOAA, the
National Oceanographic and Atmospheric
Administration. He seems to be aggressive, and
his business should grow. He looks for bargains
so we should hit him with sales notices.

    John's wife is named Mary and he has two
children: Bob, 15, and Sue, 12, as of my initial
contacts in 1981. His telephone number is 802-
435-7728.
*K
JOHN/DOE/MODEL 45/PURCHASED APRIL/1984/UPGRADE/
DECEMBER/1985/WALLA WALLA/WA/SALES BROCHURE *E
```

Screen 9

customer and client file kbase into the computer as soon as you came into the office, this information would be on the screen within seconds after entering the keywords JOHN and DOE. Or you may be getting ready to make some customer calls and want to know which of your customers bought the Model 45 and will be ready for upgrades in December. To get this information you would enter the keywords:

```
MODEL 45 and UPGRADE and DECEMBER 1985
```

SUPERFILE would then retrieve not only the entry for John Doe with the telephone number, but all other entries with those keywords.

If you want to list all your customers who should receive sales brochures and will be ready to upgrade in December, 1985, except those who live in Washington, you would enter the keywords:

```
SALES BROCHURE and UPGRADE and DECEMBER and 1985 and
/NOT WA
```

SUPERFILE would then list all such customers except John Doe and all others who live in Washington.

Combining Knowledge Bases

By themselves, each of these individual kbases can serve as useful tools in your business. But integrating several of them results in an even more powerful sales tool. With SUPERFILE it is simply a matter of adding an additional keyword to each of the items in each kbase describing the nature of each item: CUSTOMER for your customer and client list, PRODUCT for your product descriptions, CONTRACTS for your contract items, INCOMING for incoming correspondence, and OUTGOING for outgoing correspondence.

With such an integrated kbase, if John Doe called, you would first enter CUSTOMER and JOHN and DOE. If he wanted to discuss a letter you sent him in September 1985, you would enter OUTGOING and JOHN and DOE and SEPTEMBER and 1985. If he wanted to know about a particular product, you would key in PRODUCT and the appropriate model number.

Depending on the number of keywords, the size of your customer list and product list, your disk capacity, and how much experience you have with manipulating and searching a SUPERFILE kbase, the needed information will flash onto the screen of your personal computer within 5–30 seconds, giving you that extra bit of information that might clinch the sale.

Additional Uses

The ways in which a free-form knowledge-processing program can be used are limited only by your imagination and include:

Business and Professional	Educational
Action lists	Bulletins
Catalogs	Class notes
Inventory lists	Computer-aided instruction
Legal briefs	Course catalogs
Medical records	Course outlines
Minutes of meetings	Lesson plans
Product analyses	Question-answering systems
Resumes	Student records
Schedules	Test-item files

In addition to writers, virtually all professionals who are involved in paperwork of any sort are potential users of kbase-processing programs, including architects, attorneys, buyers, consultants, engineers, executive recruiters, insurance agents, marketing directors, office managers, pharmacists, physicians, professors, public relations professionals, researchers, small business owners, stockbrokers, and travel agents, to name only a few.

CHAPTER 10

Using a Knowledge Processor as a Writing Tool

Once you've had some experience with a knowledge-processing program, you'll find it can be a very effective tool in the actual process of writing. Indeed, the more complex the subject and the broader the scope of the project, the more useful you will find knowledge processing as (1) an analytical tool, (2) an automated "cut-and-paste" method of organizing and pulling together a rough draft of a document, and (3) a relearning tool.

In writing or ghostwriting articles on various scientific and technical subjects, including computers, I've found kbase-processing programs to be of enormous benefit in the organization and collation of material collected from diverse sources—interviews, internal documents, and manuals. Such programs have reduced from weeks and months to days and hours the time required to pull together information into rough draft form.

The Knowledge Base Processor as an Analytical Tool

All the general-purpose programs surveyed in Part II can be used, with varying degrees of effectiveness, as cut-and-paste tools for generating a rough draft from computerized source files of research notes and interviews. Where they vary is in their usefulness as analytical tools. A pecu-liarity of programs designed for the storage and retrieval of textual infor-mation is that the more structured they are, the more you need to know about the subject stored in the kbase.

A limitation of programs such as NOTEBOOK, Sci-Mate, and Datafax is that although they place few or no limits on the amount of text you can store (within the memory capacity of your system), they do require that you define the structure within which the text will be placed. With NOTEBOOK, for example, you must structure the text into fields of spe-cific types. With Sci-Mate, you must define the templates of the cards into which you enter information. With Datafax, it is necessary to give some thought to how you divide the information into "folders." Again, in order to define the structure, you must be reasonably knowledgeable about the subject you want to store in your kbase.

A particular strength of SUPERFILE and SYSTEM-ONE is that they impose no such structure on the information to be stored. They are designed to retrieve information on the basis of selected keywords, the choice of which depends on the information contained in each block of text stored. As your kbase increases both in size and in diversity, structures evolve on the basis of content, not on the basis of some predefined frame-work you must impose beforehand.

Suppose, for example, you wanted to do an article or paper on "The Mating Habits of the Minor Mongoose During the Stone Age." When you start, you may know little or nothing about the minor mongoose, much less its mating habits during the stone age. However, as you build up your writing kbase and sift through it using selected keywords, certain trends and structures will become apparent.

Organizing an Article with a Knowledge Base Processor

As far as article organization is concerned, no one kbase program is better than another. Your choice of such a program as a cut-and-paste writ-ing tool is more a function of the kind of writing professional you are.

If you are the kind of writer I am, putting together the rough draft of an article is a very fluid process in which the source material moves around the top of your desk like the sands of the desert—first here, then there, from one stack to another stack, until some shape or form begins to emerge. For this kind of writing professional, the most effective kbase program is one like SUPERFILE or SYSTEM-ONE.

The vast majority of writers—at least the ones I know—are much more organized than this, and they manipulate their thoughts and source material in a more structured manner; organizing it into logical groupings, placing it in the appropriate folders and files, working their way through each folder in an organized step-by-step manner, and extracting what they need for use in the rough draft they are writing. For this type of writer, one of the more structured free-form programs, such as NOTEBOOK, Datafax, or Sci-Mate, might be appropriate.

Using SUPERFILE as a Writing Tool

In many respects, a kbase organized with SUPERFILE reflects, logically, the top of my desk, and the process by which a document is put together with this kbase mirrors the manual process.

Recently, for example, I wrote a series of articles on 16-bit microprocessors that involved analysis and comparison of all aspects of their design and performance, including register structure, instruction sets, input-output (I/O) addressing schemes, memory protection schemes, direct memory access organization, execution time for various instructions, multiprocessing modes, data types, data structures, control operations, and addressing modes. This involved interviewing engineers and designers at ten companies that were manufacturing microprocessors and extracting pertinent information from piles of documentation and interviews with actual users of these devices, including how they were using them, their assessment of various features of each CPU, and how they decided which was best for particular applications.

Writing an article of this type with a mechanical typewriter is an almost insurmountable challenge, and a job that would require months to complete. Even with a word processor such an article involves an enormous amount of computerized cutting and pasting, moving blocks of data back and forth within files and between files. Using a kbase-processing program such as SUPERFILE reduces the chore of organizing an article of this type significantly. There are several steps involved in organizing such an article with SUPERFILE, including:

1. Turning your research notes into entries in a "writing database."
2. Creating the writing database dictionary and index.

3. Searching the writing database, looking for patterns and trends.

4. Determining the right keyword search sequence.

5. Building your rough draft files.

Creating Writing Base Entries

The particular advantage of SUPERFILE is the fact that with the use of three or four simple markers it is a simple matter to create a writing database. For example, after an interview has been transcribed using a word-processing program, all that is necessary is to go back and partition the notes of an interview according to subject, adding the appropriate markers and incorporating it into a special kbase using SUPERFILE.

In an interview with an engineer at McDonnel Douglas on how he or she used the Z8000, all comments relating to, say, I/O addressing could be organized into a single entry or several entries, one for each type of addressing mode. Such a file would have a keyword listing such as the following:

```
MICROPROCESSOR/INTERVIEW/I-O/ADDRESSING/Z8000/
MCDONNEL DOUGLAS/SMITH
```

Similarly, any source documentation, such as manuals, conference papers, data sheets, or application notes, would be organized in the same fashion. For example, all information on I/O addressing from a paper that Smith gave at a conference on Z8000 design and included into a single file would have a keyword listing such as the following:

```
MICROPROCESSOR/DOCUMENT/CONFERENCE/I-O/ADDRESSING/
Z8000/MCDONNEL DOUGLAS/SMITH
```

Building a Writing Base

If you are planning to construct a rough draft file based on an organized search of the working database using the outline you've developed, some care should be given to the structure of your keyword sequences in building a kbase with SUPERFILE. This is especially true when you use it in the actual writing process. The keywords for each entry should range from the general to the specific. With general keywords, you can retrieve all of a group or category of entries. The specific keywords let you narrow down the results of a search. It is important in this application of SUPERFILE to include one keyword that is absolutely unique to that entry. This is helpful during a search in that it allows you to specify which particular items should *not* be included in the search.

Searching the Writing Base

Before beginning your search, first print out a listing of the keyword dictionary SUPERFILE has created on the basis of your keyword entries. Then develop a reasonably detailed outline of the article, either by hand or using one of the programs described in Part V. Under each subheading, list the subjects you wish to include, basing this list on the keywords entered in the dictionary.

Before using those keywords as the basis of the search sequence, it is important to conduct a series of preliminary searches to make sure the list includes all the entries you need and excludes those you don't. If, for example, I wanted to search my 16BITTER writing base to get a feel for how the various CPUs handle I/O processing, I'd select the Search database option, as described in earlier chapters, and enter a keyword sequence something like the following:

MICROPROCESSOR and DOCUMENT and I-O and ADDRESSING

SUPERFILE would then search the kbase for all references to I/O addressing, regardless of CPU type.

If you're still in the preliminary stages—analyzing the knowledge you've collected, comparing it, and looking for trends and patterns—you should search with SUPERFILE in its Continuous Output mode, but directing it to display each record in its short form. In this mode, each item that meets the criteria set by your keyword search string is simply flashed on the screen.

If, however, you're in the process of selecting and categorizing, you should use the Optional Output mode, which first flashes the item on the screen and then gives you the choice of sending it to another file or to the printer.

Building Your Search Sequence

In the process of analyzing the knowledge you've collected in your writing database, using the continuous short-form display, you'll no doubt find some entries you believe should not be included. Note the unique keywords associated with those entries and, after your preliminary search, make up a new search sequence that exlcudes those entries using the NOT mode.

For example, in the search of my 16BITTER writing base for information on I/O addressing, I found that while I wanted to include those items discussing TI's 99000 CPU, I did not want to include the company's older TI9900 or its single-chip 9940. My search sequence would then be altered as follows:

```
MICROPROCESSOR and DOCUMENT and I-O and ADDRESSING
and /NOT 9900 OR /NOT 9940
```

Building Your Rough Draft

Depending on the extent of the information you've built up in your writing base, you may want to pull together a rough draft in one sitting or break it up into separate sessions. My writing base for the 16-bit microprocessor article consisted of almost 4000 entries and 400 keywords. Thus I found it necessary to work through the outline subheading by subheading. When I was working on the section of the article on how the various CPUs handled multiprocessing, I searched my working knowledge base using the keywords MICROPROCESSOR and DMA with Default Search option—display only. Assured that it did indeed contain all of the items I wanted under that section, I entered the same keywords and used the Continuous Output mode. Prompted by SUPERFILE, I entered the name and type of disk file: 16BITDMA.TXT. The output then went continuously to the printer or disk.

For this particular article the outline I developed had 20 different subheadings. Using SUPERFILE, I stored information on a disk under 20 separate filenames. With WordStar, I created a new file called 16BITTER.DOC. Then, using WordStar's Read External File command (Control KR), I entered each of the 20 separate files into the new rough draft file, one after another, according to the outline. I could have also used the CP/M operating system's PIP command to combine them into a single file. The result was a 50-page rough draft of unedited but properly organized interview and document entries.

Using a manual typewriter, developing such a rough draft using cut-and-paste techniques would have required several days. With a word-processing program, I was able to reduce the time required to about a day. With SUPERFILE, this process required only three hours.

Using SYSTEM-ONE as a Writing Tool

SYSTEM-ONE can be used with the same degree of ease as a cut-and-paste writing tool. However, it requires that you modify the way you store abstract records of your raw text as well as the thesaurus records containing the keywords.

As described in Chapter 5, SYSTEM-ONE requires that you create thesaurus records consisting of keywords describing the contents of a particular file, with the keywords grouped according to meaning. When the program scans the abstract and thesaurus records in your kbase, it numbers the new records, adding them to the listing contained in its dictionary and index files. It also numbers each of the records in each type of file sequentially. However, with this approach there is no relationship between specific records in the thesaurus and those in the abstract files. For example, thesaurus record T7 in this type of structure has no connection with abstract record A7.

What is necessary, then, is to construct your kbase keyword/descriptor records in the thesaurus file so that they parallel the structure of the associated abstract file in both content and location. The abstract file containing the transcript of, say, an interview with an engineer who used a particular microprocessor in his or her system would have to be modified in the following way. First, the notes would have to be organized according to subject. Second, the SYSTEM-ONE record delimiters would be added, breaking up the blocks of text into separate subject groups. Third, although the program adds them in automatically, I would add the record numbers manually with my word processor while transcribing the interview. Fourth, I would add some sort of header information with each record, describing the type of information, its source, and its location sequentially in that particular file. A typical record entry would look something like this:

```
~A7 Roy L. Jones, Intel Corp. Interview-J1
As in the 8-bit 8086, all instructions are byte-
oriented. A bridge processor between the 8- and 16-
bit worlds, most of its basic intruction—95 in all—
are only 8 bits long. In its few 16-bit instructions
only the first 8 bits are used for operation codes.
```

The keywords in the thesaurus record that parallels this particular abstract record would be chosen according to the same rules used in building a similar descriptor with SUPERFILE; that is, it should contain at least one general word that describes its type (INTERVIEW) and at least one that uniquely identifies that particular record (INTERVIEW-J1, for first record in Jones Interview). However, unlike SUPERFILE, the order in which these are listed in the thesaurus record is unimportant. The thesaurus record for the abstract record above would look something like this:

```
~T7 byte operation codes displacement 16-bit Intel
    interview J1 instructions 8086 Jones
~T8 .............................................................  ...
```

In this cut-and-paste application of SYSTEM-ONE, the most useful feature is the D(isplay) function. For one thing, since the thesaurus files are smaller than the abstract files, it is easier and faster to scan through the various descriptor records to pinpoint a record of particular interest than would be the case in reviewing abstract text files. Using the information gained from a search of the thesaurus makes it possible to be much more specific when using the D(isplay) or I(nquire) options to search through the abstract files and records.

For example, suppose you are reviewing your microprocessor writing base, looking for patterns in the material that might indicate the ultimate structure of the article. Using the G(iven word) option from the D(isplay) T(hesaurus) Menu, you would enter a particular topic—say, 8086 or INSTRUCTIONS. SYSTEM-ONE would then search through the thesaurus looking for all mentions of the 8086, the other keywords it is associated with, and the records in which they are located.

If you've constructed your thesaurus so that the overall structure parallels that of the records contained in the associated abstract files, this information will also tell you that the abstract records with the same numbers contain the information you want.

More often than not, the information contained in the displayed thesaurus records is enough to tell you whether they will be useful in the article. If they will, simply note the thesaurus number and the subjects and proceed through the listing. From this it is usually possible to develop a good idea of the order in which the information should appear. Taking this reordered listing, you would then call up the D(isplay) A(bstracts) display and choose the O(ne record) option. As you enter the abstract numbers in your reordered squence, SYSTEM-ONE will display the text records one at a time. If they are in the correct order, you may change the Default Output option from CONSOLE to the filename of your choice and again enter the reordered sequence.

The Knowledge Base Processor as a Relearning Tool

Though knowledge-processing programs such as SUPERFILE are useful and powerful as writing tools, you haven't taken advantage of their full power and utility until you begin to build specialized kbases from the writing bases used on specific projects. For if knowledge is power, *organized* and *easily accessible* knowledge is power plus freedom. With a specialized kbase you have taken time to keep up to date, you no longer have to go back and dig out the old paper files, magazines, and reference books when you've been assigned to write on a particular subject.

Over the many years I have spent as a free-lance writer on science and technology, I've built up specialized kbases on such diverse topics as biotechnology, photochemistry and photosynthesis, computer-aided design, computer-aided publishing, artificial intelligence research, video disk technology, expert systems, and, of course, kbase creation and text retrieval.

All of these various specialized kbases had their start as writing bases on particular projects. To each I have added pertinent items from my archival files, as well as abstracts and notes on articles and books I have read on these various subjects in the normal course of my work.

So when I'm assigned a new writing project, my "relearning curve" on a particular subject is considerably accelerated and increases as the content of that particular kbase is enlarged.

No longer do I have to depend on my memory or, even worse, on cryptic notes and taped interviews that I may have saved. In every real sense, these various kbases, constructed with keywords that reflect my own particular thought processes, are an extension of my own memory on which I can draw with almost the ease of thought.

The less time I need to get back up to speed on a particular subject, the more time I can devote to the creative process involved in writing. And through using material extracted from a particular kbase, the new information can be presented in a context that makes it much more meaningful.

Part IV

BIBLIOGRAPHIC AND INDEX CARD PROGRAMS

CHAPTER 11

VisiDex

A Card File with Vision

One of the most popular forms of text storage and retrieval is the so-called index card program. Unlike the free-form, general-purpose knowledge-processing programs surveyed in Part II, most index card programs are basically customized versions of traditional database management programs configured to allow entry of text files and to hide as much of the data-oriented structure from the user as possible.

VisiDex, described in this chapter, is one example of this kind of program. Three others that illustrate various alternative approaches to designing such programs are CITATION, PCFILE, and CARDFILE. They are discussed in Chapter 12.

VisiDex Overview

VisiDex is an electronic index card program, part of Visicorp's high-visibility Visi series. Versions are available for use under the Apple II DOS, the IBM PC-DOS, and the Microsoft MS-DOS. It requires the use of at least two disk drives, one for the program and the other for the text files. On the Apple II, only 48K bytes are required; on the PC-DOS and MS-DOS systems, 96K bytes are required.

In VisiDex, each card consists of a single screen of up to 20 lines, with a maximum of 800 characters on an Apple system (twenty 40-character lines) or 1600 characters on PC-DOS or MS-DOS system (twenty 80-character lines). Each card can be cross-indexed with up to 32 six-character words. Each kbase is limited to the amount of space available on the text file diskette. On an Apple II diskette, this is about 131,000 characters, or about 150 screen-sized "cards."

Creating a Knowledge Base with VisiDex

After you load VisiDex, pressing any key will place you immediately in the editing mode, with a list of editing commands at the top of a blank screen something like this:

```
EDIT: / <--> CTRL (QCI WASZ BV ODEX RKY)
```

Except for the slash (/), each option in the menu represents an editing action, where pressing the appropriate control key and any one of the following characters within the parentheses initiates any of a variety of cursor movements and editing functions. The left and right arrows and the Control Q, I, W, A, S, or Z, for example, move the cursor around the screen. The Control C, O, D, E, or X adds and deletes characters, lines, and screens of text.

Control B and V change the display to reverse video and back. Control R directs VisiDex to read one line at a time from an external file and display it on the screen. Control K creates a keyword from the characters to the left of the cursor. Control Y invokes a Command prompt that describes each of these editing commands and their associated symbols. It cycles through the options until one of the commands is executed by pressing the Return key or the appropriate command symbol, or until the Escape key is pressed to return to the Edit mode.

Pressing the / key will put you in the Command mode, allowing you access to the other functions of the VisiDex program, including Print (/P), Store (/S), Calendar (/C), and Create Keywords (/K).

Entering Text into VisiDex

As with a word processor, text is entered into a VisiDex kbase via the keyboard in wrap-around fashion. By using the various control character commands, it is possible to move around the screen at will, inserting and deleting characters and lines.

Loading External Files

If you already have standard ASCII text files created by your word processor, they can be entered into a VisiDex kbase in blocks of up to 20 lines.

To do this first break the ASCII text file into 20-line blocks. Then place the VisiDex text diskette on one drive and the source ASCII text file diskette on the other. Then enter the Edit mode and invoke the Control R command.

After the Return key is pressed, VisiDex will prompt you to enter the name of the text file with the following message:

```
FILENAME, D #
```

In response, type in the name of text file to be entered and the disk drive number. Then press Control R as many times as is necessary to get a block of information onto the screen (up to 20 lines). Then position this information according to the format you may have set up for each sereen/card.

Regardless of the mode of text entry, to save each screen and store it in your VisiDex kbase, it is first necessary to create at least one keyword that can be associated with that screen, followed by one of the Create Keyword commands, /KP. New text is then entered on a new screen either by typing normally, if you are in the standard Edit mode, or by pressing Control R repeatedly if you are entering text from an external ASCII file.

Creating Keywords

Using a scheme somewhat similar to that used with Datafax, keywords are used in VisiDex like labels on file folders. Storing a screen puts it in a folder. The program puts the screen in a folder for each keyword on the screen. Retrieving by keyword pulls out all of the screens in a given keyword folder.

VisiDex allows you to create a keyword in two ways. The simplest and most direct way is by entering the Edit mode by pressing Control K, which creates a keyword from the characters to the left of the cursor. The second method is less direct, but much more powerful. As with Datafax, you enter keywords that are not necessarily contained in the text of the screen you are editing. This involves entering the Command mode by entering /K followed by Return. VisiDex then presents the keyword command status line at the top of a blank screen. It looks something like this:

KEYWORDS: <--> C D E G P

With VisiDex, a keyword can contain up to 253 alphabetic or numeric characters. A given screen can contain no more than 30 keywords. The keyword limit for each VisiDex kbase is about 1900 per diskette.

Keywords are created by placing the cursor on the first character of the word you want to make into a keyword and typing in a C (/KC). The selected keyword then appears in the keyword area at the bottom of the screen in the first position on the left, pushing any previous keyword to its right. To move back and forth through the text, the left and right arrow keys on your screen are used. They automatically place the cursor on the first character of the next or preceding words.

In this mode, the program lets you create multiple keywords for each screen of text by entering two or more keywords per screen. Compound keywords composed of two or more words can also be entered by placing the cursor on the first letter of the first word and then entering the /KC command sequence as many times as is necessary to include all the words in the compound keyword.

Using the Enter Keyword command (/KE), you can create a keyword that is not part of the screen text. However, no keyword can be longer than 38 characters long.

VisiDex also includes some keyword commands that allow you to manipulate the keyword list displayed at the bottom of the screen. Selecting the right arrow scrolls the keyword list to right, whereas the left arrow scrolls it to the left. The Drop Keyword option (/KD) deletes the keyword in the upper-left corner of the screen from the area, and, of course, from the keyword index altogether.

A unique feature of VisiDex is its Keydate option, using a special set of calendar commands (/C). It allows you to store screens with unique dates as keywords via the Put Date Screen option (/CP). The program calculates the day of the week for all dates from 1970 to 1999. All prompts for month and day have default values based on the information given when loading the program. This date feature is useful when you are using VisiDex as a tickler file to display the appropriate screen at some future date on the basis of the information given when loading the program. The

Get Date option (/CG) allows you to examine a saved Keydate screen. Finally, there is a Display Month option (/CM) that displays a calendar on the screen.

Once you've modified the text on the screen to your satisfaction and selected the appropriate keywords, the Put Screen option (/KP) is used to save the contents of the current screen on the diskette.

Searching a VisiDex Knowledge Base

The main method of searching through a VisiDex kbase is with the Get Screen option (/KG). When this command is entered, the editing screen clears and the status area prompts you with the message:

ENTER KEYWORD

In response, you enter any search sequence of up to 38 characters, including (1) a keyword, (2) a string of characters in the actual text on each screen, (3) a combination of keywords or character strings, or (4) abbreviated versions of the previous three using wildcard characters (– and *).

The wildcard characters are most useful when searching by keyword, especially if the keyword is a compound exceeding 38 characters. The dash (–) symbol is a multiple-character wildcard and can stand for any character or series of characters in a keyword except for the first two characters and the last. The asterisk (*) is a single-character wildcard. Wildcards can be used more than once in a search sequence and in combination within the same keyword.

By entering the ampersand (&) in response to the /KG prompt, VisiDex searches the text, screen by screen, rather than the keyword index. If the & is used by itself, the search process becomes slower as the number of screens on the diskette increases. A better strategy is to use it in combination with keyword searches. If you enter a keyword followed by the search character and a character string, the program will first search the index to select the screens with that keyword and then the text of each of the selected screens for the character string.

Additional flexibility can be added to your search process if you use numerical rather than alphabetical characters in the search string following the &. This allows you to retrieve screens by numbers or ranges of numbers using the standard mathematical comparison operators, including the "equals" (=), "less than" (<), "more than" (>), "less than or equal to" (≤), "more than or equal to" (≥), and "not equal to" (≠) signs.

The numbers for which VisiDex searches may be any numerical sequence in the text or a special numerical sequence you have determined to be unique to that screen. Under VisiDex, a number is a string of characters that may include any of the 0 to 9 digits, the dollar sign ($), the comma, and the decimal point. The operators may only be used with field names that conclude with either a colon or an equals sign.

For example, in a kbase consisting of information about microprocessor architecture, one of the fields may be the word length—4, 8, 16, 32, or 64 bits. For the NSC 16016, the word length is 16 bits; for the NSC16032 it is 32 bits. Thus the field containing this information would start with the field name and a colon, as in WORD: 32.

To use one of these comparison operators with the /KG option, it is necessary to enter three items of information: an optional keyword, the search character, and the field name on which to operate. These should be followed by the comparison operator and a value, as in the following example:

```
MICROPROCESSOR&WORD =32.
```

Retrieving Text from VisiDex

A more sophisticated way to use VisiDex is via the Print command (/P), which allows you to search for and then retrieve text in a single operation. It allows you to send specific text to the printer, to the screen for display, or to an external text file.

Once invoked, the Print command status area sends the following message:

```
F OR PRINTER SLOT #
```

If you select F (for file), VisiDex will ask you for the name of the file to which you wish to send the screen of text.

To send the output to the screen, enter 0. To sent it to a printer, enter the name of the slot number of the printer card in your Apple II. After choosing where you want the file to be sent, you have eight Print-command options:

Calendar (/PC)	Line (/PL)
Dump (/PD)	Page (/PP)
Index (/PI)	Sorted Listing (/PS)
Keyword (/PK)	Title (/PT)

Before you select a keyword for a particular screen or conduct a search, it is a good idea to search the index of keywords and keydates by using the /PI option. This gives you the choice of three categories of indices: keywords beginning with a letter; keywords beginning with a number, punctuation mark, or special character; and keydates. Although each keyword can be up to 253 characters long, the Print Index option allows you to see only the first 15 characters, followed by a number. The number following each keyword or keydate is the number of screens referenced by that keyword or keydate.

Searching through a VisiDex kbase is faster with the /PK option than with the /KG command, because the /PK option allows you to select the number of lines you wish to send to a particular output device. After you've entered any valid keyword and/or search string, VisiDex will ask you for document length. If you are still in an investigative mode, select any number from 1 to 22, the maximum number of lines on a screen.

If you've constructed the "cards" in your VisiDex kbase properly, you should be able to tell whether or not you want a card from the first five or six lines. If you want to see the whole screen, leave the option set at its default value of 0. If you want to send the text of a card to a printer, determine the number of screens per printed page (up to three). If you want only a single screen per page, select 22; if you want two per page, select 44; and if you want three per page, select 66.

Using the Print Line (/PL) and Print Page (/PP) options allows you to be even more precise in determining which portions of a VisiDex kbase to print or send to a disk file. The /PP command allows you to print all the lines of the page being displayed, whereas the /PL command allows you to move line by line through the screen being displayed, sending each line either to an external file or to the printer. The /PS command prints keyword or keydate screens in one of three sorted listing categories: keywords beginning with a letter, keywords beginning with a number, or keydates.

Comments and Evaluation

Compared to some of the other index card and bibliographic programs in this book, such as CITATION and CARDBOX, the search methodology allowed by VisiDex is much less sophisticated. It searches by matching characters to either a keyword list or the actual text and does not allow you to use Boolean operators such as AND, OR, and NOT, as a result of which there is no way to easily narrow or expand your search range. It is also not very easy to exclude particular character strings or keywords from the search. Somewhat disconcerting is the fact that although VisiDex allows you to specify keywords up to 253 characters in length, you can only search for keywords that are up to 38 characters long.

Counterbalancing these limitations is a text retrieval capability that, in its ease of use and number of options, is far more flexible than the text retrieval capabilities of the other index card programs evaluated.

CHAPTER 12

Three More Index Card Programs

CARDFILE, PCFILE, and CARDBOX

ProTem Software's CARDFILE

Developed by ProTem Software, Inc. and distributed by Digital Marketing Corporation, CARDFILE creates a "card file environment" in which you can use your word processor to create the cards, so you don't have to learn any unfamiliar editing and cursor movement commands.

New cards are read into a CARDFILE kbase automatically when you run the program. Although the text must be entered in a highly structured manner, preceded by key or descriptor lines containing words that CARD-FILE uses to search, this structure can easily be modified using your word processor.

Each distribution disk contains a long-form version of the program, allowing three descriptor lines and 18 text lines, and a short form allowing 6 lines of text. Using the long form, you can store between 100 and 110 cards on a double-density, single-sided, 5.25-inch diskette. With the short form, you can store 300–320 entries. Whereas some of the other electronic index card programs take an hour or so to learn to use, learning to use CARDFILE takes no more than 10–15 minutes.

CARDFILE Overview

CARDFILE requires three things: an 8080/8085-, Z80-, or 8086/ 8088-based computer with at least 48K bytes of RAM; CP/M 2.2, MP/ M, CP/M-86, or IBM PC-DOS (MS-DOS); and a standard word processor/text editor, such as WordStar, Spellbinder, Peachtext, Select, or EasyWriter II. CARDFILE contains the following files:

- The long CARDFILE program, called CF.COM under CP/M 2.2, CF.CMD under CP/M-86, and CF.EXE under MS-DOS.
- The prompts program used by CF, called CF.PRM.
- The data file for CF, which contains three sample cards, called CF.DAT.
- Examples of alternative prompt and data files.
- SCF.COM (or .EXE or .CMD), SCF.PRM and SCF.DAT, the program, and prompt and data files for the short version.

In addition to these files, the CP/M 2.2 version also contains CFINSTAL.COM, which creates the environment program.

The cards created by CARDFILE are stored in fixed-length record files, regardless of how much is contained on each card. In the CP/M 2.2 version, each CF record requires about 1.5K bytes and each SCF record takes up about 500 bytes.

Installing CARDFILE

For 16-bit computers operating under MS-DOS or CP/M-86, the installation procedure for CARDFILE is relatively straightforward. It involves moving the short and long versions of the program to separate working diskettes to allow room for the data files to grow. It is also a good idea to move a copy of your word-processing program to the same working diskettes if you have enough capacity—usually more than 180K bytes. If you have less capacity than that, keep the word-processing program on a separate diskette.

For 8-bit systems using CP/M 2.2, it is also necessary to install a text editor environment program that makes it possible for CARDFILE to read in new cards automatically. To do this, log onto the drive containing the CARDFILE programs, call up the CFINSTAL routine, and answer the questions as they appear on the screen. This routine asks which word-processing program you are using, the name you use to call it up, and the name you may want to give the program that will automatically run the word processor. If you name it, say, WSCF, CFINSTAL will create a new program called WSCF.COM. This program should be located on the same diskette as your word processor.

Creating a Card

Each card created for inclusion in a CARDFILE kbase must have the same basic format:

First line	Has keywords that identify the subjects discussed in the text.
Second line	Lists the title of the article.
Third line	Lists author or editor and publication information.
Fourth to twenty-first lines	Text containing notes or abstract of article.

Each line of text in a CARDFILE card can hold no more than 72 characters. If a line has more characters than that, the program will either omit them or read them incorrectly. To be safe, ProTem recommends that you set the right margin at 65 characters—the default setting on many text editors and word processors.

Modifying the Card Format

If the above default format for the cards in your kbase does not suit your needs, it can be changed by modifying the prompts contained in the CF.PRM file. This file determines the name and location of the data file. An ordinary document file, CF.PRM can be easily changed using a word processor. As configured by ProTem, the file looks like this:

```
Subjects:
Title:
Author:
Text:
CF.DAT
```

The last line of CF.PRM has the name of the data file where the cards are stored. It has been given the name CF.DAT, but you can give it any name you want as long as it is compatible with CP/M or PC-DOS/MS-DOS naming conventions. The prompts can also be renamed to conform to the information contained in the kbase.

For example, before some of the disk catalog programs described in Chapter 18 appeared on the market, I reconfigured CF.PRM to serve as a way of keeping track of what was in the various files on my many diskettes as follows:

```
Filename:
Subject:
Magazine:
Descriptors:
```

On the first line, I list the filename as stored on the diskette. But instead of a .TXT, .DOC file type extension, I substitute .D## where the latter locations can be any number up to 9. This tells me the disk location of a particular file. For example, suppose the microprocessor article described in Chapter 10 is stored on Diskette 12 under the name MICRO.TXT. In my reformatted card, I would list it as MICRO.D12. Under Subject, I would list a general description of the article, such as Motorola 68000. Under Magazine, I would list the magazine the article was written for. Under Descriptors, I would list the keywords that describe the essence of the article.

Entering Text

To enter text into CARDFILE, all you do is call up your word processor via the environment program and proceed to enter text into each of the fields created earlier. When you call up the text editor environment program, it loads itself into memory, then loads the text editor or word processor and monitors its operation while you are creating a card. When you save an edited document under WSCF, an empty or dummy file is created having the same filename but a different file type or extension (.Y). For example, if you create a card called INTEL88 containing information on the 8088 microprocessor, it will automatically create the file INTEL88.Y. When CARDFILE is used in the Search mode, it will look for all files with the extension .Y, reading the corresponding document file into the data file and deleting the dummy file.

Searching a CARDFILE Knowledge Base

Almost as soon as CARDFILE is loaded into your computer, it is ready to perform a search. In the CP/M 2.2 version, a Subjects prompt is immediately displayed. In the 16-bit versions, the program first asks for the name of the next file to be read into the program. Pressing the Return key in response causes the Subjects prompt to be displayed. Following Subjects three additional prompts appear: Title, Author, and Text. Pressing the Return key in each case causes CARDFILE to display the first card in the kbase. To continue browsing through the kbase sequentially, press C (to continue).

Each time a card is displayed, CARDFILE displays a set of prompts at the bottom of the screen instructing you at the appropriate time to enter:

N to start a new search

X to exit the program

Escape to skip succeeding prompts

Control Z after the first entry to search the top three lines

A to invoke an auxiliary menu

Via the auxiliary menu, you are prompted to (1) print the displayed card, (2) write the displayed card to disk, (3) erase a card, and (4) continue the search.

Search Strategies

In response to the system prompts, it is possible to search the CARD-FILE kbase in a number of different ways.

To search for a subject or subjects, all you need to do is enter the appropriate word or words after the Subject prompt and press the Return key for the other three prompts. The program doesn't care what order the keywords are in, as long as they are separated by commas. Nor is any limit placed on the number of keywords listed. However, for practical purposes, entering more than two or three keywords slows down the search considerably.

To search for all cards with a particular word in the title, simply type the word in on the title line. It is also possible to search the top three lines at once by simply entering the keywords and pressing Control Z. This is useful in cases where there are descriptive words in the title that are not listed in the subject line or when you cannot remember on which line the keywords occur.

It is also possible to search the main text. This is done by pressing the Return key for the first three prompts and, after the Text prompt, typing in the keyword you want to find. Unlike the case with searches at the higher levels, you can only search the text for one word or phrase at a time. Search times are also much longer, since the program searches sequentially through the text for a particular word. For this reason, text searches should be used only as a last resort.

It is possible to start a new search at any time by pressing the N key or, leaving the program, by pressing X followed by Return.

Retrieving Text from CARDFILE

Via the auxiliary menu, you have the choice of sending a card displayed during a search to the printer or to a external disk file. During any search sequence, when a card appears that you may want to use, you can call up the auxiliary menu and select either the P(rint) or W(rite to disk) option. CARDFILE will then flag the card and continue the search without printing or writing to the disk. When you have completed all searches and Exit (X) the system, CARDFILE will automatically print out the selected cards or send them to separate disk files.

Although there is no limit on the number of cards that can be printed out, you are limited to 26 cards for output to a diskette file. This is because CARDFILE assigns unique filenames to each cared, starting with A.CFD and ending with Z.CFD. You must then use your word-processing program to combine them into a single file.

TexaSoft's PCFILE

Designed for use on the IBM PC or any MS-DOS–compatible computer with a minimum of 64K bytes of internal RAM, PCFILE allows you to store textual information of up to 200 lines per entry.

PCFILE Overview

The number of records per kbase using PCFILE depends on (1) the size of each record entry and (2) the storage capacity of the diskette being used to store the information. If you are using a single-sided, double-density diskette with about 140,000 characters of space, and if each record requires a minimum of 160 characters (two 80-chatacter lines—one for keywords, one for text), the maximum number of entries will be 875. If your entries are 5 lines long, PCFILE will allow you to store up to 290 records. The number of keywords per kbase is unlimited, but the number of keywords per entry is limited to the number that can be entered into a 65-character key line.

PCFILE is menu-driven. When you enter the program by entering PCFILE, a menu with the following nine options will appear on the screen:

```
(1) Print all entries
(2) Help
(3) End
(4) Delete
(5) Edit
(6) Create
(7) Restart
(8) Pick by entry number
(9) Pick by keyword
```

Entering Text into PCFILE

There are two sections in any PCFILE record: the Keyword section, a single 65-character line, and the Text section, with up to 199 eighty-character lines.

To enter text into a PCFILE kbase, select option 6 from the menu and enter the keywords at the Keyword prompt. With 65 characters, you can enter as many as 6–8 words, enough to describe even a 200-line record. Next enter the text, prompted by a line number and a question mark.

This can be done in two ways. For short records, you can use PCFILE's built-in line editor. For long records, you should first create the entry on a word processor. To merge this external ASCII file with your PCFILE kbase at a specific entry location, enter the command "GET filename."

Modifying an Entry

By selecting option 5, you can make changes in the keywords or text or replace an old entry with a new one of the same length. PCFILE first lists the keywords and then the text, line by line. If you wish to change a line, reenter it. If you don't want to make any changes in a particular line, press Enter and the prompt will advance to the next line.

Searching a PCFILE Knowledge Base

A PCFILE kbase can be searched in two ways: by the entry number (option 8) or by keyword (option 9). The latter option allows you to search according to a match with a single keyword or several keywords linked by the Boolean operators AND and OR. It searches for the first occurrence of your search string, displays it, and asks if you want to continue.

If you answer yes, the next matching entry will be displayed, with the options to send the display to either a printer or a file. If you simply want to browse, select option 1. It allows you to send the entries to the terminal for display, to print directly to a printer, to write to a file, or to send the entries to the terminal with options to send to a printer or file.

Caxton Software's CARDBOX

Designed to be used on any 8-bit computer operating under CP/M 2.0 (or later CP/M programs) or MP/M, CARDBOX requires at least 48K bytes of RAM, two disk drives, and a 24 line × 80 character video display. With CARDBOX, your text is organized into records resembling pre-printed index cards at the top of the screen. It lets you create records containing up to 1404 characters each, with as many as 26 fields. The maximum number of records per file is 65,600. Each file can be as large as 8M bytes; the only limit is the size of your disk storage. You are prompted at all times by a menu at the bottom of the screen. The menu contents change according to which mode you are operating in; they are usually displayed at the bottom of the screen.

Creating a Card

Before you can store information in a CARDBOX kbase, it is necessary to create a card structure. Each card is divided into rectangular fields, each of which must be defined according to five criteria: (1) the start position,

(2) the end position, (3) the name or type of field, (4) the title or field name to be displayed, and (5) whether or not it is to be an index field.

In the Index mode, you can determine the degree of indexing in any field via four basic commands:

All	Makes all words within a field keywords.
None	Prevents any words in the field from being keywords.
Auto	Assumes that each word is a keyword during text entry until told otherwise.
Man	Assumes that none of the words entered are keywords until told otherwise.

Entering Text into CARDBOX

Although you are restricted to a single page/screen per form, CARD-BOX allows you to enter text and move the cursor much as you would with a word processor. However, the program also includes keys for moving to the beginning or end of a field as well as to the next field. Via a single keystroke, specific words in a field, if allowed, can be tagged as keywords. Although there is no limit on the number of keywords you can specify, remember that when you wish to search the entire text, the larger the number of keyboards, the slower the search.

Searching a CARDBOX Knowledge Base

You can search through the cards in a CARDBOX kbase one by one, by keyword, or by nonindexed word. In the first mode, specific keys allow you to move to the next card, to the previous card, to the last card, or to the first card. Keyword searches are performed using three commands: Select (AND), Include (OR), and Exclude (NOT). Special versions of the Select and Exclude commands are available that allow you to search all text in your cards, not just keywords. Searching is performed in levels or stages, narrowing and expanding the search as appropriate, with criteria applied at each. At each level, the program searches only those records that meet the combined criteria for all previous searches. Up to 100 levels can be searched at any one time.

To let you move around the search tree relatively freely, CARDBOX includes Back and Clear commands, which let you undo a selection one record at a time or in groups of records. Also included is a History command, which tells you the search history of your current selection of cards, and Listindex, which allows you to predict the effect of a Select command.

Once the program has selected the appropriate cards from the database, you can read through them using the browse functions, printing or sending cards to a separate disk file one at a time or in groups.

Comments and Evaluation

Although roughly equivalent in terms of card capacity, each of these index card programs has its own particular strengths. CARDIFILE uses the most primitive form of searching—searching by simple character string matching. But of all of the index card programs in this section, CARDFILE is the easiest to use. Whereas the other programs take as much as an hour to learn to use, this one requires no more than 10–15 minutes. PCFILE, of course, is not that much harder to learn, and it also allows you to perform multikeyword searches using AND/OR operators. At the other extreme is CARDBOX, with its very sophisticated—and demanding—search methodology, requiring several days to master.

If all you require is a program you can use as a research aid or for such business applications as tickler files—indeed, for any application for which you'd normally used regular index cards—any of the programs in this section are adequate. Aside from the differences above, the choice is a matter of personal preference based on your compatibility with the way a particular program "thinks."

CHAPTER 13

Three Bibliography Programs

CITATION, BIBLIOTEK, and Find It Quick

Almost as common as the ubiquitous electronic index card programs surveyed in the previous two chapters are the numerous bibliographic citation programs available.

Whereas programs such as VisiDex, CARDFILE, CARDBOX, and PCFILE are more efficient and easier to use in the maintenance of card file–type information than general-purpose kbase programs, bibliography programs are better at doing the specific job of maintaining magazine and book references.

In general, these programs work by imposing additional levels of structure onto the already relatively structured index card format. In addition to limits placed on field and record length, bibliography programs place further limits on what can be placed in various fields. Illustrative of the many such bibliography programs available are CITATION, BIBLIOTEK, and Find It Quick.

Eagle Enterprises' CITATION

Of the three bibliographic citation programs covered in this chapter, CITATION from Eagle Enterprises has by far the most sophisticated keyword definition and search capabilities.

CITATION Overview

CITATION allows you to store text in blocks of up to 800 characters in length, with up to six 20-character keywords per item. Searches can be conducted, however, with multikeyword sequences of up to ten words.

For each entry it is possible to store text in any of three formats: periodical/citation, publication, and name/address. Any item can be accessed within seconds, with the results displayed or printed in descending order of keyword matching score. In addition to an implicit AND operator, CITATION allows you to qualify your choice of keywords using NOT, ALL, and FROM/THRU.

CITATION is available in two versions, one for 8-bit CP/M systems, requiring at least 56K bytes of RAM (48K available for program use) and another for 16-bit PC-DOS/MS-DOS systems, requiring 96K bytes of RAM. Both require dual floppy or hard disk storage with a minimum of 85K bytes per drive (250K bytes are recommended). About 800 entries can be stored on a single 500K byte disk when the keyword index is stored on the same diskette, and 1000 can be stored when the index is on a separate drive. On a hard disk system, about 1600 fully indexed entries are possible for each megabyte of storage, assuming an average of 300 characters and three keywords per entry.

The minimum program disk capacity for running CITATION with all the programs on a single disk is 227K bytes. If your system disk capacity is less than 227K bytes, it is necessary to separate these programs into several logical groupings, including a primary system diskette and one or more secondary system diskettes. The primary system diskette contains the program modules that control the Main Menu, Print Citation, Keyword List, and Index programs as well as files containing date information and CRT control codes. The secondary system diskettes contain program modules concerned with the printing and display of the results of keyword searches, the updating and browsing of CITATION entries, and various file management functions. When CITATION is run with multiple program disks, the user always begins by inserting the primary program disk, with the secondary system disks inserted when requested by the CITATION Main Menu program.

Creating a CITATION Knowledge Base

In operation, CITATION automatically creates three additional types of files for each new kbase you use: a parameter file, contained on the main system diskette; a master data file, which stores the text entries; and an associated keyword index file. The master data and associated keyword index files are both contained on a separate working text file diskette.

For most of the CITATION program operations you are prompted via the Main Menu, which is displayed when you first invoke the program. It is then redisplayed after each required function is completed, prompting you to enter one of the following function codes:

```
*Update/browse CITATION entries (menu function 11)
*Multikeyword selection, print/display results (21)
*Print CITATION file (31)
*Print/display keyword index (32)
*Print/display keyword list (33)
*Recreate CITATION file (41)
*Recreate CITATION index (42)
*Update parameter file (43)
*Load from external file (44)
*Merge CITATION files (45)
*Reset data/file ID (90)
*Exit CITATION (99)
```

Defining a CITATION Knowledge Base

Before the Main Menu is displayed, CITATION asks you for the current date and a two-character file ID, which it then uses to open a kbase parameter file. Before you can enter text into your kbase, you msut select Main Menu function 43 to define the parameters of your kbase.

When selected, this option asks you for a file description up to 48 characters in length. This description is displayed on the screen each time the kbase is accessed. It also appears as the heading of all reports generated from this kbase. Via this submenu you also store this kbase on up to six disk drives and direct the program to pause after printing each entry to change sheets of paper. You can also direct the program to treat the author name as a keyword.

Entering Text

To enter text into a CITATION kbase or to add new information, just enter code 11 for the update/browse function. In response to your choice, CITATION will ask you if you want to Add, Change, View, or Delete. If you select the Add function, you will be asked to choose one of three types of text entry formats:

Type 1—Periodical Citation: Consisting of fields for information source (48 characters), authors (48 characters), title (48 characters), volume (4 characters), date (6 characters), and page (4 characters).

Type 2—Publication: Consisting of fields for title, authors, chapters and publisher (each of which is 48 characters long); page (4 characters); and date (6 characters).

Type 3—Name/Address: Consisting of 48 character fields for the name and three address lines, 19 characters for the city, 3 for the state or province, 11 for the ZIP or International Postal code; 28 for the salutation, and 12 for the phone number.

All three types have the same amount of space for keywords (120 characters, or six 20-character lines) and comments (800 characters or ten 80-character lines).

Data and/or text is entered within each field, and the cursor is moved the same way as with a word processor, except for tabbing back and forth between fields. In the comment field, CITATION supports a number of word-processing functions, such as word-wrap, cursor up and down, line insert, line delete, tabbing, and line clear, to simplify lengthy entries.

Loading External Files

To simplify entry of text into a CITATION kbase, particularly if you have a lot of information, the best procedure would be to use your word processor to construct your text according to the above rules and then enter the text using Main Menu function 44. The external files can have any name you want, but they must not have any of the special control characters that might have been inserted by a word-processing program. The files should then be marked with special control characters recognizable by the CITATION program.

Searching a CITATION Knowledge Base

There are three ways to search through a CITATION kbase, depending on whether you are looking for (1) a particular citation or name, (2) records that contain references to a single keyword or portion of a keyword, or (3) records that meet multiple keyword criteria. If your requirements fall into category 1 or 2, select menu function 11. However, instead of selecting Add, enter the code letter for View (V), as a result of which

CITATION will ask you to select one of the following access methods: S(pecific), K(eyword), F(irst), or N(ext).

Single-Keyword Searches

If you enter K, you are telling the program you want to access items on the basis of single keywords. The program will prompt you to enter the keyword you are looking for. Your kbase of CITATION items is then searched for the first item with a character sequence equal to or greater than what you requested. For example, if you are looking for all items containing the keyword "microprocessor," you could enter M and CITATION would begin by showing the first item beginning with the letter M. Or you could enter a portion of a word, such as "micro," and it would search for all items with keywords beginning with that partial sequence. The search string can be as short as one alphabetical character or as long as you want, but it must consist of a single keyword or phrase. In general, however, the shorter the search string, the faster the search. This faster search speed must be balanced, however, against the time you may have to spend browsing through items that are not related to what you are looking for.

Search by Title/Name/Date

If you select S, the program will prompt you for the specific name or title of the entry you want and for the date, where appropriate. You can enter all or any portion of the above fields, up to their maximum length.

If you select F or N, you are asking the program to obtain the first or the next item on the basis of the current selection method. If you are searching by keyword, the program will find the first or next item for the most recently requested keyword; if you are searching by title, name, or source, it will find either the first item of the kbase or the next item in alphabetical order from your current location.

A similar procedure is followed if you want to change or delete an item.

Multikeyword Searches

To perform searches for items that satisfy multikeyword criteria, you must use Main Menu function 21. When this function is selected a special keyword selection screen is displayed with blank keyword fields for up to ten keywords and their keyword qualifiers (NOT, FROM, THRU, and ALL). When you have finished entering the keywords, two more columns are displayed, one for Hits and the other for Items Found. Below these two columns is another field indicating Items Selected. Blank during keyword entry, these columns are filled in after you press the Return key to terminate keyword entry and begin the search phase.

The program then accesses your kbase's keyword index file on the basis of requested and excluded keywords and determines the degree to which each entry in the master file matches the keywords requested. The maximum match is a 7 and the minimum is a 1.

As the search progresses, statistics are displayed on the screen showing the number of items found for each keyword (Hits) and the number of items found and selected according to the number of matching keywords in the item (Items Found).

During the search process you can specify the minimum number of matching keywords an item must have to be selected. Index pointers are sorted in descending order on the basis of their keyword match scores, with the best-matching items shown first.

Retrieving CITATION Lists

If matching items are found, an option screen will be displayed, asking you to indicate how the found items are to be processed. The options include displaying, printing, displaying and then printing, and displaying and then writing the items to another file. Via this screen you can also select to print/write either all the items or only those you select after viewing them on the screen.

If you want to write the item or items to an external file, the program will ask you for the name of the file and the drive to which you want to send it. Similar alternatives are available for a CITATION-type file output, except that the program asks for a new two-character file ID number.

If you want hard copy of the contents of your kbase, select Main Menu function 31. Items are listed in sequence by source, title, or name and then by date and page number.

Main Menu function 32 allows you to Display/Print or Display/Write to file the index for any keyword or set of keywords in your CITATION kbase. The report is in alphabetical sequence by keyword, with summarized references under each keyword in sequence by source, title, or name and then by date and page number.

Via Main Menu function 33, you can direct the program to Display/

Print/Write a listing of your kbase keywords, starting at whatever word or alphabetical letter you ask for.

Scientific Software Products' BIBLIOTEK

Designed for operation on Apple II+ and Apple IIe computers, Scientific Software's bibliography manager, called BIBLIOTEK, requires at least 48K bytes of RAM and two disk drives. Once a collection of citations has been stored in a BIBLIOTEK kbase, searches can be conducted using author names, title phrases, publication titles, dates, phrases in comments, or keywords as criteria in any combination using AND, OR, and NOT Boolean operators.

BIBLIOTEK Overview

The program allows the storage of up to 480 citations per single-sided, single-density diskette. Maximum title length is 224 characters; maximum author length is 25 characters. The text or comment field is limited to about 200 characters per entry. Up to eight keywords per citation can be specified in the keyword field, and even more can be specified if the comment area is used for keyword storage.

As a tool for researchers and writers to control and manage their collection of reprints, literature references, and research notes, the program is menu-driven, instructing the user step by step as to what information needs to be entered and in what order. Most operations of the program can be selected from the Main Menu, which allows you to choose from the following options:

```
(A) Edit a bibliography
(B) Search a bibliography
(C) Edit citation lists
(D) Print citation to paper or to disk
(E) Define print formats
(F) Edit keywords
(G) Start a new bibliography
(H) System hardware setup
(I) Copy
(J) Exit BIBLIOTEK
```

Setting Up a BIBLIOTEK Knowledge Base

After properly configuring your hardware and software to run the program and making a backup copy of the distribution disk, the first step in setting up a bibliographic kbase is to select Main Menu option G, with which you are asked to assign a name to the diskette containing your kbase and specify the length, in characters, of the reference field provided for this particular bibliography.

The reference field can be anywhere from 4 to 12 characters long and contains a unique identifier (either numbers alone or letters and numbers) for each entry; this identifier is used by the program to find the entry's location on the diskette. The size of this field should be considered very carefully, for if it is too short, you will not be able to uniquely identify each entry. If it is too long, it will take up extra disk space and require more processing time than is necessary.

Entering Bibliographic Information

Selecting Main Menu option A moves you into the Bibliographic Editor mode, in which you can enter, edit, and delete text at the prompting of the program. Whenever information is required, a prompt is generated, explaining to you what response is to be made in the following underlined field. After entering your response, push Return, signaling to the program that you have finished and want to move to the next blank field.

Until you push the Return key, you can edit text by using different control key codes to insert characters, delete single characters, cancel an entry and restore the default entry, if any, erase all characters from the cursor position to the end of the blank, move the cursor to the right, and move the cursor to the left. Additional control character commands allow you to move forward and backward page by page in a BIBLIOTEK kbase.

Among the various fields presented to you for completion in this mode are (1) the reference field number; (2) the work type; (3) the subtype; (4) the title; (5) the author; (6) the year, month, and day of issue; (7) the volume; (8) the issue; (9) the edition; (10) the first and last pages of a citation; (11) the publisher; (12) the location of the publisher or conference; (13) the opening and closing date of the conference; and (14) up to eight keywords and comments with up to a total of 200 characters. The comment area can be used either for ordinary text/abstract information or for additional indexing capability by entering keywords and searching the comment.

Editing Your Citation Lists

Selecting Main Menu option C puts you in the Citation List Editor mode, where you can control the order and content of your citation lists. Among the operations you can perform in this mode are selection, deletion or review of a list, changing list order and content, and selecting lists from other bibliography disks for insertion in the current list. In this mode you can sort citation lists by author, date of issue, or manually, whereby you reorder them according to your particular requirements. It is also possible to move a citation within a list, delete it, add it to the end of a list, or insert it at a specified position within a list.

Editing/Modifying Keywords

In addition to allowing you to enter keywords via the bibliography editor, BIBLIOTEK also provides a keyword editor (Main Menu option F) that allows you to add, modify, and delete keywords. In addition, you can combine keywords. Another useful feature is the ability to print an alphabetized list of your keywords so that you can easily find the keyword number to use when you are entering citations into your bibliography.

Keyword editing functions include View, which displays all keywords on the screen for review; Modify, which allows you to change keywords; Delete, which allows keywords to be removed from the list; Merge, which allows references to any one keyword to be changed to a reference to a second keyword (especially useful if you accidentally enter the same keyword twice); Print; and Exit, to the Main Menu.

Searching a BIBLIOTEK Knowledge Base

Using menu selection B, you can search for citations by specific keywords, authors, ranges of dates, phrases within the specific title, phrases within the comment section, or any logical combination of these. After a search is completed, a list of all the citations that meet the specified criteria is saved on the bibliography disk.

In addition to searching a single bibliography and creating a citation list, this option allows you to select citations from several different bibliography disks and transfer them to another bibliography disk. It also allows you to merge or split bibliographies as well as create a new one from subsets of existing ones.

Retrieving Citations with BIBLIOTEK

One of the most powerful features of BIBLIOTEK, one that makes it unique among the bibliographic/card file programs reviewed in this book, is its ability to construct print formats. These are templates or patterns that describe the content of a citation or list of citations to be printed. The "Define print formats," selected via Main Menu option E, allows you to specify not only what citation information will be printed, but the order in which it will be printed and the punctuation to be used.

Formats are defined using "tokens" to represent each of the items of information to be stored. In BIBLIOTEK, the various characters of the alphabet (upper- and lower-case), numerals, and special characters represent particular pieces of information stored for a citation. With this feature, it is possible to reduce the detailed and complicated style and format guidelines recommended by a journal's editors to a single one-line mathlike formula.

Instant Software's Find It Quick

A tightly structured program, Find It Quick (FIQ) is configured into a journal/magazine format and requires a minimum system consisting of a TRS-80 Model I, Level II with 16K bytes of RAM, an expansion interface with at least 16K bytes of additional RAM, and at least one disk drive, with two disk drives preferred. One single-density, 40-track diskette can store up to 1080 bibliographic citations, with 12 journal names and 230 keywords, or, alternatively, 20 journal names and 210 keywords.

Find It Quick Overview

The distribution diskette containing the FIQ program also contains Instant Software's Tiny DOS operating system, allowing you to be up and running with the program as soon as you insert the diskette in drive 0. Once the program has been loaded, single–disk drive users will be prompted to remove the program/DOS diskette and insert the data/DOS diskette. On dual-drive systems, users are directed to insert the data disk in drive 1. Upon entering the command Run, the Main Menu of the system will be displayed:

```
(1) Write new citations into the library
(2) Read citations in library in sequential order
(3) Review the list of keywords already in file
(4) Review list of Journals currently in file

Obtain selected citations according to

(5) Given keywords
(6) Journal title and date
(7) Selected by author          Press (E) to End
(8) Keyword or phrase in title        choice?? >
```

If you have entered a blank data diskette, the program will first ask your name and the name of the bibliographic kbase, both of which will be displayed on the screen before the menu appears.

Entering Text into Find It Quick

Selecting option 1 from the menu places you in the Data Entry mode. The first two fields displayed are the Author and Title fields, with asterisks at the edge of each field to mark the maximum admissible length. The Author field may contain 21 characters, and the Title field may contain 30 characters. Pressing the Enter key after typing in the author information, and again after the Title field, causes the display to be replaced with three more fields: Journal Title (28 characters long), Date (5 characters long), and Page (5 characters long). The Enter key is pressed after each entry. At the time of entry, the left arrow can be used to erase any mistakes.

Entering Keywords

Following the citation entry, the program asks how many keywords you wish to tag the article with; you may choose up to nine. As each numeral appears on the screen, enter a keyword. After each keyword is entered, the keyword list will be searched. If the one just entered is not in the list, you will be asked to indicate whether you wish to add it to the list.

Since there is a limit of 280 keywords per FIQ kbase, it is best to choose non-unique keywords, words that can be associated with a group of items.

After the last field has been filled in, the program will direct you to press X if there are further corrections or L if it is the last item, followed by Enter to continue.

Up to 12 bibliographic items can be entered at a time. Moreover, with each batch of 12 items, the computer remembers the information entered in the previous items. So if all 12 articles come from the same journal or magazine, the magazine title need only be entered once. The same is true for the date. The same field entry can be assigned to all other entries in the group just by pressing the Enter key when those fields appear.

Browsing through Find It Quick

Selecting option 2 from the menu allows you to read items entered into a FIQ kbase in sequential order, starting at whatever point you specify. The title section tells you how many items there are in the list and asks you to enter a number from which to begin reading. The program searches the FIQ list and loads the items into RAM 12 at a time. To return to a previous item, you simply press the B key. Pressing A will allow you to alter the fields in the entry, and pressing D will delete the entire entry.

Selecting option 3 displays the current keyword list, and selecting 4 displays the journals list. The keywords are displayed 40 to a page in four columns, whereas the journals are listed ten to a page in a single column. If you want a hard copy of a particular item, press P at the time of display.

Locating Specific Find It Quick Entries

You can search through the FIQ kbase in four ways: by keyword, by journal, by date, and by author or keyword-in-title.

Option 5 places you in the Keyword Search mode, whereby you are asked to type in the number of keywords you want to use in the search. Any number can be listed. However, FIQ "ANDs" the keywords together. That is, if you list, say, three keywords, FIQ will select only those articles having all three keywords After giving you an opportunity to correct your search sequence, FIQ searches sequentially through all items that match. Options 6 and 7 allow you to search by journal title and/or date.

Option 7 (author search) and 8 (keyword-in-title search) operate slightly differently than the other search options in that both make use of an INSTR function. This allows you to search a string for any sequence of characters, not just complete words. Thus, if you were searching for an article written by BERNARD C. COLE, you could enter, B, BER, NARD, NARD C, COLE, or OLE. The keyword-in-title search is best used when you recall a word in the title that was not general enough to be included in the keyword list.

In the Search mode, you have all the options available in the option 1 mode: Print, Page Forward, Page Backward, Alter, Delete, and End.

Comments and Evaluation

These three programs are good illustrations of the diverse approaches taken to meeting the need of writing professionals for a computerized method of maintaining bibliographic citations. Whereas general-purpose, free-form knowledge-processing and even index card programs can be adapted to perform some of these functions, only specialized programs such as CITATION, BIBLIOTEK, and FIQ can meet the particular requirements of the writing professional.

FIQ has the most limited search methodology of the three. But its particular strengths are ease of use and the greatest capacity, not only in numbers of citations per kbase, but also in number of keywords. BIBLIOTEK is the most limited in capacity, but its strength is in the power of its unique template approach to citation retrieval. More than any other such program I have looked at, it allows the user to customize its output to the particular requirements of specific publications and journals. CITATION falls into the middle ground between the other two in capacity. It is also more difficult to learn to use than the other two. But it shines in the number of ways the user can search through a kbase of citations.

Part V

TREE-STRUCTURED KNOWLEDGE-PROCESSING PROGRAMS

CHAPTER 14

QUESTEXT

The Electronic Wordsheet

Information Reduction Research's QUESTEXT, version 3.6, is a tree-structured knowledge-processing program of wide-ranging flexibility and power. It is to programs such as ThinkTank, FirstDraft, and EAZYFILE what general-purpose, free-form programs such as SUPERFILE are to more limited index card programs such as VisiDex and CARDFILE.

In QUESTEXT, textual information is organized into a hierarchical structure consisting of four levels: major category, subcategory, heading, and text. Each level consists of lines of text that can contain up to 65 characters. Every line is numbered and can be selected as a menu choice. However, QUESTEXT does not formally distinguish between text and menu structures. Any line of text can be a menu selection, since it is automatically connected to the next-lower level by the system.

At each level there can be up to 99 lines of menu/text. But this is not as serious a limitation as it might appear, since QUESTEXT allows any subcategory to be broken down into further subcategories. In other words, with QUESTEXT you can organize a kbase with up to 99 major categories, each of which can have up to 99 subcategories. Each subcategory can have up to 99 headings, and each heading can have up to 99 lines of text.

At a minimum, QUESTEXT can be used to perform all the basic functions of an outline processor—outlining, boilerplating, and templating. But because of its capacity, it is also capable of serving as a full-function knowledge-processing program equivalent in power to most of the free-form knowledge processors surveyed in Part II. Within the constraints of this hierarchical structure, kbases of substantial size can be stored.

For example, the information in this book was easily organized into the QUESTEXT format with chapter titles as major categories, subsections as subcategories, and paragraph titles as headings.

Accessing any piece of information is very quick, since you need only make three choices to gain access to an individual heading and the associated text. When this is combined with a new keyword capability, a wide array of search and retrieve strategies is possible.

QUESTEXT Overview

QUESTEXT is available for use on both 8- and 16-bit CP/M-based systems as well as the MS-DOS–based IBM PC and other similar 16-bit systems. It requires 60K bytes of RAM on CP/M-based systems and 96K on computers operating under PC/MS-DOS.

QUESTEXT is distributed with three programs: (1) QU.COM, (2) QF.COM, and (3) QTXT.MSG for CP/M systems and QU.EXE and QF.EXE for the IBM PC and MS-DOS–based systems. These give full access to all of QUESTEXT's features as well as numerous application examples, including QUESDOC, an electronic minimanual describing its features.

QF is the file manipulation module used to create, delete, and copy QUESTEXT application files. It will also allow you to alter the descriptive header material at the front of every QUESTEXT application base. QU is the utilization module. It is used to retrieve, add, delete, and edit information in QUESTEXT application files already created using QF. The two programs function as a single unit and contain the main menus: Menu 1 in QF and Menu 2 in QU. You can go to either program from the other without leaving QUESTEXT. QTXT.MSG is used for storage of help information and large menus.

Four other program modules—QI, QB, Q, and QOB—provide for limited access to system features and autoactivation of frequently used applications. QI is an inquire only module; QB is the build, print, or inquire module; Q is the autoactivate inquire only module on logged drive; and QOB, the autoactivate inquire only module on B drive.

Although QUESTEXT can be used on single-drive systems, having at least two disk drives is recommended—one for the various system programs and the other for disks with each of your application bases. Every QUESTEXT application consists of five files. All are assigned the same filename, but each has a unique extension: .XP, .CLS, .SCL, .QLS, or .ALS. For example, an application base of information on knowledge processing, named KBase, contains the following five files: KBASE.XP, KBASE.CLS, KBASE.SCL, KBASE.QLS, and KBASE.ALS.

Within these five files, QUESTEXT organizes your kbase in a hierarchical manner; that is, it forces you to establish classes of information, each of which may contain subclasses, each of which in turn may contain sub-subclasses. As mentioned earlier, QUESTEXT organizes your text into four levels: major categories, subcategories, headings, and finally text, where the desired information is stored. Each QUESTEXT application is created with an obligatory major category called *+GENERAL+*, with a similarly named subcategory. These are present when each new XPERT Kbase is created, and neither can be deleted, changed, or duplicated. Information can be put into them as with any other category, and they are useful for storage of comments and suggestions pertaining to the operation of the particular XPERT application.

Operation of QUESTEXT involves the use of no more than a dozen or so basic commands, all of which are performed within the context of two menus. The main function of Menu 1 is to aid you in defining the purpose and basic parameters of your kbase—in QUESTEXT terms, building the XPERT shell—and in performing the backup file manipulation associated with managing a kbase, as shown in Screen 1.

After you have defined the XPERT shell, it is necessary to (1) give the kbase a structure by defining the categories, subcategories, and headings; (2) enter text into your kbase; and (3) search for specific information. This is done via Menu 2, shown in Screen 2.

Via these two menus, operations of this program are directed through the use of no more than a dozen or so basic commands, the most important of which are

H(elp)   Used to view explanations of commands and
                settings of variable features and to change those
                settings.

```
MENU 1 (File Operations)

Which mode of operation do you want?

(I) Introduction
(H) Help
(E) Editor instructions
(C) Create an XPERT shell
(M) Modify an XPERT description
(U) Use an existing XPERT
(B) Back up an XPERT
(D) Delete an XPERT
(X) Exit to system
```

Screen 1

S(how)	Displays complete information concerning your location within a QUESTEXT-generated kbase.
R(eview)	Allows you to redisplay on the screen text that may have been scrolled off.
U(p)	Used to move from a lower, more specific level to a more general one of your choice. Pressing Return takes you up one level.
T(op)	Takes you back up to the major category level you entered when the kbase XPERT was activated.
N(ext)	Usable only at the lowest level, it causes a display of the next heading and allows users to sequence

```
MENU 2 (System Utilization)

Which mode do you want to use?

(H) Help
(A) Activate an XPERT
(I) Inquire only
(B) Build, Print, or Inquire
(R) Revise (all functions available)
(F) File operations (MENU 1)
(X) Exit to system
```

Screen 2

	through a series of headings or subcategories with a minimum of keystrokes.
Q(uit)	Used to exit from an activated XPERT. It causes text files to be closed and changes made during the session to be saved.
P(rint)	Causes all or a portion of a kbase to be printed or sent to an external disk file.
A(dd)	Used to add lines of text to the end of the display at any level.
I(nsert)	Used to add a line of text in the position preceding some other line of text at any level.

D(elete)	Used to remove any numbered line of text displayed at any level.
M(ove)	Used to remove a line of text and reinsert it in another position within the same level.
E(dit)	Allows changes to be made in any line of text.
G(et)	Allows you to read a properly formatted external text file into a QUESTEXT-generated kbase.

Creating a Knowledge Base with QUESTEXT

Before you can store information in a QUESTEXT kbase, an XPERT shell must be created. This is done by selecting the C(reate) function from Menu 1. At the prompting of the program, you must supply the following information:

1. The disk drive on which the text files of your application kbase will be written.
2. The name of your XPERT application kbase (all caps, 1–8 characters without extension).
3. Name of the person creating the application kbase.
4. A short description of the application kbase, no more than three lines with a maximum of 65 characters each.
5. A set of notes or preliminary instructions, also no more than three 65-character lines.

If it is necessary to change or correct this descriptive material, this can be done by using the M(odify) function from Menu 1.

Creating Categories and Subcategories

Your newly created kbase XPERT remains a bare shell until you provide it with all the layers of category and textual information that you've determined it should include.

If you are using this program as a kbase rather than as an outline processor, you should spend a great deal of time developing a detailed outline before filling in the detailed descriptive text. This will save you time in the long run and involve less reworking and modification later on.

For example, suppose I wanted to organize the material in my microprocessor kbase (as described in Chapter 10) into a hierarchical structure with QUESTEXT rather than according to the AND/OR structure used in the free-form programs. The easiest way of doing this is to assign major category status to specific product types—Intel's 8088/8086, Motorola's 68000, Zilog's Z8000, and so on—and create another category containing comparison information about the various features and designated, naturally enough, Comparison. The various subcategories and headings beneath each structure are identical, delineating the various architectural features of each microprocessor. The overall outline I came up with for my QUESTEXT kbase, including each major category down to the heading level, looked like this:

MICROPROCESSOR TYPE
    Process Technology
        Execution Time
        Clock Speed
    Instruction Set
        Number
        Instruction Execution Time
        Data Types
        Data Structures
        Control Operations
        Control Structures
        System Structures
    Development Tools
        High-Level Languages
        Assemblers
        Compilers
        Debuggers
    Physical Design
        Bus Structure
        Memory Organization
        Register Structure
        I/O Addressing Modes
        Protection Schemes
        Multiprocessing Capability

Peripherals
Floating Point
Memory Management
Bus Arbiter
Dynamic RAM Controller
I/O Interface Processor
Interrupt Controller

Once you've come up with at least a rough outline of the structure of your kbase, you can then call it up (if you've created the shell via Menu 1) using the A(ctivate) command in Menu 2. The next step is to initiate the process of filling in the information by selecting the R(evise) function from Menu 2, which allows you to use all the features of QUESTEXT. Alternatively, if you want to safeguard against making mistakes, you can also use the B(uild) function, which includes only the A(dd), P(rint), and I(nquire) functions. In either case you should then see the following display:

```
MAJOR CATEGORY level:/S(uspend) or any key to
interrupt

TYPE H(elp), S(how), A(dd), D(elete), I(nsert),
    M(ove), E(dit), R(eview), G(et), Q(uit), or
    number (Max = 0)
```

Since you are developing a new kbase, no major categories are listed. After selecting the A(dd) command, you are given the opportunity to enter text in the first numbered line. Once entered, QUESTEXT redisplays "MAJOR CATEGORY level," but with your first entry. As categories are entered via the A(dd) command, each is numbered in the left-hand column. At any time it is possible to go to the subcategory level of any category by selecting its number. QUESTEXT automatically takes you to the subcategory level within that particular major category. Again, since this is a new kbase, QUESTEXT will display "SUBCATEGORY level—NONE FOUND." By using the A(dd) command in the menu at the bottom of the display, you can sequentially enter the subcategories under a particular major category. A similar procedure is followed at the HEADING and TEXT levels.

Entering Text

At the TEXT level, information is entered and organized differently than at upper levels. First, the lines are not numbered. Second, QUESTEXT allows continuous text entry without repeated entering of the A(dd) command. Like a word-processing program, QUESTEXT has a word-wrap feature that automatically starts a new line as soon as the sixty-fifth character has been entered. QUESTEXT searches for the most recent break and moves the unfinished word to the next line.

Revising with QUESTEXT

At all levels, whether using the A(dd) command or continuous text entry, new lines are added to the end of the text displayed. It is not possible to (1) add or delete lines and/or categories or subcategories at other points, out of sequence; (2) move lines from one location to another; or (3) add or delete characters in a line in the same manner as with an ordinary word processor. As you may have noted earlier in the review of the basic QUESTEXT commands, this is done by using the I(nsert), D(elete), M(ove), and E(dit) commands listed in the prompt line at the bottom of the screen.

Accepting External Files

Using the G(et) command, it is possible to incorporate external text files into a QUESTEXT-created kbase at any level. This is particularly useful for those who find the method of text entry in QUESTEXT somewhat awkward and would feel more comfortable using a standard word-processing program.

To conform to the structure of QUESTEXT, the external text files you wish to read into your kbase must:

1. Contain no more than 65 characters per line
2. Contain no more than 100 lines per file
3. Have the .TXT extension
4. Reside on the system disk in the logged drive

QUESTEXT reads the lines of the external text file, adding them to the end of the lines already in the system at the level in which G(et) is executed. As the lines are added they are displayed on the screen.

When G(et) is selected, the user is shown a directory of available .TXT files on the logged drive and asked to select one for input, specifying whether it is a WordStar document or not. As described in earlier chapters, WordStar uses the eighth bit of its ASCII code to structure the text file for formatting. Before incorporating a WordStar document, QUESTEXT removes this eighth bit. Since this is a time-consuming process, a better alternative would be to remove the eighth-bit settings beforehand. As discussed in Chapter 17, under CP/M this can be done by using the PIP command to transfer the text files to the logged drive disk and using the Z parameter setting to strip off these settings.

Searching a QUESTEXT Knowledge Base

Once you've read the appropriate XPERT kbase from disk files into computer memory by using the A(ctivate) command from the utilization menu, (option 2), you can begin a category search by selecting any of the following three options: B(uild), I(nquire), or R(evise). Again, the basic difference among them is the degree of protection you are given from making mistakes.

Searching by Category

Whichever option is chosen, QUESTEXT will respond with a listing of the major categories. For example, the display of major categories for the Micro kbase would look something like this:

```
MAJOR CATEGORY level:        /S(uspend) or any key to
                                           interrupt
1       Intel 8088/8086
2       Motorola 68000
3       Zilog Z8000
4       NS16000
5       TI99000
6       TYPE NUMBER OF YOUR CHOICE (1-5 or 7) or Q to
        exit
7       * +GENERAL +*
TYPE    H(elp), S(how), R(eview), Q(uit), or number
(Max =7)
```

As described earlier, QUESTEXT always numbers the lines in an XPERT menu on the left of the screen. The numbers are used to identify and select a category you are interested in and want to work with. For example, selecting MAJOR CATEGORY 3 would result in the automatic display of the subcategories:

```
SUBCATEGORY level: /S(uspend) or any key to interrupt
1       Process Technology
2       Instruction Set
3       Development Tools
4       Physical Design
5       Peripherals
6       TYPE NUMBER OF YOUR CHOICE (1-5) or U to
        continue
TYPE    H(elp), S(how), U(p), T(op), R(eview), Q(uit),
        or number (Max =6)
```

You may continue to make choices in narrower and narrower categories until you've located your specific area of interest. For example, selecting option 4 results in a display of the headings under that category:

```
HEADING level:      /S(uspend) or any key to interrupt
1       Bus Structure
2       Memory Organization
3       Register Structure
4       I/O Addressing Modes
5       Protection Schemes
6       Multiprocessing Capability
7       TYPE NUMBER OF YOUR CHOICE (1-7) or U to
        continue
TYPE    H(elp), S(how), U(p), T(op), R(eview),
        P(rint), Q(uit), or number
```

At any point you can move back and forth between various levels using the T(op), U(p), or N(ext) commands, or you can find out where you are in the kbase by selecting S(how).

Searching by Keyword or Character String

In addition to searching by category, it is possible to search a QUESTEXT XPERT kbase at any level for any occurrences of a word, phrase, or title—in fact, any character string with up to 65 characters (including spaces).

To access the Keyword Search option, first select the S(how) command, whereby, in addition to displaying the names of the categories you are in, QUESTEXT will ask for the search string. QUESTEXT will then look for all occurrences of the string in the level at which the Search command has been executed.

Designed intentionally to search only on the level at which the Search command is executed, this allows a variety of sophisticated search and retrieval strategies combining both the category and keyword approaches. For example, if you're not sure which level the string you're looking for might be on, the most direct strategy is to start at the highest level—a major category—and descend the tree until the string has been found.

Once executed, a QUESTEXT keyword search continues until it finds the first occurrence of the string and moves the display to its location. The material found can then be sent either to a disk file or to the printer.

When a successful search has been made, QUESTEXT tells you, "STRING FOUND" and displays the line in which the string is found. As soon as any key is pressed, you are shown the display containing the line. If you then execute another search without changing the search string, QUESTEXT will locate and move to the next occurrence, and so on indefinitely until the entire level has been searched. If you change the search string, QUESTEXT will automatically return to the first record in the level being searched and begin again. The same thing occurs when the Q(uit) command is executed or when a search is begun at a new level. Each time, QUESTEXT will tell you how many lines (records) have been searched.

The particular advantage of this level-by-level character string search is that it allows implementation of more than one search strategy, with varying degrees of selectivity and search/retrieval speed. This is particularly so when you combine the character string/keyword search with the category menu–based search and retrieval method unique to QUESTEXT.

For example, using the category search procedure, you can narrow down your field of search by selecting the appropriate major category and subcategory. At the heading level, at least three strategies are possible. The first and most powerful is to place text titles at the heading level with as many auxiliary keywords as necessary in the lines just below the title, also at the heading level. A second alternative is to store text titles at the heading level, with the full text below them at the text level. This allows full or partial title searching at the heading level and a full text search at the text level. The third alternative is that keywords can be located at the heading level, allowing structured keyword vocabulary searches in tandem with full text searches at the text level, although the entire text needs to be searched to find the location of specific keywords and the associated records.

Sorting with QUESTEXT

With the QS.COM utility (QS.EXE on the IBM PC), QUESTEXT also allows you to sort a kbase by category, subcategory, heading, or text line.

As with QF, movement between QS and QU is done without leaving QUESTEXT via a simple menu selection. QS adds an in-memory sorting algorithm to the XPERT shell of your kbase that provides very fast response regardless of the order or disorder of the records. As with the rest of QUESTEXT, there is no distinction between upper- and lower-case characters. In addition, the hierarchical structure of QUESTEXT is maintained during sorting, which means that subcategories are moved when categories are sorted.

Sorting is initiated via the O(rder) command in the QS menu, displayed at the bottom of the screen. After a short display (at most less than a second), the items reappear on the screen in sorted order.

Retrieving Text from a QUESTEXT Knowledge Base

At any point, by choosing the P(rint) option, it is possible to send parts of a particular QUESTEXT-structured kbase to the output of your choice. At the prompting of the QUESTEXT program, you will be directed to choose whether you want to print (1) what is currently being displayed on the screen, (2) the entire level in which you are located, or (3) the whole kbase. The last option is particularly useful if you're using QUESTEXT as an outline processor.

It is also possible under P(rint) to direct the output to an external text file, which can then be edited and formatted into the appropriate form by using a word-processing program.

Comments and Evaluation

Within the limitations of its hierarchical structure, QUESTEXT rivals in flexibility and sophistication any of the free-form knowledge-processing programs surveyed in Part II. It should be the program of choice for any user who is not comfortable with Boolean AND/OR search strategies, but wants a kbase program of similar capacity and capability. It can perform most of the functions of these free-form programs and outline processing, as well. Used as an outline processor, it allows you to build outlines of a complexity and detail rivaled only by FirstDraft (see Chapter 15).

There are two basic limitations to the QUESTEXT system. First, it is not capable of managing a kbase that consists of multiple floppy disks; in other words, one disk equals one kbase. This program is thus most effective on high-capacity systems, particularly those with hard disks. Second, when QUESTEXT is being used as an outline processor, you cannot directly view on the screen the entire structure of your outline; it can be viewed only by category and subcategory. The way to get around that is to use the P(rint) command to print out a hard copy occasionally to get an overview. Although this is a definite drawback when compared to outline processors such as ThinkTank and FirstDraft, it is a small enough price to pay for the many other features QUESTEXT offers to the writing professional.

CHAPTER 15

FirstDraft

The Quintessential Outline Processor

Illustrative of a new trend in programming aids for writers are two programs from PromptDoc, FirstDraft and DocuMentor, which are designed to work in conjunction with your word processor.

As with QUESTEXT, EASYFILE, and ThinkTank—all of which point to outline editing as one of their functions—FirstDraft is hierarchical in structure, allowing the organization of text files into categories and subcategories. Unlike them, these two programs do not claim to allow you to store text for retrieval. FirstDraft is designed specifically as a word-processing support program. Its focus is to help the writer organize his or her thoughts into an outline and manipulate and reorganize text files in the context of that outline. FirstDraft's companion program, DocuMentor, is designed primarily as a template generator, deriving outline structures from previously written documents and then allowing you to reorganize your text files on the basis of these templates.

FirstDraft Overview

Designed to operate on all computer systems (both 8- and 16-bit), running under the various versions of CP/M from Digital Research, First-Draft requires a minimum of 56K bytes of memory.

FirstDraft is aimed at creating outlines and skeletons for three general types of documents:

M   Memo or short report consisting of up to 98 subjects with subordinate topics.

R   Report consisting of 98 sections with subordinate subjects and topics.

B   Book consisting of up to 20 chapters, each of which contains up to 98 sections with subordinate subjects and topics.

The FirstDraft software recognizes three logical drives: System, Library, and User Text. You can assign these logical drives to any of your physical drives via the configuration program. This program also allows you to configure FirstDraft to the word processor you are using. If you decide to put all the files on a single physical drive, you will be able to ignore all FirstDraft prompts for loading disks into certain drives. However, your text files will eventually fill up the system disk, so if you have more than one disk drive you should follow PromptDoc's recommendations for disk configuration; for single-density systems, the Library and Text logical drives should be on physical drive B and the System drive on physical drive A. On double-density systems, the System and Library drives should be on physical drive A and the Text drive on physical drive B.

Creating a Document with FirstDraft

Organization and creation of a document with FirstDraft is a simple process. It is initiated via the program's Main Menu, which offers you the following options:

```
(1) Define a document
(2) Edit a document outline
(3) Add/edit a standard outline/template
(4) Print/display an outline
(5) Print/edit a document
(6) Change document status/definition
(7) Assemble a skeleton document
(8) Delete notes from document outline
```

```
 (9) Create a table of contents
(10) Create an index
```

Above and below this listing on the screen, which is called the *scroll window*, are the *heading window* (above) and the *prompt window* (below). The information in the heading window tells you about the display in the scroll window, whereas the information in the prompt window tells you about your entry options and the result of selecting each option.

All FirstDraft screens conform to this format. Thus using the program is simply a matter of following the instructions in the prompt window and watching the heading and scroll windows to see the results of the entries.

The various options available via the Main Menu can be categorized into three main groupings: 1–6, which generally involve the definition and creation of the document outline and structure; 7 and 8, which involve the actual creation of the text to fill in the outline and preparation of the document/outline for final printout; and 9 and 10, which involve the creation of the table of contents and the index.

The program also categorizes the document outlines according to their stage of completion, including:

O	Outlined: no document or template exists.
D	Draft template is being processed; this outline is frozen until DocuMentor has made a template.
T	Template exists.
f	Frozen: documents exist and this outline cannot be altered.
F	Frozen: template and documents exist and this outline cannot be altered.

Defining Your Document Structure

The first step in building an outline is to define your document. This is done via Main Menu option 1, which prompts you through the process of creating the structure of a new document, directing you to enter the document ID (up to four characters), the document name, and the document type—book, report, or memo. It gives you the choice of using an existing standard outline or generating a new document from scratch by listing its sections, subjects, and topics in free-form fashion.

Within any memo, book chapter, or report, FirstDraft maintains six different standard outline labeling styles. If you need to work out the structure of your document, it is recommended that you use the generic outline structure, which has no preassigned content and allows you to set up a dummy document or chapter free-form and then produces a structured outline when you're finished.

If you already have a good idea of the basic elements you want to include in your document and of their order and sequence, then you should use one of the other labeling styles.

In either case, FirstDraft forces you to organize your thoughts. For example in the writing of this book, the program first directed me to list my chapters (no more than 20) and their titles, then the main section titles and details of each section in each chapter, and then the subject headings under each section in the order in which I wanted them to appear.

Modifying an Existing Outline

At any time during the preparation of a document using FirstDraft/ DocuMentor, it is possible to edit an outline—either one of the standard ones provided with the program or one you may have created previously from another document. Using option 2 from the Main Menu, you can (1) add a section, (2) resequence sections or subjects within sections, (3) change an outline heading name, (4) insert a new subject, (5) delete a line or block of lines, (6) change a label option; or (7) duplicate lines or portions of the outlines.

Adding New Outline Structures

Via option 3, you can add other outline choices to FirstDraft. This can be done in any of three ways: (1) using another standard outline and altering it to suit your purposes, (2) using an existing outline from some external document or template generated via DocuMentor, or (3) using the generic outline and editing it to suit your needs.

Option 3 is more restrictive than option 2. Your document outline, standard outline, and template files must be structurally consistent. In other words, every section, subject, or topic in the document file must have a corresponding file in the template. Whereas with the previous option FirstDraft would simply warn you in the event of an inconsistency, here the program forces consistency by controlling how and when you change an outline associated with a template.

In essence, FirstDraft freezes a standard outline once you create a document with associated text files from it. You cannot edit an f-type frozen outline because you've made documents from it and may want to create a template from it in the future. In the case of an F- or T-type outline, a template has already been made, so editing is prohibited to keep your standard outline consistent with its template.

In writing this book, I found this particular feature an invaluable aid in maintaining the parallel structure from chapter to chapter. For this task, none of the outline structures available within FirstDraft were suitable. The structure of the chapters came from the nature of the material I was working with. After writing my description of two or three of the programs, the structure used in Chapter 4 of this book evolved, and it became the template for most of the other chapters.

Displaying Your Outline

As you are developing an outline with option 2 or 3, it is possible to see only one section at a time—the one on which you are working. Main Menu option 4 allows you to print or display an entire document, chapter, or standard outline. This is useful when you need to get a clear idea of the overall structure of your outline.

Defining Document Filenames

As discussed in the system overview, FirstDraft creates a variety of different files and file types for each document. For example, in the creation of this book and this chapter, I used the ID KBMP (for knowledge base management program). In response, FirstDraft, at various stages of the assembly process, automatically assigned the following filenames:

KBMPSTAT.TBL	For the chapter status file on the library disk.
KBMP$14.OTL	For the chapter 14 outline file on the library disk.
KBMP1401.TXT	For the assembled skeleton section 01 on the raw text user disk.
KBMP1402.TXT	For the assembled skeleton section 02 on the raw text user disk.

KMP$14.TOC   For the table of contents of Chapter 14 on
                        the raw text user disk.

KBMP$14.IX   For the index entries for Chapter 14 on the
                        raw text user disk.

With option 5 from the Main Menu, it is possible to keep track of
these various files and their associated document names. When invoked,
FirstDraft displays and/or prints the document section names and the corresponding skeleton text filenames for an assembled document or chapter.

Such listings are very important during the later stages of document
preparation, when it may be necessary to combine a document's various
section files into one print file before the final printout.

Viewing Document Status

To view the status of the various documents on which you are working
with FirstDraft, you would use option 6 from the Main Menu disk. The
FirstDraft library status display would look roughly as follows:

ID	TYPE	NO	TYPE	DATE	STATUS	NAME
MP	R	1	O	6/1/83	Rough draft	Microprocessors
KBMP	B					Beyond WP
HLL	M	2	F	11/15/83	Reassembled	HiLevel Lang.

As noted, this status display contains the outline type as well as the
document ID and name. For memos and reports, the date of the last document outline update and the document status are listed. To obtain more
detail on the specific status of various chapters in more complex documents, such as books, you must call up, at the system's prompting, the specific chapter letter and name. This status display includes various messages
about the document or chapter, including:

Defined   Created by Main Menu option 1 and
                 automatically assigned.

Outlined   Created by option 2 and automatically assigned.

Assembled   Created by option 7 and automatically assigned.

Reassembled   Created by option 7 and automatically assigned.

In process	Means the actual process of writing and filling in the skeleton has begun.
Rough draft	Means that a draft has been completed.
Final draft	Means that the rough draft has been polished into publishable form.
No assembly	Means that a document originally assembled from a template has been resequenced using DocuMentor and it is not possible to reassemble it with the current template.

Preparing Your Document

Now that you've edited and reorganized your outline to your satisfaction, you are ready to begin preparation of your document.

The first step in this process is to build a skeleton of your document in text files your word processor can work on. This is done via option 7, which creates either blank files or files containing editing comments for each section and/or subsection of the document you are going to write. For example, an article I am writing on microprocessors might contain as many as 20 or so sections, for which FirstDraft will create 20 or so files of the .TXT type, each of which will contain comments on the subject matter and the location in my note and interview source files of the raw text information I want to enter under each heading.

With menu option 8 you can delete all the instructional comments you may have added to your outline files during the organizational process. These notes should be deleted before you create a table of contents and print your final document. Usually, these are eliminated during the writing process. However, it is a good idea to pass all your text files through this option before printout.

Although FirstDraft can be used with just about any CP/M-compatible word processor, it is most effective when combined with one of the multiscreen/multibuffer word processors described earlier. Using FinalWord, for example, I assign five or six of the buffers to my source files, assign the others to each of five or six .TXT section files, and move the raw research and interview text to the appropriate locations. I continue this process until I have assigned all the source text to the appropriate locations. I then reassign the buffer files, one to each of 10 or 11 of the various subsection

.TXT files, saving one or two as "wildcard" files to be assigned and reassigned to the other .TXT files in the skeleton document as appropriate.

Generating Contents and an Index

Via option 9, you can add page numbers and page prefixes to an existing document outline and write this file to disk, using your word processor to format it into a presentable table of contents for your document. With option 10, you can create a subject index from your table of contents entries and write a formatted index text file that can also be edited and printed with your word processor. The Table of Contents for this book, for example, was generated using this option.

Using DocuMentor

A useful complement to the FirstDraft program, DocuMentor allows you to turn any group of text files into a document database. Along with various other functions, it can:

- Extract outlines from existing documents.
- Create templates from existing documents.
- Build tables of contents and indices from existing documents.
- Renumber out-of-sequence paragraphs following a cut-and-paste session with your word processor and update the outline and table of contents.
- Reorganize a document according to changes you make in its outline.

In combination with your word processor, FirstDraft and DocuMentor allow you to manipulate and restructure text files in an almost database-like fashion.

Comments and Evaluation

As an outline processor, the FirstDraft/DocuMentor combination is a strict taskmaster in a number of respects. First, unlike ThinkTank, which allows entry of text descriptions up to several hundred words in length, FirstDraft limits text entry descriptions of each level to no more than a half-dozen short, succinct words. Second, it limits you to half a dozen or so outline structures and about 20 or so variations. Third, once you have developed an outline and used it as a template, it does not allow you to vary considerably from this structure.

For writing professionals who are comfortable only with a more fluid environment in which the development of a document is a much more dynamic process, this is not the program to choose. The more flexible structure of a full-function hierarchical knowledge-processing program such as QUESTEXT or the looser format of ThinkTank or EAZYFILE might be more appropriate.

For the individual user, FirstDraft is most valuable in the development of large documents, such as a book, where it is necessary to bring some structure to a large body of information. It is also the program of choice for those writing professionals who feel that they need help in organizing their thoughts into a formal outline.

FirstDraft is also a useful tool in the corporate environment, where there is usually some sort of standard for company documentation, particularly for user manuals.

In general, then, the effectiveness and usefulness of FirstDraft and DocuMentor increase with the size of the document and with the complexity of the subject matter. Writing professionals who normally deal with short documents such as memos, articles, and reports of not more than a few thousand words might well consider EAZYFILE or ThinkTank instead.

CHAPTER 16

Two Tree-Structured Index Card Programs

ThinkTank and EAZYFILE

Just as the tree-structured QUESTEXT represents an imaginative and powerful divergence from Boolean-logic–oriented, free-form knowledge processors such as SUPERFILE, so ThinkTank and EAZYFILE represent a similar divergence from the other, more traditional card file programs described in this book. Although less powerful than their tree-structured big brothers, these two programs make up for that in ease of use and faster access. The basic difference between the two programs has to do with what they were designed for and what they can actually do.

ThinkTank, for example, described as an "idea processor" by its developers, is designed for use as an outline processor and idea organizer. But it can also be used as a card file in which short text items can be stored and retrieved by category and subcategory. By comparison, EAZYFILE, designed basically as a category-oriented text file program, can also be used as an outline editor and article organizer.

Living Videotext's ThinkTank

Designed to run under the Pascal operating system (P-SYSTEM), the 8-bit version of ThinkTank requires two disk drives and 64K bytes of

RAM on Apple II, Apple IIplus, and Apple IIe, and 96K bytes on the Apple III. The program uses the familiar outline format to help you generate, organize, store, and retrieve text within a category structure consisting of headings, subheadings, and paragraphs. In systems using floppy disks, ThinkTank limits you to one outline per diskette to allow room for expansion.

ThinkTank Overview

Unlike QUESTEXT and FirstDraft, both of which differentiate among categories, subcategories, and headings and allow up to 100 levels or branches for each, the *total* number of categories and subcategories available on ThinkTank is limited to 100. Under each heading or subheading within a ThinkTank outline, it is also possible to store text in paragraphs no more than 2048 characters long (about 25–50 lines of text) on the 8-bit version.

When you are operating the ThinkTank program, the screen of your computer is divided into two parts. At the top is the text area, about 18 lines deep, which displays the outline you are working on, or as much of it as will fit. The bottom four lines constitute the command area.

Into the top 18 lines of the screen, text and headlines are entered in outline form, with some indented under others. Headlines with additional text at lower levels are preceded by a plus sign (+) leader. A minus sign (−) leader indicates that there is no additional information beneath the headline. For example, suppose you are writing an article on cosmology, focusing in particular on how rapidly scientific theories evolve and are replaced by others. A partial display of this outline while in the Editor mode would look something like Screen 1.

ThinkTank makes use of a bar cursor that you can move about the screen with the appropriate cursor movement keys. The position of the bar cursor in your outline is important, because it determines where the various program commands will take effect.

Most of the functions of ThinkTank are controlled via one of the three menus displayed at the appropriate times in the command area at the bottom of the screen. When a menu is displayed, you can select a particular command for execution by moving the cursor to its location at the bottom of the screen and pressing Return. To tell the program how many times the command should be executed or how many levels of the outline the command applies to, a numerical command prefix can be used. Many of the

```
+The Sky Is Falling In
------------------------------------------------
   The universe as the scientist sees it seems
to always be on the verge of coming apart at the
seams as a result of the logical dilemmas
inherent in most theories. But it is in
investigating these logical inconsistencies that
progress is made.
------------------------------------------------
+Quasars, How Far or How Near?
-The Red Shift: A Shifting Yardstick?
+Black Holes and White Holes
+Tacyons, Tardyons, and Photons
-Quarks and Charmed Particles
+Magnetic Monopoles
+Missing Matter
+Missing Neutrinos
+Reversed Time


ENTER NEW PARAGRAPH (ESC) WHEN FINISHED
(LEFT ARROW ERASES LAST KEYSTROKE)
```

Screen 1

commands on all three menus have submenus that offer additional subcommands.

ThinkTank's most important commands are listed in the Main Command Menu and are accessed by entering a single slash (/). These commands are

C(ollapse) and E(xpand)	Allow you to hide and then reveal various material, including both paragraphs and subheadings, only subheadings, or only paragraphs.
M(ove)	Moves the bar cursor outline in whatever direction you specify—up,

	down, left, right, and either a step at a time or in a series of moves.
D(elete)	Deletes either the bar cursor headline and all subheadings and paragraphs or only the paragraph beneath the cursor and not its subheadings.
E(dit)	Allows you to edit either paragraphs or headlines.
K(eyword)	Allows you to search through your outline for a particular word, phrase, or pattern of characters. At each match you stop, keep searching, or replace it with an alternative.
W(indow)	Allows you to adjust the position of the outline structure within the window of the screen.
P(ort)	Allows you to print an outline, transfer information from one outline to another, back up your outlines, and send outlines.
F(iles)	Allows you to change old outlines, create new ones, or select one when you first load the program.
N(ew)	Allows you to add material to an outline.
E(xtra)	Moves you to the Secondary Command Menu.

Additional ThinkTank commands are listed in a Secondary Command Menu, which you can display by selecting E(xtra) from the Main Menu or by pressing the slash key twice (//). These commands include:

C(opy)	Makes a duplicate copy of the bar cursor outline and places it just below the original and at the same level.

A(lpha)	Alphabetizes the first-level subheadings of the bar cursor outline.
P(romote)	Promotes subheadings to the same level as the bar cursor headline.
M(erge)	Combines two paragraphs into one as long as the two together do not exceed 2048 characters.
D(ate)	Stamps the current date on your outline when it prints or saves it.
U(tilities)	Allows you to change some of ThinkTank's command keys.
S(pecial)	Contains routines to format, copy, and list the contents of the floppy disk.

The command keys for these options are also selectable from the top level, but only when the Secondary Command Menu is being displayed.

Creating an Outline with ThinkTank

To enter text into an outline or to modify an existing outline, it is necessary to gain access to one of ThinkTank's two text editors (one for paragraphs and one for headlines). This can be done via the Main or New command menus or via the New subcommand in the Files Command Menu. Once in the Edit mode, you can call up the paragraph editor by pressing the P command key or the headline editor with the H command key.

The functions available to you in the Headline Edit mode include the ability to (1) enter new text at the flashing cursor position, (2) move the flashing cursor through the headline one character or word at a time, (3) erase characters to the left and right of the flashing cursor, and (4) move up and down the outline from headline to headline. Once you've completed editing the headlines on an outline, press the Return key. You can also cancel any changes by immediately pressing the Escape key, which restores the original headline.

In the Paragraph mode, ThinkTank operates much like a standard word-processing program, allowing you to insert, delete, type over, backspace, or select a block of text to copy, delete, or move. If the paragraph under a heading or subheading occupies more than one screen page (about 18 lines), it is also possible to move from page to page as well as GOTO the top or bottom of the text.

Filling in the Outline

If you are using ThinkTank primarily as an outline editor, you can squeeze in additional levels of categorization by making use of the 25–50 additional lines available in the paragraph area under each heading and subheading. If you are using it primarily as a card file and you need to enter more information, you must split the text into two or more smaller paragraphs and place them under adjacent headings, suppressing the headlines so that the paragraphs appear to be consecutive on the screen or on the printer. However, each paragraph with a blank heading means that there is one less level available for outlining. To search through such a structure you would use a word-processor–like Search/Find or Search/Replace function.

Searching the Outline

If your outline is a very long one with many levels, and if you also have extensive text in paragraph form, only a small portion will be displayed at any one time. In such a case, it is useful to hide not only paragraphs but subheadings by using the C(ollapse) command. If you need to go to a deeper level at any point, all that will be necessary is to move the bar cursor to that headline and redisplay the hidden material by using the E(xpand) command.

Rather than just scrolling through the outline to find a particular heading, it is better to use the F(ind) or eX(change) functions. Depending on whether you are in the Headline or Paragraph editing mode at the time, the first function searches for any pattern you enter, either forward or backward. The second function searches for the pattern and replaces it with another pattern. This can be a global change, replacing all occurrences, or it can be structured to replace just some occurrences. The F(ind) and eX(change) functions are particularly useful if you've used the 25–50 additional lines available in each paragraph to add more subheadings to your outline.

Retrieving Outlines and Text

To print an outline, transfer information from one outline to another, back up an outline, or send an outline to another ThinkTank user, you would invoke the P(ort) command from the Main Menu and select one of two options: T(extfile) or P(rint).

A number of different styles are available to you if you are printing an outline or sending it to a text file:

Plain: Used primarily in porting paragraphs of an outline to a text file that will later be edited with a Pascal word processor. It arranges the outline material according to a set of minimal-format settings, including single-space; left and right margins of 0 and 79; flat indentation; and no section numbers, table of contents, page headers, or footers.

Structured: Used primarily in porting an outline to a text file with information about the organization of the outline.

Formatted: Used primarily in printing an outline, it arranges the outline according to 16 different format settings.

P(ort)/T(extfile) also allows you to transfer an external copy into ThinkTank and place it directly below the bar cursor headline indicator. The external text can be either an outline or any text written using a Pascal text, a word processor, or ThinkTank.

Because the P(ort) command does not operate in the Block mode, but only on material below the bar cursor headline, it is difficult to port just portions of an outline. This is not impossible, however. To do this, you would invoke the C(opy) command and create a duplicate just below the original. Then use the S(elect) command to move the block of text to the bottom of the outline. Repeat this process for as much material as needed, move the bar cursor to the beginning of the duplicated material, and port it to the output you desire. Finally, invoke the S(elect) command and delete the duplicated material.

Miracle Computing's EAZYFILE

EAZYFILE Overview

Designed for use on the IBM PC, EAZYFILE constructs a file for each major category of information, under each of which a number of different subcategories can be entered. The number of lines of text that can be entered under each subcategory is limited by the amount of space in the file, with a maximum of 3000 forty-character lines requiring 128K bytes of disk storage per file. Some thought should be given to the structure of the particular kbase—the number of major categories, the number of sub-categories in each file, and the number of lines of text to be entered under each subcategory.

All operations of this program are selected by letter from a Main Menu of available functions, including:

```
(A) Display file
(B) Add to file
(C) Copy file
(D) Print file
(E) Erase/build file
(F) Status report
(G) Select new file
```

Creating and Defining Files

After you have booted up your system under PC-DOS, enter the com-mand to start BASIC and place your EAZYFILE diskette in the system drive, typing in "RUN EAZYFILE."

When the menu appears on the screen, select the Erase/Build File function, which sets up the files where your text is to be stored. Then select the G option from the menu, which asks you the purpose of the file—the major category—and the number of the subcategories to be stored under this file.

Entering Text into EAZYFILE

To enter text into the EAZYFILE kbase, use Main Menu option B, first entering the names of the subcategories (40 characters maximum) and then the text under each subcategory. If each file can be considered the rough equivalent of a file cabinet, each subcategory can be viewed logically as a file folder heading under which text can be filed.

Text is entered in the same way as with a word processor, with approx-imately the same cursor controls.

Searching EAZYFILE

Files can be searched in EAZYFILE in two ways—by category and by text—via Main Menu option A (Display File). Regardless of which method is chosen, the program then displays a record selection screen and requests that a "search argument" be entered; this is used to scan the kbase contained in the file. If a match is found, the appropriate subcategory or text is listed on the screen. When searching the text, you also have the option of making changes to the text by pressing the C key.

When you select the Print File option, you have the same alternatives. You also have the choice of sending what is displayed to the printer or to an external file. Selecting the Copy File option allows you to move portions of other files into a new file.

Comments and Evaluation

One of the most heavily advertised and promoted of any of the text-oriented knowledge-processing programs covered in this book, the 8-bit version of ThinkTank for the Apple series is both more and less than its developers and promoters represent it to be.

Compared to QUESTEXT, it is considerably less powerful. However, it is much easier to use. Compared to EAZYFILE, it is a much more powerful category-oriented program, but it is harder to learn.

Compared to FirstDraft, it is less capable as an outline editor and "idea processor." However, unlike FirstDraft, it is also able to operate as an electronic card file, using a categorical tree structure rather than AND/OR Boolean logic as the primary search mode.

The truth about ThinkTank is that it represents an ideal compromise for the user who wants a little of each of these various capabilities.

Although it is less powerful than either ThinkTank or QUESTEXT, EAZYFILE is certainly much easier to learn, requiring no more than ten minutes whether or not you read the user documentation.

Technically, EAZYFILE allows an unlimited amount of text to be entered under each category. However, for most practical purposes there is a trade-off between the number of categories and subcategories, the amount of text to be entered, and the amount of disk space available.

Part VI

MAKING THE MOST OF WHAT YOU'VE GOT

CHAPTER 17

Making the Most of Your Operating System

One of the most underused resources of your personal computer is its operating system. Indeed, proper use of the operating system and its various internal commands and utility programs can go a long way toward turning your personal computer into an effective writing and knowledge-processing tool. Although less powerful and less automated than a full-fledged knowledge-processing program, the internal capabilities of your operating system will let you perform most of the basic knowledge-processing functions outlined in Chapter 1. These internal facilities allow you to perform fairly sophisticated cut-and-paste operations on your text files, pulling together, combining, and organizing not only files, but also specific paragraphs and lines of text into whatever order you want. These are then stored in rough-draft form in a file that can be polished and reorganized with your word processor.

The various features of an operating system that can be of use to you as a writing professional include:

- Internal file and screen management commands
- The structure of the filename and file type extension
- Wildcard or ambiguous file reference characters

- The system's built-in line-oriented text editor
- Programming and file management utilities
- The operating system file structure itself

In this chapter we'll look at how each of these features can be used for knowledge processing.

Internal Commands as Knowledge Base Tools

Most of the operating systems in common use on personal computers are roughly comparable in certain ways. The internal file commands list files contained on a diskette and how much disk space each takes. The screen commands control and manage a file when it is displayed on the computer's CRT screen. All use the same file-naming protocol, in which each file is described by a filename that can be up to eight or sixteen characters long and an extension or file type up to three characters long. Finally, all allow you to search and sort through the files on a disk by using a wildcard character, usually either a question mark (?) or an asterisk (*).

CP/M Internal Commands

Illustrative of the power of these features as writing and knowledge-processing tools is the CP/M operating system, in wide use on numerous 8- and 16-bit personal computers.

Three of the most heavily used internal commands, employed by novice and sophisticate alike, are DIR, which displays a directory of files on a diskette; STAT, which allows you to display the amount of memory space required by each file and the total amount of memory space remaining; and XDIR, which combines features of the first two.

These commands are useful in letting you know at all times what is on a disk and how much space is left for new files. But what if you have several tens or hundreds of diskettes, or a hard disk with thousands of files? Unless you invest in one of the many diskette-cataloging programs available, some of which are discussed in the next chapter, you will probably end up keeping a typed or hand-written list of the files and where they are located.

Making use of one additional internal command automates this whole process, allowing you to generate a printed listing of what is contained on each disk and to easily update that list. That command in the CP/M operating system is the Screen Print command—Control P—one of several command line editing commands that is immediately executed by the computer. It allows you to turn your printer on and off at will and to selectively print or not print what is appearing on the screen of your CRT.

Where you would normally type in one of three internal commands—DIR, STAT, or XDIR—and press Return to see a listing, you can insert a Control P command between the internal command and the Return. The computer will then print out what appears on the screen—the listing of the diskette contents and the space required by each—in seconds.

The Control P line command is also useful when you want a "quick and dirty" printout of a file and do not want to go through all the hassle of inserting your word-processing program. This is done by combining it with the operating system's TYPE command, which displays the contents of a disk file on your CRT screen. Suppose, for example, you want a quick print of a file containing a story about Motorola's 68000 microprocessor, with the filename M68000TA.TXT. Using your word processor, this would require at least six to ten different key entries, in addition to typing in the filename. Doing this at the command line level would require entering only the TYPE comand, the filename, and Control P followed by a Return.

Using Structured Filenames to Simplify Searching

If you are like most users of personal computers, you are haphazard in the way you structure your filenames. However, by giving a little thought to the way you assign names to your files and disks and combining the DIR, XDIR, and STAT commands with the use of ambiguous wildcard characters, you can design a search strategy that allows you to differentiate among various files with a great deal of precision.

In CP/M, the asterisk and the question mark are used as wildcard ambiguous file reference characters. The asterisk can be used to replace an entire filename or file type/extension on either side of the period. The question mark represents a single character within a filename or file type/extension. For example, DIR B:*.DOC would list all files on a disk drive

B with the .DOC file type/extension whereas DIR B:QBXTA.* would list all files with the filename QBXTA regardless of file type. On the other hand, DIR B:Q???????.DOC would search for all .DOC-type articles with filenames beginning with the letter Q.

When I first started using my personal computer as a writing tool, I was more than a little capricious in assigning filenames. For example, a typical diskette contained such cryptic names as QBXCAETA.TXT, NSC16000.DOC, NCGATA.TXT, INTLPRRW.TXT, and ZLGMI-CRO.TXT. As working filenames—that is, for files and diskettes containing current projects—these posed no problem, since they were usually related to some familiar aspect of the job at hand. However, for files that may be months or years old, or that contain extensive research relating to many different subjects, such cryptic names can be highly mysterious. Trying to search through such cryptically named files for particular items is extremely difficult, even using the wildcard characters.

The first level of differentiation can be achieved by segregating your files by types and grouping them together onto similarly named diskettes. For example, all magazine articles can be assigned to diskettes with the common disk name MAGART, technical articles TEKART, press releases PRART, and brochures BROART. Then each diskette can be assigned to a group with a unique file type. For example, MAGART.D01 would be magazine article disk 1. In addition to writing this disk name on the cover, it is useful to give it a number your computer will be able to recognize when you put it in the disk drive. This is done by simply saving a blank file on the diskette with a filename beginning with a unique character that can be always recognized as indicating a diskette name or title. This should be a nonalphanumeric symbol of some sort. Care should be taken not to use symbols that the operating system itself uses for various purposes. I use a dash symbol (–) at the beginning of the filename. When I see, for example, -TEKART.D01, I know that this is technical article diskette 1.

Saving a blank file can be done in two ways. The most complicated way is to use your word-processing program, open up a blank file, and give it a filename. A more direct way is to use another of the CP/M operating system's internal commands, SAVE, which saves the contents of the computer memory as a file on the disk. For example, the command:

```
SAVE 0 B:-TEKART.D01
```

creates a blank file on the disk with that filename and type.

By properly structuring your filenames, it is possible to obtain up to eight levels of differentiation. A filename with two levels of differentiation would look something like QBX077, where QBX stands for the company for whom the article was written and 077 stands for the seventy-seventh article. This is an improvement over using no method, but it still requires that you maintain an extensive list somewhere telling you what the subject of the article was, who it was about, and its source. A code of this sort is used by one public relations company I know of, and it requires 50–100 pages of comments to catalog a hard disk.

If you wanted a filename structure with eight levels of differentiation, each of the eight character locations would be assigned a particular meaning—location 1 might hold the company or magazine for whom the article is being written, location 2 might hold the source, and so on. The filename structure I prefer uses five levels:

Location 1	For up to 62 unique company or magazine identifiers, A–Z, a–z, 0–9.
Location 2	For up to 62 unique date identifiers for the month and year.
Locations 3 and 4	For up to 1500 primary keyword codes, such as 01, 0a, 0A, A1, and 1B.
Locations 5 and 6	For up to 1500 secondary keywords.
Locations 7 and 8	For up to 1500 tertiary keywords.

More levels can be added by making better use of the file type extensions. Instead of using the standard DOC for document, .NON for non-document, and .TXT for text, you can more precisely characterize the nature of the document with such extensions as .INT for interview notes, .NOT for library research notes, .RGH for rough draft, .SEC for second draft, and .FNL for final draft.

To direct CP/M to search for all final drafts of documents or magazine articles written on the subject of *knowledge processing* on *Apple computers,* with each subject having *A1* and *1C* as keyword codes, respectively, you would enter the following command sequence:

```
A> DIR B:??A11C??.FNL
```

If you wanted to find any reference regardless of document type, you would enter the following search sequence:

```
A> DIR B:??A11C??.*
```

Even with the increased precision with which you can search for the files that meet your keyword specifications exactly, this is still somewhat tedious if you maintain your files on numerous floppy disks instead of a high-capacity hard disk. The time-consuming process of inserting diskette after diskette in a particualr category can be eliminated by creating a special index disk for each category—MAGART.NDX, TEKART.NDX, and so on. On each index disk, blank files are created for each file using the Save command, with identical filenames and file types.

The number of uniquely identified blank files that can be stored on a single index diskette varies with the amount of storage capacity and the number of sectors into which it has been divided. CP/M allocates space in 1K- or 1024-character blocks; that is, when you save a file, it saves the text and breaks it up on the diskette into 1K blocks, no matter how much text it contains. If the last 8-character word of an article were to fall into a new sector, an entire block of 1024 characters would be saved, not just 8 characters. Thus a 400K index diskette would allow you to save 400 uniquely named blank files.

The names of the files are retained unchanged. However, to indicate their disk location, the file type or extension of each is altered. Instead of .INT, .NOT, .RGH, .SEC, and .FNL, only the first letter is used, followed by the disk number, such as .I01 for interview notes, .N01 for research notes, .R01 for rough draft, .S01 for second draft, and .F01 for final draft, all located on diskette 1.

If you have a word-processing program that allows you to perform search and find operations using wildcard characters, as with the CP/M operating system, the capacity of your index diskette could be even higher. Indeed, an all-encompassing index diskette could be created containing unique files for each diskette category, within which would be the structured filenames and file types for your archival files. For example, the file TEKART.NDX would contain all the names and extensions for each file in that diskette category.

Although this system still requires that you maintain a listing of the meaning of the codes, it is certainly less voluminous, taking up perhaps no more than five or six single-spaced typewritten pages.

Evaluating the Operating Systems

Similar strategies can be used with most of the other personal computer operating systems in popular use. Where they begin to differ is in the sophistication of their file structuring, the number of housekeeping utilities supplied as part of the operating system, and the flexibility and power of the internal text editors they contain.

File Structures

Many personal computers use operating systems with flat file structures, whereby data on a disk is directly accessed in a random manner in much the same way a record player needle can be moved to any location on a record. Into this category fall such operating systems as CP/M, Apple DOS, MS/PC-DOS 1.0, and the UCSD P-SYSTEM. More recently introduced operating systems for use on personal computers use hierarchical tree-like file structures. Included in this category are various implementations of UNIX, MS/PC-DOS 2.0, and ProDOS, the new operating system developed for Apple II computers. The chief advantage of a tree-like file structure for a writing professional is that it allows related text files to be linked together into groups, which simplifies and speeds up their location and retrieval.

Housekeeping Utilities

Operating systems serve two functions. One is to perform the various supervisorial operations involved in keeping your computer functioning. The other is to serve as a "programming environment" in which various housekeeping utilities are supplied to make it easier for the programmer to develop applications software. Many of these programming utilities can also be used by the writing professional to turn his or her personal computer into a more effective knowledge processor.

At the top of the list in terms of the number and sophistication of such housekeeping utilities is UNIX. Following it are the newer hierarchical operating systems for the Apple and PC clones: ProDOS and MS/PC-DOS 2.0. Of the nonhierarchically structured operating systems, the one most useful in the quick and efficient search and retrieval of text files is CP/M, followed by the P-SYSTEM. At the bottom of the list in their usefulness to the writer are MS/PC-DOS 1.0 and Apple DOS.

Internal Text Editors

Most operating systems incorporate internal text editors for use in writing programs. From the point of view of the writer who has used any standard word-processing program, most of these internal text editors are rather primitive. Their chief drawback is that they are character- and/or line-oriented rather than screen-oriented. They also contain very few of the automatic editing features that are standard on a word-processing program. And most of them do not have any print-formatting capabilities. There are exceptions, however. The UCSD P-SYSTEM, for example, has a fairly sophisticated screen editor, as well as a separate print-formatting program.

Another exception is UNIX, especially in its most recent implementations. Early versions were line-oriented, whereas its latest revisions include a powerful screen-oriented text editor, called VI, that rivals standalone commercial word-processing programs in its sophistication. Text formatting is handled by a separate and very powerful program, NROFF, that formats text for printout on the basis of commands embedded in the text of a document. Other features of NROFF include full footnote processing and automatic table-of-contents generation. Also included as part of the basic UNIX package are (1) SPELL, which checks the spelling of words, reports spelling errors, and maintains a history file of spelling errors, and (2) TYPO, which examines a text file and reports possible typographical errors or unusual words, giving an "index of peculiarity" derived from the usage of the words in the document itself and from known statistics about the English language. Finally, many versions of UNIX also include the famed Writer's Workbench, a set of programs that examine a document for split infinitives, clichés, excessive use of passive voice, sexist phrases, readability, and other flaws.

UNIX as a Knowledge-Processing Environment

Due to its many housekeeping utilities and sophisticated command structure, the UNIX operating system has the reputation within the computing industry of being the "ideal programming environment." For many of the same reasons, UNIX can also be characterized as an ideal environment for knowledge processing.

Tree-Structured Files

Originally developed for use on large mainframes and minicomputers with disk storage capacities in the hundreds and thousands of megabytes, UNIX's hierarchical tree structure was designed to ease the difficulty involved in managing and organizing literally tens of thousands of files. This capability has been retained in the versions of UNIX that have been moved to the personal computer environment. It should be most useful for those systems with 5- or 10-megabyte (5M or 10M) hard disks, which can have as many as 2000–10,000 files; it requires as many as 100 or so screens of information to review an entire directory. However, the tree structure can also be of enormous use on floppy-based systems, where your archival files can take up 100 or so diskettes.

You do not have to build the tree structure from scratch. The operating system itself is already structured with a number of directories designed for easy access to the various programs and utilities. To this preexisting tree is added an additional directory, the *home directory*. Starting from the home directory, you can build the various subdirectories and branches to your various files. The entries in each directory can be either files or other directories. Each subdirectory can reference files and sub-subdirectories, each of which can also contain sub-sub-subdirectories, and so on.

The directory in which you are located at any time is referred to as the *working directory*. Associated with each file, in addition to its filename and type, is a pathname, which is formed by stringing together all the names of the directories through which you passed to get to a particular file. It can take two forms: *absolute,* which locates a file absolutely by tracing a path from the root directory to the file, and *relative,* which establishes the location of a file relative to a particular working directory. To aid you in organizing your files and moving about the branches you have created, UNIX provides a number of useful utility programs, including:

MKDIR	Creates new directories.
CHDIR	Allows you to change to another working directory.
MVDIR	Allows you to move a file or group of files from one directory to another.
COPY	Copies one file to another or several files from one directory to another.
RMDIR	Allows you to remove directories.

LN	Establishes links between various files and is used to establish connections with other files that are related to one another but are members of different directories.
PWD	Displays the pathname of your working directory from the root to the user through the various subdirectories.
LS	Lists the contents of any particular directory in the tree, displaying the contents of all files and subdirectories, file size in kilobytes and blocks, and other status information.
DU	Lists all the paths and directories that exist on a disk and summarizes the amount of disk space taken up by each directory and file.

Cataloging Diskettes with UNIX

On systems that use limited-capacity floppy disks for file storage, many implementations of UNIX on personal computers incorporate an additional program utility called MOUNT/UNMOUNT. It establishes logical connections between the primary tree structure on the system disk and various directories and files on each of the disk-storage volumes. This command essentially tells the operating system that other file systems exist that should be incorporated into the file structure, indicating to it the disk drive location and the disk volumes to be included. In operation, the fact that some files are not located in the same disk as the main portion of the system tree is transparent most of the time, except for those occasions when you are directed to insert the correct disk volume. In organizing my files, I establish the main directories and subdirectories on the diskette and then link these to the files on the various diskettes using the MOUNT command. Alternatively, additional subdirectories could also be located on each diskette. The advantage of the first approach, however, is that it allows you to keep track of the contents of dozens of diskettes, even those that are frequently altered.

Knowledge-Processing Utilities

In addition to the utilities that allow you to manipulate and move around the file structure with some ease, UNIX contains many programs and commands that allow you to perform some fairly sophisticated search-and-retrieve knowledge-processing functions, including:

FIND: Searches through specific branches on user-specified pathways for one or more occurrences of a file that meets various criteria (includng filename, group ID, user ID, and so on), both individually and in combination, using AND/OR operators.

GREP, EGREP, and FGREP: A family of commands that can be used to search for a specified string of characters in one file or in several files simultaneously. Among other things, these commands will display the names of the files in which the pattern is found or copy every line in the files being searched that matches the selection pattern to a separate file. GREP (for Globally find Regular Expressions and Print) is the simplest and locates all lines matching a single search pattern. EGREP accepts multiple search patterns, and FGREP accepts only fixed strings, which must be matched exactly.

SORT: Sorts or merges files in ascending or descending alphabetical or numeric order, and which allows the use of multiple keys to sort files.

LOOK: Searches through a presorted file and locates all lines starting with a string of characters you have defined.

PTX: Creates a sorted keyword index from a text file constructed from significant words. Word lists control what is included in or excluded from the index. An extensive word exclusion list is supplied, but it can be edited using a word processor to add or delete words to be excluded from the index.

CAT: Successively displays the contents of one or more files, directing them to the CRT screen, to another file, or to a printer.

SPLIT: Splits one file into several files, the size of which can be controlled.

CSPLIT: Splits files on the basis of ranges of line numbers or context, with the latter specified using regular editor-style expressions.

COMM: Reads two presorted files and identifies common or unique lines.

CMP: Compares two files and locates any differences, reporting the line numbers of the differences.

DIFFDIR: Compares all of the files in two directories, identifying differences by line number for similar files.

DIRCMP: Compares two directories and identifies files that are unique to each; where common filenames are found, it indicates whether the files themselves have the same contents.

HEAD and TAIL: Print the first few or the last few lines of a file.

The one drawback of most UNIX implementations is that there are few versions available for 8-bit personal computers. However, as discussed in the next chapter, there are a number of shell utility programs that make many of these features available to users of 8-bit personal computers.

MS/PC-DOS 2.0 and Apple's ProDOS

Created in the image of UNIX, both of these programs use a similar tree-structured file system and incorporate many of the same commands to allow the user to move about and manipulate the files and directories. Both are much more sparing in the number of housekeeping utilities and commands supplied, particularly those of use to the writing professional in the quick and efficient search and retrieval of text files and records. Of the two, DOS 2.0 does a better job, providing some additional knowledge-processing utilities that are similar in most respects to those provided by UNIX, including COPY, DIR, PATH, TREE, FIND, and SORT.

Using CP/M for File Search and Retrieval

Of the flat-structured operating systems being used on personal computers, CP/M has the most potential as a text file search and retrieval tool.

First of all, CP/M has in common with Apple DOS and MS/PC-DOS 1.0 a TYPE command that allows you to scan through candidate files selected via the wildcard technique outlined earlier. It takes no more than a few seconds to determine whether they contain needed information. The one drawback of TYPE is that it limits you to scanning only one file at a time. Each time you want to scan another file, you must reenter the command, followed by the name of the new file.

However, unlike the other similarly structured personal computer operating systems, CP/M can also scan through multiple files on a single command as well as (1) concatenate multiple files into a single larger file; (2) send the results of such a file search directly to a printer/file or to your console and then to the printer/file; (3) send any portion of a file beginning or ending with a specified character string to a printer, console, or another file; and (4) selectively display, print, or send to another file any portion of a file between and including two selected character strings.

All of these functions are performed by a single housekeeping utility, PIP.COM, one of CP/M's best-kept secrets. The most common use of PIP.COM is to copy files from one disk to another. It can be invoked in one of two ways. If you wanted to perform only one operation, you would enter the PIP command followed by the command line immediately after the CP/M prompt, as follows:

```
A> PIP pipcommandline (Return)
```

If you had several operations to perform, it would be best to invoke PIP.COM after you've called up the PIP program and the PIP prompt (an asterisk) has appeared.

For example, PIP B: = A:MICRO.TXT copies a file with the filename MICRO.TXT from disk drive A to disk drive B and gives it the same name. PIP B:NEWMICRO.TXT = A:MICRO.TXT copies the file named MICRO.TXT from disk drive A to a file on disk drive B and assigns it the name NEWMICRO.TXT.

It is also possible to concatenate several files together and direct them to any output device you desire. These output devices can be disk drives, printers, or your console/CRT.

For example, if you wanted to scan through three or four files—say, MICRO1, MICRO2, and MICRO3 on disk drive B and MICRO5 and MICRO6 on disk drive A—in rapid succession and see these displayed on your CRT, the PIP command line would take one of two forms:

```
A> PIP CRT: =B:MICRO1,B:MICRO2,B:MICRO3,A:MICRO5,A:MICRO6
```

or

```
*CRT: =B:MICRO1,B:MICRO2,B:MICRO3,A:MICRO5,A:MICRO6
```

Under CP/M, each command line can be up to 127 characters long, so you can display as many files as will fit in that space, which is partly a function of the length of the filenames. In this case, about ten or so filenames can be fitted into this space.

If you wanted a printout of these files, you could obtain it in one of two ways. First, you could enter a Control P at the end of the command line. Then everything displayed on the screen would also be sent to your printer. Second, you could substitute the device name for your printer (usually LST:, for list device). Then all of these files would be sent in succession directly to your printer.

Using a somewhat similar command structure, you can concatenate any number of such files together in whatever order you want. Suppose, after you've scanned ten or so files (MICRO1 to MICRO10), you want to merge five of them into another file on disk C: in the following order: #7 from disk A followed by 1 and 4 from disk B, 8 from disk A and 9 from disk B. This command would be as follows:

```
PIP C:MERGE.TXT =A:MICRO7,B:MICRO1,B:MICRO4,A:MICRO8,B:MICRO9
```

By assigning special control parameters to the basic PIP command, a wide range of other functions can be performed. These control parameters are set off in square brackets following the file or files they reference. If you wanted to assign a particular parameter to a whole set of files, the parameters would be entered following the first filename. You may also mix files with and without control parameters in the same command line.

There are about 20 such control parameters. However, there are only 2 that perform any useful knowledge-processing functions. These are [Sstring^Z], which specifies that PIP start copying a file after the unique character string following S is encountered, and [Qstring^Z], which tells PIP to stop copying (Quit) after the unique string following the Q is encountered. Used with the PIP CRT: header, a command line including one or the other of these parameters will allow you to scan the beginning and ending of a file, making the command similar in some respects to the TAIL/HEAD commands used under UNIX. Using them both allows you to display only text that falls between the two character strings. Alternatively, you can also send the selected text to your printer or to another file.

When using these two parameters, you must be careful about two things. First, to make sure that you are copying the exact portion of the file you desire, you should carefully select the keyword to make sure that it is the only one of its type in the file. Second, you should use the form of PIP in which you enter the command line after the asterisk prompt. It will select exactly the character string you enter: STRING, string, and

String would be treated as three different sequences. The other form of PIP converts all the characters in the search string to upper case.

One way I use this command is to quickly search through files without scanning the full text. I do this by listing at the head of my text file a set of keywords that reflect the contents and end this with the phrase "TEXT FILE KEYWORDS." To view only this keyword area at the top of a series of files, I enter the following PIP command:

```
*CRT: =A:MICRO7 [QTEXT FILE KEYWORDS^ Z ],
       B:MICRO1 [QTEXT FILE KEYWORDS^ Z ],
       B:MICRO4 [QTEXT FILE KEYWORD^ Z ]
```

In response, the top portion of each file ending in that unique character string is then displayed on the screen in sequence.

Another way PIP can be used is as the search-and-retrieval mechanism in an electronic scratch pad containing notes related to a specific research project. Each note entry begins with a unique character string consisting of the capitalized word NOTE followed by a number that identifies a specific entry, such as NOTE#1, NOTE#2, or NOTE#3. Using either the TYPE or PIP CRT: command, I scan through the files, identifying the files I need and the sequence in which I wish to retrieve them. I then enter the following PIP command sequence:

```
*B:RESULTS =A:FILENAME [SNOTE #1^ ZQNOTE #
   2^ Z ],A:FILENAME [SNOTE #7^ ZQNOTE #
   8^ Z ],A:FILENMAE [SNOTE #3^ ZQNOTE #
   4^ Z ],A:FILENAME [SNOTE #8^ ZQNOTE #9^ Z ]
```

The program then retrieves these specific note entries and combines them into a file in the order I have specified.

COPY and CAT

The only other commands in other operating systems that perform comparable functions with the same degree of sophistication are the COPY command used under MS/PC-DOS 2.0 and the CAT command used under UNIX.

COPY allows you to copy one or more files from one disk to another, concatenate files, and send files from one device to another—say, from a disk to the console.

The UNIX CAT command is even more powerful, especially when combined with the ">" symbol, which directs the output of one or more files to a terminal or another file. Among the possible variations are:

CAT FILENAME	Displays the contents of the named file on the CRT.
CAT FILE1 FILE2 ...	Displays the named files in sequence on the CRT.
CAT FILE1 FILE2 > FILE3	Concatenates the first two files and places the result in a third.
CAT > FILENAME	Accepts lines from the keyboard and writes them to the named file.
> FILENAME	Creates an empty file with the designated name.

Your Built-In Electronic Card File/Notebook

As mentioned earlier, most operating systems include a line- or character-oriented editor that is used primarily in the writing of programs. Although somewhat awkward to use for the generation of long documents, it has more than enough capability as a card file/scratchpad editor.

Actually, for generation of short files, using your operating system's line editor is a much more efficient and speedy process, even though some of the editing commands are less automatic than with a full-function word processor. The other unique feature of line editors—insertion of a number at the beginning of each line—is a drawback for the generation of long text files but an advantage in generating card file entries, which are typically relatively structured, with specific types of information on each line.

In a bibliographic card file, for example, I usually put the name of the author on the first line, the title of the article or book on the second, the magazine on the third, the date on the fourth, and the abstract on the next four. Although most line editors also contain a range of commands that allow you to edit character by character, I find it simpler and faster to edit at the line-command level, and even then only very selectively.

Since the notes I am taking are quickie, scratchpad-style entries that I will likely edit more extensively with a word processor, I leave misspelled words for later editing. When I am working with a line editor, I alter a particular line entry only when there is a major error, such as a wrong page number or a wrong word in the title or abstract that changes completely the meaning of the entry. Even then I use only the line-editing commands, writing over the line completely, rather than the character-editing commands.

Typical of such line editors is the MS-DOS program EDLIN.COM, which includes the following line-editing commands:

[line #] I	To insert new lines of text.
[line #]	To edit a particular numbered line.
[line #][line #]L	To list numbered lines of text.
[n]A	To append lines of text to file in memory.
[line #][line #]D	To delete numbered lines in memory.
[n]W	To write lines in memory to output file.
E	To exit editor and close files.

To write text into a file, you would call up the edtior by entering its name and the filename of a new or existing file. For example, suppose I am gathering information on a particular type of microprocessor and name each file on the basis of its subject and its file type, according to the sequence of entry. If this is my sixth entry and the information in the file is related to the processor's instruction set, I will open a file as follows:

```
A> EDLIN B:INSTRUCT.N06
```

Calling the editor opens a file with that filename. If the file does not exist, a directory entry is created with the above filename and a NEW FILE message on the screen. To begin entering text, type an I and a Return. Then type in text line by line, ending each line with a carriage return. A typical sequence would look something like this:

```
*I
    1:* ZILOG Z8000 INSTRUCTION SET DESCRIPTION
    2:* By Hank Brineen
    3:* IEEE Spectrum Magazine
```

```
4:* This micro executes in sequences of machine
    cycles
5:* These cycles vary from 3 to 10 clock periods
6:*
```

After entering the text you want into your electronic card file, type in a CONTROL/BREAK, which puts you back in the Command mode, where the console will again display an asterisk. Typing in "1L" will redisplay your entry from the beginning. To correct line 5, enter "5," which will display line 5 with the cursor in position for entering the new text.

You can then type in either "1L" or a "5L" to see the new entry. If the information is satisfactory, enter an E at the EDITOR prompt. This writes the lines of text in memory to a disk file. To confirm this, enter a DIR command, get a listing of the directory, and check to see whether INSTRUCT.N06 has indeed been created.

Although most implementations of UNIX on personal computers have similar line editors, a quicker way to enter text is to use the CAT command combined with the file redirection symbol (>). To create the same INSTRUCT.N06 file, you would enter the following command sequence:

CAT > INSTRUCT.N06

This causes CAT to read whatever you type at the computer keyboard and place it in the file INSTRUCT.N06. Since CAT is not an editor, you can't back up and fix errors. However, for simple one- or two-line entries, this command is very useful and speedy. To save a file created this way, all you do is enter a Control D at the end of the text. This causes CAT to close the file and exit, returning you to the primary system prompt.

CHAPTER 18

Low-Cost System Utilities as Knowledge-Processing Aids

Whereas many features of your operating system can be used to enhance your personal computer's capabilities as a writing tool and knowldge processor, this strategy has its limits. Often much more is needed. But what if you don't want—or can't afford—to invest in one of the knowledge-processing programs described in earlier chapters? A way to enhance your computer's capabilities at a relatively low cost is to purchase one or more of a number of system-level utility programs originally designed to aid programmers. Utilities that might also serve as writing aids fall into several categories, including:

- Disk-cataloging programs
- Search/Index/Retrieve utilities
- Operating system "shells" and "overlays"

Where such programs differ from the full-featured kbase-processing programs discussed in Parts II and III is that they are narrowly focused on one or two functions, whereas the latter combine many of these functions into a single program. In exchange for this narrowly focused functionality, such utility programs have four basic advantages.

First, they are low in cost, typically no more than $15 to $150. Second, they require very little program space, from 5 to 15K bytes, and so can fit on your system disk with the operating system and your word-processing program. Third, they allow you to "jury-rig" together, in piecemeal fashion, a knowlege-processing system that performs only the knowledge-processing operations you want. Fourth, they allow you to build up your computer's knowledge-processing capabilities in an incremental fashion, adding features as you can afford them.

Disk-Cataloging Programs

One of the basic problems facing the writing professional who has used a computer for any length of time is keeping track of the location and content of his or her disk-based text files. This is especially true if you have accumulated several tens of diskettes with several megabytes—millions of words—of text files. Two kinds of programs are available to solve this problem: simple disk catalogers and more sophisticated disk catalogers that allow you to add comments to describe what is in each file.

Simple Catalogers

One of the most common programs available, the simple cataloger automatically assigns names to your diskettes; notes the names, locations, and sizes of the files; and creates a catalog on a separate diskette. When searching for the location of a file, such programs will display your text files by filename, by extension/type, or by diskette. If you construct your filenames according to the conventions outlined in the previous chapter, you should be able to pin down the location of any text file and its contents with a great deal of precision. Some of the many such programs available are:

- DISK LIBRARY (Apple IIplus) from Instant Software
- MASTERDISK (Apple II) from Sensible Software
- MULTIDISK CATALOG III (Apple II) from Sensible Software
- CATALOG (CP/M) from The Software Store
- MASTER CATALOG SYSTEM #2 (CP/M) from Elliam Associates
- FLOPPY DISK LIBRARIAN (PC/MS-DOS) from Little Bit

- PROLOG (PC/MC-DOS) from ProSoft
- DISKETTE CATALOG (PC/MS-DOS) from N. F. Systems, Ltd.

Catalogers with Comments

Even using the strategies outlined in the last chapter, the filenames allowed by most operating systems are still somewhat cryptic. Thus you might want instead to consider programs that combine this cataloging function with a limited ability to store a line or so of comments that give you a more complete description of each file's contents. Typical of this enhanced cataloging approach are:

- EUREKA! from Mendocino Software
- SYNOPSIS from ProTem Software
- MicroLIB from Advanced Micro Techniques
- SIMPLIFILE from Durant Software

EUREKA!

This program can operate either as a simple cataloging program or as a more sophisticated program that allows you to incorporate some comments that describe the contents of each text file. Each catalog disk can hold data for as many as 250 of your text file diskettes. The exact number depends on your hardware configuration, the number of files on each disk, disk storage capacity, and the extent to which you have put comments in your files.

The first step in setting up your disk files is to give each disk a title. The disk title is just like any other CP/M file except that when you view it outside the program, the filename is only seven characters long, preceded by a dash. Putting a title on the disk involves creating a blank file that the program will recognize as the filename. This can be done in one of three ways. The first is to use the CP/M SAVE command in the manner described in the last chapter to create a blank file with the name you may want to give the disk. The second is to open a file with your word processor, using the same filename and saving the blank file. The third way is automatically performed by the program. If there is no title on the disk, it will ask for one.

If you wish to use the program as a simple cataloger, simply follow the menu prompts given you by the program and proceed to index your disk files. If, however, you wish to incorporate descriptive comments into the listing created by EUREKA!, you must add a set of four label/comment fields at the beginning of each text file with your word processor, including:

1. A file description field that consists of a label of up to four characters and a colon, followed by 90 characters describing the contents of the file.

2. A date field, which can contain up to 8 characters.

3. Two user-defined, 4-character labels, followed by fields up to 10 characters in length.

The first two fields come with default labels—Desc: and Date:—that can be changed during installation on your system. The other two can be anything you want. The only permanent feature of each label is the inclusion of the colon to separate the label from the field. For the purposes of my technical-article kbase, the labels I chose were:

Keys:	Lists five or six words describing contents of file
Mag:	Abbreviated name of the magazine for which the article was written
Sorc:	Source of material for article
Corp:	Company that assigned job

Once these preliminaries are out of the way, cataloging files and searching for them is simply a matter of following the menus and inserting and removing the appropriate diskettes when prompted by the program. The center of activity in this program is the Main Menu, which allows you to select which of the basic operations you wish to perform:

U	Update catalog
A	Access catalog
P	Put program on new disk
E	Erase disk from catalog
D	Change date
C	Select catalog drive
Q	Quit and return to operating system

The U(pdate) command is used to enter a new diskette into the catalog or to update the entries on an old one. Before it scans your raw text file diskettes and adds them to the catalog, the program asks whether or not you want to put comments into the catalog. The submenu that appears gives you the choice of:

1. Renaming your diskette
2. Showing the disks currently in the catalog
3. Showing the directory of the current text file diskette
4. Entering the library disk to update it

If you are entering files into the catalog, the program will direct you to enter the name of the text file disk drive and then put the disk in the drive. Once the program has cataloged a disk, it will display a message telling you the number of files cataloged with or without comments.

With the Main Menu A(ccess) command, you can find any file in your catalog by its name, by the disk it is on, or by any information in the comment fields. This command has its own submenu with ten options and three toggles, including:

E Exclude comments: this toggle determines whether or not the comments in your files will be shown along with the file titles.

P Printer selected: this toggle is used to send reports to your printer or to the screen.

W Wait on screen full: when this toggle is on, reports will pause when the screen or printed page is full; pressing any key will allow the report to continue.

H Help, giving a brief description of all the other options.

Q Quit, which returns you to the Main Menu.

D Disk title, which allows you to narrow your search to specific disks or groups of disks to be searched.

F File title, which allows you to narrow your search to specific files or groups of files.

t Text, which allows you to select text to be searched for in the comment fields in your cataloged files (you may specify up to four groups of characters that either may or must be found for a file to be selected).

A   Shows files alphabetically.

S   Shows files by disk.

L   List of disks in catalog.

I   Disk information, which shows you, for each selected file, the title along with the user number cataloged, the size of the disk, the space free, the space used, the number of files cataloged, and the date the disk was last updated.

SYNOPSIS

Compared to EUREKA!, SYNOPSIS is a much more limited (or more focused, depending on your point of view) cataloging program. It is designed to automatically create, update, search, and display an index containing the filename, disk ID, and four lines of comments—30, 40, 60, and 75 characters long, respectively—describing any CP/M file you wish to catalog.

Unlike its counterparts, SYNOPSIS does not concern itself with file sizes, number of files, or used and unused disk space. Its one and only aim is to provide you with a brief synopsis of what is contained in each file.

The program has two parts. One is SYNSTALL, which creates an "environment program" under which your word processor or text editor runs, automatically and simultaneously updating the index. The second part is a set of programs designed to work together. The most important of these programs are (1) TOP.WS, TOP.SP, and TOP.MW, which contain default nonprinting comment headings for WordStar, Spellbinder, and Magic Wand, and (2) SYN.COM, which creates and updates two index files, SYN.DAT and SYN.KEY, and provides a menu that links a set of programs together to create, maintain, access, rename, and erase files and indices. Operation of the program is a four-step process.

The first step is assigning disk IDs. This is done as was discussed in the last chapter, using the SAVE command.

The second step is installing the environment. When called up, the program asks for the brand name of your text editor or word processor, the name you ordinarily type in to run it, and the name you want to give to the environment program. For example, if you use WordStar and enter WS to call it up, you might give the environment program the name WSE or WSN. Thereafter, when you wanted to create a new text file or edit an older one, you would enter WSE or WSN instead of WS.

The third step is entering comments into the SYNOPSIS index. After calling up your word processor via the environment program designation, enter text in the usual manner. However, at the beginning of each file, read in one of the appropriate TOP files containing the comment headings. The default headings supplied in the TOP files as well as in the SYNOPSIS program containing the system prompts (PROMPT.SYN) are:

```
Date:
Author:
Addressee:
Subject:
```

The headings on these fields can be changed at any time by using your word processor to edit them in the TOP and PROMPT.SYN files to your satisfaction. Whatever headings are assigned, when the TOP file has been read in, enter the comments as you wish. When you've finished editing a file and have saved it, the environment program will automatically and simultaneously signal the SYNOPSIS index. Once you've returned to the CP/M operating system, call up the main SYN.COM file by entering SYN X:, where X is the drive containing your document file. The program will then update the SYN.DAT and SYN.KY files by reading in the comment lines from these files.

The fourth step is searching the SYNOPSIS index. After SYN.COM updates the index, it displays a submenu from which you select the Search Index command. In response, the program displays six prompt lines that correspond to the name of the document file, the disk ID, and the four lines in TOP. After you make your response, in letters, words, or phrases, SYNOPSIS searches the index entries for matching letters, words, or phrases. If you key in a Return, the program will search without regard to the information on that line. If you end any line with the Escape key, the program will begin searching without regard to the information on any succeeding line. The program will display the complete entry of every file that meets your requirements and the disk on which it is located.

MicroLIB

Designed for use on CP/M 2.2 and MP/M 1.0 or 2.0, MicroLIB is both more and less powerful than either of the two previous cataloging programs. Offering at a minimum the same disk-cataloging features, MicroLIB is less powerful in the sense that only a single 50-character comment field is available for the storage of descriptive material and keywords. However, it is more powerful in that it offers a number of features not available on the other two programs.

From the writing professional's point of view, a key feature of MicroLIB is that it allows you to organize your text files into a quasihierarchical tree structure by consolidating groups of files within a logical structure that its developers call a library, or within a group of libraries. Moreover, files within a library may also be associated with other files in the library through relationships established by MicroLIB. This allows a single command to be used to search through a related group of files.

A MicroLIB library is viewed by the operating system as one large file into which the program packs the contents of many files. These files are tagged with their original names, access dates, grouping keywords, and descriptions. The libraries are stored in a compact format to reduce the amount of disk space required to save files. They can also be protected from unauthorized access through the use of a password protection scheme and data encryption for sensitive data.

MicroLIB consists of five programs: MLIB, a menu-driven program used to manage the libraries, and MPUT, MDIR, MSTAT, and MGET, all of which execute actions from the CP/M command line.

MLIB: Used to create a library and assign its characteristics, including the maximum size it can reach, whether the files in it are to be protected by passwords and/or encrypted, and whether descriptions are required with them. It is also used to alter these choices, to edit the descriptions of the files, to print a report on all or only selected files, to display files on the screen or the printer, and to delete files or entire libraries.

MSTAT: Used to display all the libraries on a particular disk volume, including name, attributes, and disk allocation statistics.

MDIR: Allows you to scan the directory of a particular library.

MPUT: Used to save a file into a library initially and also to return a file to a library once it has been retrieved and updated.

MGET: Used to retrieve a file from a library once the file has been saved into a library.

SIMPLIFILE

Designed primarily to make the file-handling and command execution tasks of CP/M simpler, SIMPLIFILE also allows you to add up to 42 characters of descriptive information on each file. Essentially, this program acts as an umbrella under which CP/M is invoked and operates. Instead of using the unfamiliar system commands, the program allows you to select commands from a menu that are more like English.

Each time SIMPLIFILE is invoked, a split screen appears on the display. At the top is the Disk Area, which contains information on disk status and the amount of file space left on the disk. At the bottom is the File Area, containing the basic commands: V(iew), C(opy), B(ackup), L(ist), R(ename), E(dit), S(ort), and H(elp).

The first time you call up the program, you are asked to give the disk a six-character ID. After that, each time SIMPLIFILE is called from CP/M, it asks for the current date, which you can enter or ignore by hitting Return. When the SIMPLIFILE Menu appears, the cursor automatically appears at the top of the screen in the Disk Area. To move from the Disk Area to the File Area and back, simply hit the Escape key.

The file area contains information about the files on the current drive. The cursor is moved up and down through the files using the cursor arrows, and action can be taken on any file by moving the cursor to that line.

When the cursor is on a filename, you can enter the 42-character description of the contents of the file. To move the file list up and down, hit N to go to the next screen, P to go to a previous screen, or T to move the cursor to the top of the screen. The files can be sorted according to filename, file type, or size by using the S(ort) command.

Search/Index/Retrieve Utilities

One step up in sophistication from the disk catalog programs are a wide range of search, index, and retrieve utilities. Typical of programs of this type are:

- Search from Micro Alliance
- KWICINDX from Miracle Computing

Search

A useful program to have once you've narrowed down the search of your disk-based text files for information about a particular subject, Search is designed for use on CP/M or MS/PC-DOS systems. It performs simple sequential searches for any sequence of ASCII characters on any or all drives and in any or all CP/M user areas with a single command. On the basis of these searches, separate files are created containing the names of the files holding the words, phrases, or character strings.

The program is called up by entering its name at the SYSTEM prompt followed by your search criteria, as follows:

```
SEARCH (first argument), FOR (second argument),
(options)
```

The first argument contains the name of the file or files you want searched. It allows you to use ambiguous filenames that incorporate the standard CP/M wildcard characters (? or *) and is extremely useful if you've constructed the filename and its extensions carefully, as described in Chapter 17. The word FOR is used to separate the files to be searched from the character string you want to search for. The second argument contains the character strings for Search to match. If you want to search a text file containing the character string, enclose it in quotes. If the character string is in a data file, do not use the quote signs.

Search can be used to look for up to 16 different character strings, incorporating any or all of the following special characters as wildcards:

#	Match any number from 0 to 9.
|	Match any upper- or lower-case character.
?	Match any character.
/	Tells the program not to interpret the next character as a wildcard. This is to be used when you want any of the above three characters to be taken literally.

Various options can be specified within brackets, which condition the command sequence in the following ways:

U	Search for both upper- and lower-case characters.
W	Search for whole words only.

P	Send output to printer.
K	Kill display and detach (used only with MP/M).
F	Put names of all files being searched into Directory file.
R	Put names of files where string is found into Results file.
N	Eject to a new page every time Search uses a new drive.
C	Count the number of occurrences of each string.
DIR	Search only directory files.
SYS	Search only system files.
DRIVE	Used to specify which drives to search.
USER	Used to specify which user areas to search.

With this small repertoire of commands, it is possible to search your text files in a number of different ways. Here are some typical command sequences:

SEARCH MICRO.TXT FOR "INTEL"	Searches a single file (MICRO.TXT) for a single entry (INTEL).
SEARCH MICRO.TXT FOR "INTEL" [W]	Searches only for whole words.
SEARCH MICRO.TXT FOR "INTEL" [U]	Searches for both upper- and lower-case characters, that is, both

	INTEL and Intel.
SEARCH MICRO.TXT FOR "INTEL" [U,W,]	Searches for upper- and lower-case characters and for whole words.
SEARCH *.TXT FOR "INTEL" [U,W,]	Searches all files of the type .TXT for all references to INTEL.
SEARCH *.TXT FOR "INTEL", "8088" [U,W]	Searches all files of the type .TXT for the word INTEL and the alphanumeric string 8088.
SEARCH *.TXT FOR "INTEL" [U,W,P]	Sends the results of the search to the printer.

To specify more than one drive, enclose your instructions within square brackets. For example, the sequence:

```
SEARCH *.TXT FOR SIXTEEN.TXT [U,W, DRIVE = (A,D)]
```

tells the program to search only drives A and D, whereas:

```
DRIVE = (A, E-G)
```

directs the search to drive A and drives E through G.

```
DRIVE = ALL
```

directs the program to search all drives currently logged onto the system. Under CP/M, USER may be specified in the same way, with user numbers instead of drive letters.

To search for multiple words or strings of characters, up to 16 in number, the most direct way is to list them after the FOR qualifier, separated by commas. However, this is a long, drawn-out process, especially if you are searching a number of different diskettes. Search allows you to automate this process somewhat by putting them all in a separate data file, listing each word or phrase on a separate line. For example, if you want to search your files for all references to 16-bit microprocessors produced by Intel and National Semiconductor, create a file named, say, SIXTEEN.TXT and use your word processor to enter a command string that looks something like this:

```
16 BIT MICROPROCESSORS
INTEL
NATIONAL SEMICONDUCTOR
```

To search for all of these words, you would then type in the following command sequence:

```
SEARCH *.TXT FOR SIXTEEN.TXT [U,W,P ]
```

You can add several additional strings or even several different data file names after the FOR, provided that you don't search for more than a total of 16 individual character strings. This method is a useful way to search for strings of lower-case letters, since the command line is always converted to upper case by CP/M and PC/MS-DOS.

If the command string starts getting too long, you can enter the whole sequence into a command file by any name you want. It can include not only sequences of search words, but nested files of search words as well. For example, say you created a command file named COMMAND.FIL that contained the following command sequence:

```
*.TXT FOR SIXTEEN.TXT [U,W,P, DRIVE = D, USER = 10]
```

The entire command could be executed by entering:

```
SEARCH $ COMMAND.FIL
```

where the dollar sign directs the program to look for a command file to get the information it needs.

Search time for this program is dependent on a number of variables, including the speed of the processor, the number of drives and words to be scanned, and the number of qualifying options. However, scanning for a single nine-character search sequence in four files with a total of 80K bytes (about 50 double-spaced pages or 13,500 words) takes just about 60 seconds on a Northstar Horizon with a 2-megahertz Z80 CPU. This is roughly comparable to the search time for more sophisticated knowledge-processing and card file programs.

KWICINDX

Designed for use with PC/MS-DOS–based computers, this program reads any ASCII-formatted file and produces a sorted keyword-in-context index along with a line reference based on a scan of the text and a separate stopword file containing those words you may consider to be "noise" words. Since documents that are to be processed by KWICINDX must be ASCII files, this means you cannot use the direct output produced by your word processor, because most place special control characters throughout the text. Whereas they have special meaning to your word-processing program, they only confuse KWICINDX, so it is necessary to remove them. Most word processors have a special facility for producing "plain," ASCII, or unformatted "nondocument" text. For those that don't, there is usually some operating system utility that makes it possible to strip such characters off the file. In CP/M, for example, you would use the PIP command with the Z parameter.

KWICINDX is written in BASIC, so it is necessary to load in the BASIC program first. Once BASIC is started and KWICINDX is in the system drive, the program is started by typing in "RUN KWICINDX." If everything is operating properly, you will be presented with a series of prompts asking you the name of the file to be indexed, the record length, the number of records, and the filename containing the stopwords.

This program considers each line of text to be a record, so the record length is the number of characters per line, and the number of records is the number of lines in your text file. You need not be precise in determining these numbers, but you should err on the upside, overestimating rather than underestimating.

Stopwords are those words you would like to suppress from the index. They include such common words as a, the, it, and so. You may either build your own stopword file from scratch or use the one provided with the program (STOPWD1) or some modification of it. Such a file consists of a list of words, one per line. As with the index proper, the stopword index must be a pure ASCII file.

Once all of the information has been entered, KWICINDX begins processing the file. Run time for indexing depends on line length, the number of words, and the number of lines. In most cases, indexing a text file takes no longer than the processing required with a spelling checker.

This program has no search capability, so searching is something you need to do using other programs in your knowledge-processing repertoire. A suggested strategy is to give the index file a filename extension that indicates the disk number or name the file is on. This index file and its associated stopword index with a similar extension are then stored on a separate index diskette. For example, a file on technical article diskette 3 containing a story on the Zilog microprocessors might have the filename ZMICRO.TXT, whereas its associated index and stopword files would have the names ZLOGINDX.D03 and ZLOGSTOP.D03. To find the location of text information on the Zilog microprocessor I would then use a search facility such as Search or one of my operating system's built-in facilities to scan the files to find the keywords of interest. If it happened to be in the Zilog Micro index, I would know from the extension that it was on diskette 3.

Operating System Shells and Overlays

As discussed in the last chapter, each of the operating systems in widespread use on personal computers incorporates commands and internal utility programs that perform unique knowledge-processing functions for the writing professional. Unfortunately, it is rare to find all of these functions in a single operating system. For example, there are a number of features that I like in UNIX, but not enough to give up CP/M, and likewise for MS-DOS and Apple DOS. Ideally, what one wants is an operating system that incorporates all of the various text/knowledge-processing features. No such operating system seems likely. However, there are alternative solutions, specifically in the form of *shells* and *overlays*, which give one operating system additional capabilities previously associated with another operating system.

For the writing professional, the most useful group of shells are those that add UNIX-like features to such operating systems as CP/M-80, CP/M-86, and MS-DOS/PC-DOS 1.0. Some of these UNIX-like shells are:

- CLIP from Thoughtware
- MICROSHELL from New Generation Systems
- UNICA from Knowology
- MicroTools+ from Carousel MicroTools

Illustrative of the wide range of writing and knowledge-processing tools such shells provide is MicroTools+, which combines a quasihierarchical file structure with a set of over 60 software utilities (tools); these perform such knowledge-processing tasks as text manipulation, document search and retrieval, and file organization. This shell takes advantage of the user number feature of CP/M to simulate a two-level hierarchical structure, allowing you to organize the files on a disk into logical groupings. Among the utilities most useful in performing such tasks are:

FIND	Locates text patterns in a file or set of files.
CH	Changes text patterns in a file or set of files.
SORT	Sorts and/or merges text files.
LS	Lists the filenames in a directory.

ISAM	Builds an index sequential access list.
PL	Prints specific lines in a file.
CAT	Concatenates/copies files.
TAIL	Prints the last lines of files.
COMP	Simple file comparison.
FB	Shows blocks of lines in a file containing a specific text pattern.
KWIC/UNROT	Generates a permuted index.
AR	Archive file maintenance. This tool allows you to store more bytes of data on a disk than is usually possible with CP/M. It has the added benefit of making additional levels of the filename hierarchy available.

When taken together, these utilities—combined with the program's formatter, editors, and other text-processing tools—make a powerful document and text management system.

CHAPTER 19

Word-Processing Programs as Knowledge Processors

A final but key element in turning your personal computer into an effective knowledge-processing tool is, surprisingly, the word-processing program. It can perform several important functions beyond the primary functions of text editing and formatting.

First, if you've chosen the right program, your word processor can serve as a highly effective cut-and-paste and file-management tool, taking the text records and files retrieved from your kbase and rearranging them in the proper order. Second, if it is backed up by the appropriate word-processing utilities, your program can also be used as an outline editor and a primitive, but effective, text retrieval and card file system.

Selecting the Right Word Processor

In order to perform as a knowledge-processing tool, your word processor should be able to perform certain minimum cut-and-paste operations in addition to its standard editing and formatting features. These include:

Block move: Shifts a marked block of text from one location in the file to another.

Block copy: Creates a duplicate of a block of text and allows you to place it at another location in the file for editing.

Block write to an external file: Useful when you are searching source files for information; it allows you to create separate files that can later be added or inserted into your main document file.

However, you will very quickly find that while these block move capabilities are an enormous improvement over similar operations performed on a standard typewriter, they become quite limiting, especially when compared with the way a personal computer manipulates data files. To perform as a knowledge processor, a word-processing program should also include the following file-manipulation capabilities:

Display another file: This allows you to scan other files while you are editing. It is useful when you must refer to a kbase of research material.

Insert or add one file to another: With this option, you can work in one file and at the same time call up another to be inserted or added. It can also be used instead of a block move to shift a body of text from one location in a file to another.

Insert or add portions of a file: Much like the PIP option, but easier to use, this feature allows you to scan another file, mark those portions you need, and then transfer them to your working file.

Multiple or split screens: When combined with the above features, this feature allows you to look at two or more files simultaneously on the screen, scroll and move each independently, and then move the portions you need to the working file. It is particularly useful when you are working with a long file, where one screen can be set up to view the beginning of the document and another to view that portion of the text in which you are entering copy.

Multiple buffers: This option can be used in combination with the split-screen capability to reduce the delay time required to call up a file to the screen. When you begin work on a project, you first open up a number of buffer memory locations containing the files you will probably be accessing for reference and source material. When working in a particular file, these reference files can be accessed immediately without waiting for the computer to go to your disk to access the appropriate file and bring it up onto the screen.

Run other programs without exiting document: This feature is especially useful when you find that your source files do not contain the
information you want. With this feature, you can, without exiting the
file you are working on, (1) run your card file or free-form knowledge-
processing program, (2) retrieve the text you need, (3) send it to an
external text file, (4) return to your working document file, (5) enter
the text file into a buffer, and (6) shift the appropriate text into your
working file.

Of the two dozen or so advanced word-processing programs incorporating such features, I have found three that I consider ideal for the writing
professional:

- ELECTRIC BLACKBOARD from Santa Cruz Software Services

- FinalWord from Mark of the Unicorn

- Perfect Writer from Perfect Software

ELECTRIC BLACKBOARD is a multiwindow text editor for CP/M-
based systems. It allows you to divide the screen into ten different windows, each with a separate file displayed. The windows are independent
of one another, and each has its own tab settings, page size, and cursor
positioning.

FinalWord and Perfect Writer, available for use on both CP/M- and
PC/MS-DOS–based systems, take a different tack. Both allow splitting the
screen into only two parts. This is not the disadvantage it appears to be,
since both are also multibuffer in-memory word processors, which means
that you can access several documents at one time, without repeatedly
going back to the disk to retrieve them.

By copying documents into separate memory buffers—7 in the case of
Perfect Writer and 11 for FinalWord—it is possible to switch back and
forth betweeen documents with ease. Using the split screen, it is possible
to gather parts of text from one file and insert them into the other while
viewing the process on the screen.

In practice, I find it easiest to use half of the screen as the location of
my working file and the other half to display, when required, any one of
many buffered files. Moving portions of text from one screen to the other

is simply a matter of marking the text in one file, moving to the other, and using a block move to shift material into the working file. After I have moved all the text I need from the various buffer files, I close the external file buffers and open up a new one in which I place another copy of my working file. Shifting back and forth between the two makes it relatively simple to quickly cut and paste a document into a form appropriate for final editing.

A particularly useful feature of FinalWord is its STATE-SAVE feature, which allows you to stop anywhere in a document, use your computer for another application, and return to your document as you left it, without wasting time reading files onto and off of your disk.

Another interesting word-processing program is MultiMate from Softword Systems, which, in additon to having a split-screen capability, allows you to compose a rather detailed description of a document's contents as well as time, date, and revision sequence. This description precedes creation of the document and can be used as a mini-kbase/card file reference when searching through your files for the appropriate text. Although it is designed to operate on IBM PC and compatible systems, it bypasses the operating system, which means that it is extremely fast, both in keyboard entry and in execution of commands.

Other multiple-screen/multiple-buffer word-processing programs worth mentioning here include:

- VisiWord from Visicorp
- XyWrite II from Xyquest
- LEADING EDGE from Leading Edge Corporation
- WORD PERFECT from Satellite Software International
- WORD VISION from Bruce and James Publishing
- PieWriter from Howard W. Sams and Company
- MICROSOFT WORD from Microsoft
- MEMOPLAN from Chang Labs
- SELECT from Select Information Systems

All of the above are designed to operate on PC/MS-DOS–based computers, MEMOPLAN and SELECT operate on CP/M systems as well.

Getting More Out of Your Document Indexer

A common word-processing utility, supplied either in an integrated software package or as a stand-alone facility, is a program that generates a page index and table of contents for your disk-based documents.

Falling into the first category are word processors such as FinalWord and Perfect Writer, which incorporate document indexing as part of the basic program. In the second category are such stand-alone programs as Documate and STARMATE. Falling somewhere in between the two is StarIndex, which operates independently of WordStar but is customized to operate in close conjunction with it.

In addition to the functions of generating tables of contents and indices for documents, such programs can also be used, with a little ingenuity, as a way of organizing your document files according to categories of keywords. The best way to illustrate these capabilities is to focus on one particular program, MicroPro's StarIndex. The same principles can be applied to almost any document-indexing program.

Using StarIndex as a Knowledge Base Organizer

Designed for use with WordStar, this indexing program recognizes two types of index entries: words or phrases supplied by you and words or phrases supplied in the text. These entries are marked with word-processing commands using the same dot command or control-character formats used within WordStar itself.

Supplied index entries are marked on the line preceding the one you want to reference with .II. Embedded words or phrases are tagged by entering the command ^P^P before each entry.

Using similar dot and control-character commands placed in the text file, StarIndex can also create a table of contents with headings up to four levels of emphasis:

.IA   First level

.IB   Second level

.IC   Third level

.ID   Fourth level

Once these commands have been entered at the appropriate locations in your text file, you may exit WordStar and call up the StarIndex program by entering the line command STARINDX, followed by a space and then the name of the document file containing the StarIndex commands.

Unless you have indicated otherwise, StarIndex will then generate three output files with identical names except for their file types or extensions: an index file with the extension .IDX, a table of contents file with the extension .TOC, and a copy of the text file with the new extension .SI.

After the project involving that document is completed and I have moved the file from my working project disk to my archival or library disks, I make extra copies of the index and table of contents files and move each to the keyword index and category index disks I have created, renaming them to reflect the disk location for the particular text files they reference. For example, after I have completed work on a manual on the 4-bit microprocessor family of a particular semiconductor manufacturer (FOURBIT.SI), I may move it to disk 13 in my archival kbase of technical manuals. Instead of moving the table of contents (FOURBIT.TOC) and index (FOURBIT.IDX) files to the same disk, I move them to my technical manual kbase index disks, one for category searches with the table of contents files and one for keyword searches with the index files.

Then, using strategy similar to that described in Chapter 17, I rename the files. For example, the file name FOURBIT is changed to something like AB070319, which tells me the company for which it was written, the month and year, and three 2-character codes defining specific descriptive keywords. The extensions are then changed to reflect the disk location of the file: .I13 instead of .IDX, and .T13 instead of .TOC.

When it is necessary to find particular information in my manual kbase, I use the directory and wildcard commands to narrow the search down to a few possible files. Then, using a utility such as Search or one of the operating system's built-in commands, I search the table of contents or index files to find the specific reference and its location by page. Often all that is necessary is to scan the table of contents to find the appropriate file. In particularly long documents, however, even though searching the table of contents file narrows the search down to a particular section or chapter, it may be necessary to search the index file to find the particular page on which the information is located.

Getting More Out of Your Merge-Print Utility

A common program supplied with most word-processors is the Merge-Print utility. It is designed to perform the same function as the regular Print command with the additional capabilities of form-letter production, insertion of variable data into a document during printout, insertion of other named files in the printout, and printing multiple copies of a document. Enormously useful as these capabilities are, such Merge-Print utility programs can also be used as outline organizers and electronic card files.

Again, the best way to illustrate these knowledge-processing capabilities is to focus on one particular utility, MicroPro's MailMerge option, which allows you to precisely control the print output via a few simple dot commands and symbols, including:

.AV MESSAGE	Asks you for the variable name to be inserted between the ampersand symbols.
.DF FILENAME	Specifies the name of the data file.
.FI FILENAME	Directs the insertion of a file's contents during printing and prints the contents as controlled by the commands in the command file.
.RP n	Directs the program to repeat printing of the file *n* times or, without the *n*, until you intervene, or until the form letter or document runs out of data in the data file.
.RV	Specifies the names of variables and order of values.
.DM	Displays message.
&VAR&	A variable with up to 200 characters whose data value is read in with the .RV or .AV commands.
&VAR/O&	An optional variable that is eliminated from the form without leaving a blank line if no data value is entered.

Before going to these commands for knowledge-processing applications, it is instructive to look at how they are used normally—say, in generating a form letter.

Suppose you want to send a roughly identical letter to a list of potential interviewees for an article. First you create a data file of the names and addresses (ADDRESS.DAT); this contains a number of lines, each of which contains the data to be used in one letter or document. Within the line, the data items are separated by commas and always occur in the same order—for example, company, first line of address, second line of address, third line of address, and name of potential interviewee (COMPANY, ADDR1, ADDR2, ADDR3, NAME). Two names in the address data file might appear as follows:

```
XYZ Inc.,1492 Columbus Ave.,"Alemeda, CA",94503,Mr.
Jones
ABC Inc.,1776 Washington St.,"Berkeley,
CA",94730,Ms. Smith
```

The quotes around the "city, state" items indicate that the city and state are to be read as one value, including the comma but excluding the quotes.

Second, you create the document command file—say, with the name INTVW1.LET—as shown in Screen 1.

When you execute the MailMerge option, either directly via the operating system command line or through the WordStar No-file Menu, it will ask you the name of the file to MailMerge, upon which you will enter the name of the document command file (INTVW1.LET). The program then looks for the file holding the data (ADDRESS.DAT), merges the two, and prints out form letters with the individualized names and addresses.

Alternatively, the document command file for the same form letter can be constructed so that you can key in the data as the letter is being printed or sent to a file in response to prompts, as shown in Screen 2.

When you execute the MailMerge command in this second case, each time the program runs into an .AV (ask for variable) dot command, it will ask you for the variable you wish to be entered, and it will continue to do this for as long as there is information you wish to enter.

Organizing Your Thoughts with MailMerge

To use MailMerge as an outline editor and idea organizer, a format is used that is somewhat similar to the first form-letter format discussed ear-

```
.DF ADDRESS.DAT
.RV COMPANY, ADDR1, ADDR2, ADDR3

                                APRIL 1, 1985
&COMPANY&
&ADDR1&
&ADDR2&
&ADDR3&

Dear &NAME&,

    I am writing a book for McGraw-Hill entitled
"Beyond Word Processing," and would like to
include a description of the operation and use
of programs that your firm, &COMPANY&, publishes
and markets that might be of use to the writing
professional.

                        Sincerely,
                        Bernard Conrad Cole
```

Screen 1

lier. First, determine the structure of your outline—whether you simply want to reorder topics in rough sequential order or want categories and subcategories. In MailMerge, all variables must start with an alphabetical character, so assign each topic or subject one or more letters of the alphabet, much the same way you would on paper, depending on the complexity of the outline. If it is a relatively simple outline, such as an outline for a magazine article, a simple single-letter heading (a,b,c,d,e, . . .) is appropriate. A more complex outline with three levels of categorization would begin each entry with three letters—aaa, aab, . . ., aba, . . ., adc, and so on.

Second, create a data file for your ideas—for example, OUT-LINE.DAT—using WordStar. Once the file is opened, enter randomly all the ideas you have concerning the topics to be covered in whatever order

```
.AV DATE-TODAY,1985
.AV COMPANY
.AV ADDR1
.AV ADDR2
.AV ADDR3
.AV NAME


                                        &DATE-TODAY,  1985&


&COMPANY&
&ADDR1&
&ADDR2&
&ADDR3&

Dear &NAME&,

    I am writing a book for McGraw-Hill entitled
"Beyond Word Processing" and would like to
include a description of the operation and use
of programs that your firm, &COMPANY&, publishes
and markets that might be of use to the writing
professional.

                        Sincerely,
                        Bernard Conrad Cole
```

Screen 2

they occur to you. Just as you would on a piece of paper, assign values to each topic in order of their importance. For example, in organizing this book, there were a number of major subjects to which I assigned alphabetical headings, depending on where I wanted them to appear in the book:

```
i  EUREKA
l  SEARCH
b  MINDEX
g  SEQUITUR
d  NOTEBOOK
n  SCIMATE
```

```
e  QUESTEXT
a  SUPERFILE
c  DATAFAX
f  CITATION
j  EAZYFILE
k  THINKTANK
h  CARDFILE
m  CARDBOX
```

Third, create a command file SEQUENCE.FIL, beginning with the .RV command and followed by the sequence listed in the data file and then the variable listing, in alphabetical order, as follows:

```
.RV  i,l,b,g,d,n,e,a,c,f,j,k,h,m
&a&
&b&
&c&
  .
  .
  .
&z&
```

Calling up the MailMerge command will then reorder your ideas alphabetically as follows:

```
a  SUPERFILE
b  MINDEX
c  DATAFAX
d  NOTEBOOK
e  QUESTEXT
f  CITATION
g  SEQUITUR
h  CARDFILE
i  EUREKA
j  EAZYFILE
k  THINKTANK
l  SEARCH
m  CARDBOX
n  SCIMATE
```

Creating Electronic Card Files with MailMerge

To automatically generate card file entries with your word processor, you would use the second form-letter format, using the .AV command to prompt you to enter text into a predefined card file form. Here, you would create a file command file with your word processor called, say, CARD-FILE.FRM, as follows:

```
.DM Enter the symbol and data as prompted:
.DM
.DM ————————————————————————————————————————
.AV "Main Heading", MAIN HEADING, 25
.DM ————————————————————————————————————————
.AV "Synopsis", SYNOPSIS, 30
.DM ————————————————————————————————————————
.AV "Keyword1", KEYWORD1, 25
.DM ————————————————————————————————————————
.AV "Keyword2", KEYWORD2, 25
.DM ————————————————————————————————————————
.AV "Keyword3", KEYWORD3, 25
.DM ————————————————————————————————————————
.AV "Line1", LINE1, 60
.DM ————————————————————————————————————————
.AV "Line2", LINE2, 60
.DM ————————————————————————————————————————
.AV "Line3", LINE3, 60
.DM ————————————————————————————————————————
.AV "Line4", LINE4, 60
.DM ————————————————————————————————————————
.AV "Line5", LINE5, 60
.DM ————————————————————————————————————————
.Av "Line6", LINE6, 60
.DM ————————————————————————————————————————
.Av ."Reference", REFERENCE, 60

+&MAIN HEADING&
:&SYNOPSIS&
<&KEYWORD1&      &KEYWORD2&        &KEYWORD3&
&LINE1&
&LINE2&
&LINE3/0&
&LINE4/0&
```

```
&LINE5/0&
&LINE6/0&
*&REFERENCE&
.RP
.FI CARDFILE.FRM
```

Each file card is designed to hold eight fields, each of which uses periods between each word in the field, except for the line fields containing the text. MAIN HEADING is the category or subcategory you've chosen for your report. The SYNOPSIS field contains a brief single- or multiple-word description of the text contents. KEYWORD1, KEYWORD2, and KEYWORD3 are keywords selected from the text. Lines 1 and 2 of text are always printed on the file card, whereas lines 3–6 are optional and are not printed unless text is actually entered on them. REFERENCE is a citation listing of the journal, book, magazine, or other source from which the abstracted text information is derived.

When you execute this program via the MailMerge command in the No-file Menu, you are prompted by the program and your responses are written on consecutive file cards.

The search through the file cards use WordStar's^QF Search function.

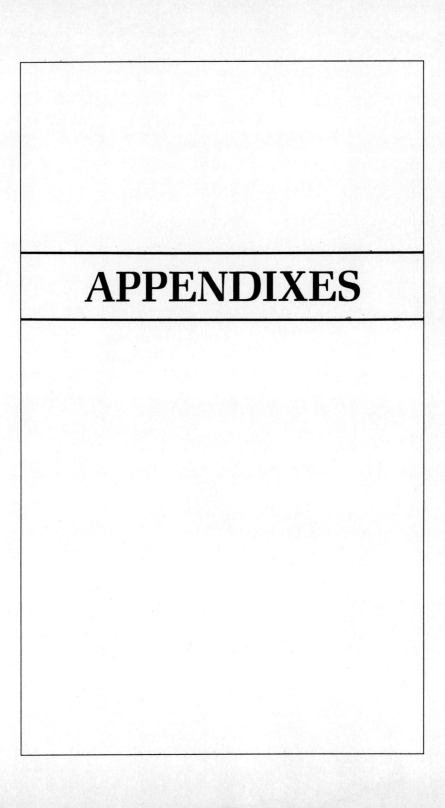

APPENDIXES

APPENDIX A

More Knowledge-Processing Tools for the Writer

After many years of neglect, the needs of writing professionals are receiving ever-increasing attention. One measure of this trend is the increased number of kbase-processing tools of various sorts that are now appearing on the market. A few of these new programs are reviewed in this appendix.

DAYFLO

Developed by Dayflo, Inc. for use on any IBM PC, IBM XT, or hardware compatible system with a hard disk and a minimum of 256K bytes, DAYFLO is designed to operate under and take advantage of MS/PC-DOS 2.0 and its hierarchical file structure.

Unlike traditional database management programs, which impose rigid limitations on formatting and using data, this program allows the use of both structured and unstructured data; that is, any data can be used without regard for prior classification or structure. No two records need look alike, any record can be changed without affecting others. In addition, information stored in the DAYFLO structure can be quickly and easily retrieved using common words and phrases.

Key to the operation of DAYFLO is the concept of the "desktop,"

261

whereby you can organize information in as many as 20 "stacks" and scan through these stacks as if they were file folders on a desk. Associated with each stack is a scratch pad by which information from one or more records in the folders can be edited or manipulated and then added to another folder to create new documents.

DAYFLO comes with a set of basic operations (including an editor, an organizer, a sorter, a find-and-retrieve processor, and a display manager) and a set of standard data types (text, numbers, and dates) that are understood throughout the system.

In DAYFLO, you create a document by simply going to the scratch pad in the stack on which you want to work and begin typing, using a sophisticated word processor. Every record you create is saved automatically when you go to another stack to work, leave the program, or begin creating a new record.

Each of the stacks is set up just like a stack of paper, with items coming to the top as you recall them and going to the bottom as you work your way through them. You can have up to 2500 records on top of your desk at one time, either all in one stack or spread out over the 20 stacks. As you collect pieces of information into specific stacks, the program keeps track of what is in each one and allows you to view a listing of the stacks and their contents at any time.

Each of the stacks can be labeled with a key that uniquely identifies the records within. If you want to be able to find a particular record in more than one way, you can specify up to 100 labels, or item names, per record.

DOCUMAX

DOCUMAX is a fully menu-driven information management system designed for use on the Apple II, IIplus, IIc, IIe, and III; under DOS 3.3 and ProDOS; on the Macintosh; on the IBM PC; and on CP/M. The program requires 48K bytes of RAM on the various Apple II versions. An in-memory resident program, it requires only one disk drive to use, although two would be more convenient.

DOCUMAX can be used to scan quickly and sequentially through full file contents or to search for files that contain one or two words, phrases, or fragments, each up to 30 characters long, linked by AND, OR, and NOT. Search speeds up to 15,000 characters per minute are possible; a full disk can be searched in less than a minute and a half.

A sort function allows you to arrange a catalog of disk files not only in alphabetical order, but into as many as ten subgroups, with the files in each group also in alphabetical order.

For storage purposes, DOCUMAX contains a proprietary text-compression scheme that doubles the capacity of any disk. For example, with this feature an Apple II disk can hold more than twice as much as it normally would (60 pages versus 27 pages of text).

DOCUPOWER!

Developed by San Francisco Computing! Inc., DOCUPOWER! represents an interesting divergence from most of the knowledge-processing programs discussed in this book. It uses none of the traditional techniques for building and organizing a kbase; it ignores keywords, categories, character-string searches, indexing, Boolean logic, and hierarchical structures. What DOCUPOWER! does is take the approach used in many of the disk-cataloging programs discussed in Chapter 18—that is, the use of a simple 50-character comment line—and carries this approach to its logical conclusion. Like the disk catalogers, DOCUPOWER! allows you to add comments to each file that are then displayed each time you search through the disk. In addition, using the same approach, numbered comment lines can be entered to describe specific portions of a file, down to the paragraph level. These descriptions can be redisplayed at any time. By scanning them, one can quickly determine the specific content of particular text files.

However, this is only the starting point for this easy-to-use and deceptively powerful program. On the basis of an index of the location of the numbered comment lines, DOCUPOWER! allows you to quickly extract the appropriate text and send it to a file in any order you desire.

A DOCUPOWER! kbase consists of four types of files: a resource file of text created by your word processor, and index files, control files, and output files—all created interactively by the program.

The resource file can be any text file that contains sections (paragraphs, entire letters, or groups of paragraphs under headings and subheadings), with each section given a unique five-digit number. These numbers and an associated 40-character comment line can be added to the text with your word processor or with a DOCUPOWER! utility called Number. By using another utility, called Index, you can create an index file listing of each of the unique numbers, its associated comment line, its file, and its location in that file. With these two utilities, an entire disk of research notes, transcribed interviews, and so on can be indexed and cataloged in less than five minutes.

When you are ready to write an article based on the information in these files, you simply scan the listing of numbered section comments, choose the sections that contain material you want to include, and send them to a control file created by the program. Another utility, called Process, will use this control file, either as created by the program or reorderd to reflect the structure of the article you are writing, to create an output file containing the sections you have chosen from the resource files.

Although unsuitable for managing large kbases of textual material, DOCUPOWER! is an excellent tool for creating and manipulating a writing kbase. Completely menu-driven, DOCUPOWER! lets you index, catalog, extract text files, reorder the material, and generate a rough draft of a 30-page report or article based on about 100 pages of research notes in less than an hour.

The Number utility alone is useful in formatting the text files from some of the other kbase programs. Using it, I was able to insert the special record delimiters required in programs such as SUPERFILE and SYSTEM-ONE as quickly as I did for the DOCUPOWER!-generated article described above.

DOCUPOWER! can be used on almost any personal computer that runs under the CP/M-80 (version 2.2 or later), CP/M-86, PC-DOS, or MS-DOS operating systems. Under CP/M-80, it requires a minimum of 56K bytes of memory. Under CP/M-86 or MS/PC-DOS, it requires 128K. Although it can be used on a system with a single disk drive, two disk drives are recommended.

FRAMEWORK

Available from Ashton-Tate, FRAMEWORK is a unique blending of several current trends in the personal computer industry. It combines the features of a multiscreen word processor, an integrated software package, and windowing and coordinates them within the "framework" of a hierarchical outline structure.

It is designed to operate on IBM PC or compatible systems with a minimum of 256K bytes of RAM and two 360K disk drives. The starting point of all the operations with this program is the outline. Selecting the outline function opens a frame containing three major section headings, each of which has three subheadings. You can add, delete, or reorder sections and fill in with text to describe the content of the section.

Used as a knowledge-processing program, FRAMEWORK allows you to develop a detailed outline in much the same manner used with ThinkTank (Chapter 16). Once you have completed your outline, you can begin to fill it in by highlighting a section, thus opening it up to form a "frame" similar to the windows used with other integrated packages. Into each window frame you may enter text via the program's word processor or call up existing text files to the window. Just as in other such programs, multiple window frames can be displayed on the screen at one time with each containing text. Text can be displayed and moved back and forth between section window frames, as with a multiple-screen word-processing program.

FYI 3000

Building on the success of FYI SUPERFILE 1500, its earlier knowledge-processing program, FYI, Inc. has introduced an enhanced version, FYI 3000, designed specifically for 16-bit systems operating under MS/PC-DOS and CP/M-86 with a minimum of 128K bytes of memory. A new version of the program for 8-bit CP/M systems is also being planned. Two disk drives are required.

Key improvements to the new program include (1) a maximum of 65,000 keywords per kbase, versus 3000 for FYI 1500; (2) linking of up to 128 keywords in a single search request (versus 64); (3) a maximum kbase file size of 2M (versus 512K bytes); and (4) a maximum search speed of 400 entries per second (versus 100–200). The most fundamental change is the addition of an automated method of cross-indexing all words in the text, similar to the method used with ZyINDEX, as well as a manual method whereby the keywords are specified as part of the text entry.

With the manual method, entries can be up to 2M bytes long, and each entry can have up to 500 individual keywords or phrases, each of which can be up to 64 characters long. The manual method gives tighter control over the keyword content in a kbase than the automated method.

With the new automated indexing scheme, FYI 3000 cross-indexes all the words in the text in two additional types of entries: single paragraphs with no more than 500 words (about 8000 characters) and 500-word entries containing blank lines marked with the standard FYI start and end symbols. The first format is useful for managing large documents that consist of many paragraphs or for individual entries that consist of one paragraph each. The second is useful for managing free-format entries that contain blank lines, such as form letters.

When indexing every word in the text, FYI 3000 allows you to exclude "noise words," in a manner similar to that used with ZyINDEX, by making use of an "omit list" that directs the program not to use certain words for cross-indexing. The program comes with an omit list containing the most obvious of the words that would not be used as keywords. Words can be added or deleted from this list with a standard word processor, or you can create your own list.

Idea Processor

With a name that only brings further semantic confusion to a still-developing area of program development, Ideaware's Idea Processor is not an "idea processor" in the same sense as ThinkTank, QUESTEXT, and FirstDraft. Whereas these three programs are tree-structured programs designed to process and organize your ideas and thoughts into categories and subcategories, Idea Processor is, in reality, more like the general-purpose, free-form programs described in Part II.

Integrating word processing, an index card capability, and graphics management into a single system, this program is designed to run on IBM PC and compatible systems with a minimum of 192K bytes of memory and two disk drives.

The kbase management portion of this program is organized like office files, with cabinets, drawers, and cards. Each card can hold up to 8000 characters, or about 1500 average-size words (100 eighty-character lines, or about four double-spaced pages). Before it can be stored, a card must be indexed with at least one keyword and no more than ten keywords. Each keyword can be up to 14 characters in length. The cards are stored in drawers, each of which can contain hundreds of cards, depending on the amount of text stored on each card and the amount of memory and disk space. The maximum number of keywords per drawer is 512. Drawers are stored in cabinets, each of which can hold up to ten. The number of cabinets in a card file kbase is limited only by disk capacity.

The central element in the program is the editor, which is used to create document files by typing in the text or by moving text from the card file. The editor and the card file program operate simultaneously, and it is through the editor that you can gain access to the card file kbase. Text can be moved from the document on which you are working to the card file kbase, from which you can retrieve specific cards and move them back into the document.

You can search a card file kbase using either single-keyword character matches or sophisticated search requests linking keywords with AND, OR, and NOT operators. This program sets no limits on the length of a multikeyword search request.

A unique feature of this program is its ability to store graphics images imported from other software, including many of the popular spreadsheets and graphics software packages. These charts and images can be embellished with titles and text using the editor and stored, searched, and retrieved in the same way that text files are.

KWICREF/1

Available from Chen Information Systems for use on CP/M-, OASIS-, and MS/PC-DOS–based personal computers that use IBM/ COBOL, RM/COBOL, or CIS/COBOL, this program is designed to cross-reference any text-based file on the basis of an externally generated index file. Like ZyINDEX and FYI 3000, KWICREF/1 automatically indexes text files using a keyword file or exclude-word file. Using this external index file, it then searches the text file, constructing a set of pointers from the index file to the text files containing the keywords. The maximum capacity of the program is 32,000 keywords and 32,000 documents. Once the documents are indexed, you can search the index by specifying the desired keyword combinations with the standard Boolean operators. The program will then inform you of the number of hits and the titles of the documents, or, alternatively, it will display the actual selected document text on the screen.

Sequitur

Although Golemics, Inc. may not have had this use in mind, Sequitur is a database ideally configured for use in the storage, manipulation, and retrieval of text- and document-based information. It is designed to operate on most 16-bit systems under either MS-DOS (including the IBM PC) or

UNIX and combines data entry, database management, word processing, report generation, form letters, mailing lists, and document and text management into a single integrated system.

Capable of running on any system with a minimum of 64K bytes of code space and 32K of data space, Sequitur creates kbases whose size is limited only by the amount of disk memory. The amount of text in each entry is limited only by the amount of data storage space available in RAM. On the IBM PC, for example, each table in a kbase can be up to 8M bytes in size (aobut 2000 single-spaced pages). And each kbase can contain over 200 tables of that size. On a UNIX system, it is possible to store about 4000 pages on each of those 200 tables.

Although similar in structure to most database management systems, Sequitur differs from them in the ease with which users can enter information. Many traditional full-function, general-purpose database programs require the use of special query programming languages. While these languages look a little like English, they require the user to conform to a rigid syntax.

Sequitur, on the other hand, uses what can only be called a "visual query language"; in other words, the screen of the computer terminal becomes a picture of the file with which you are working. Database commands are visual, too. A query is a picture of the information wanted. There is no query programming language to learn.

Currently, Sequitur allows 1000 column names and 750 tables or relations in each kbase. Each table may contain up to 16M bytes of information. Provision has been made for upward compatibility with kbases using up to 32,000 different column names in 32,000 tables of up to 2 gigabytes each.

THOR

Developed by Fastware, Inc., THOR is a tree-structured kbase program designed to operate on and take advantage of MS/PC-DOS 2.0 and its hierarchical file management structure. It is designed to operate on IBM PC, IBM XT, or compatible hardware and requires a minimum of 128K bytes of RAM and at least two disk drives The maximum size of each entry is 40,000 characters (25 full screens or 500 lines of text). The maximum size of each tree-structured kbase is 8M bytes.

Like QUESTEXT, this program allows you to use a tree structure to store text by category and subcategory. It can be used as an outline editor or as a sophisticated tree-structured kbase. As with QUESTEXT, its main method of searching is by category. However, it also allows you to do simple character-match searches. Two unusual aspects of this program are that it allows you to search (1) by date and (2) in a single-line short form similar to that used with SUPERFILE and Datafax.

A unique aspect of THOR is its attempt to use English-like commands related to the way the human mind performs similar operations. Entries are made via the New Thought command, which allows you to enter text with a primitive word-processing function. Once you've entered your text, you execute the Categorize command to assign it to any of five different categories. The Collect command saves the entry and stores it in the kbase. The Edit command allows you to update any entry. The State of Mind command allows you to set the search criteria by category or by content. Using the Brain Scan command, you search the kbase for entries that fit your search criteria. Use Collected to review, in short or long form, the entries that have been found.

ZyINDEX

Designed for use on MS-DOS/PC-DOS 2.0 systems, Zylab's ZyINDEX is described by its developers as an auto-indexing and file-content–retrieval kbase-processing program. It requires 192K bytes of memory and at least two double-sided, double-density disk drives or hard disk or RAM disk equivalent.

ZyINDEX is similar to FYI 3000 in three respects. First, it automatically generates an index of all the informational, or "content," words in what Zylab calls a textbase; that is, it includes the nouns, objects, and phrases in a paragraph but excludes "noise" words, such as prepositions, conjunctions, and verbs. Second, it allows construction of kbases that may span over multiple floppy disks. And third, it allows you to search a text file for occurrences of any word, or of any two or more words, using the standard Boolean logic operators, AND, OR, and NOT.

A search string or request in ZyINDEX can contain up to 160 characters, not including connectors, consisting of multiple key or content words, each of which can be no more than 16 characters long. There is no restriction on the number of words in a content phrase, as long as the entire search request is under 160 characters long.

The particular uniqueness of ZyINDEX is in the fact that it allows you to set "distance" criteria similar to those used in many of the programs designed for larger computers (Chapter 2). Using the Within command and a parentheses qualifier, you can specify that a matching file must contain two or more selected words within a specified number of words of one another. The program will then display relevant passages within files that meet the requirements and will either print out the files or store them on a separate disk file.

APPENDIX B

Do-It-Yourself Knowledge Processing

A Bibliography of Published Program Listings

A software package often included with the purchase of a personal computer is the high-level language called BASIC. It can be used as a low-cost alternative for writing professionals who need more knowledge-processing capability than can be squeezed out of their operating system and word processor, but who find that most of the commercial programs available are beyond their financial means.

Even nonprogrammers can build up a useful set of BASIC programs to perform many of the knowledge-processing tasks outlined in this book. This is done by taking advantage of the many program listings published by popular computing magazines. The following list offers some of the programs I have found useful as a professional writer.

Anderson, D., and Nash, J. C., "Catalog Builder," *Interface Age*, March 1982, pp. 98–99, 156–157.

Archer, G., "Magazine Article Tracking System," *Nibble*, vol. 4, no. 3, 1983, pp. 91–97.

Armstrong, J., "Rolodex Data Base Program," *Creative Computing*, March 1980, pp. 120–123.

Fant, A., "Get Your Library in Order," *Microcomputing*, December 1982, pp. 48–50.

Halten, R., "Master Catalog System for CP/M Users," *Microcomputing*, December 1980, pp. 188–190.

Hellman, J. M., "A Personal Computer Based Library Catalog," *Creative Computing*, March 1983, pp. 216–255.

Hughes, P., "Keyword Access System," *Creative Computing*, March 1980, pp. 112–119.

Lappen, W., "Free-Form Storage and Retrieval System," *Personal Computing*, November 1980, pp. 46–51.

Lesser, M. L., "Information Retrieval: Quick and Dirty," *Microcomputing*, May 1982, pp. 64–68.

Liddil, B., "A Disk Catalog for the Eighties," *Byte*, August 1981, pp. 404–407.

Myers, F. E., "DATBAS, A Data Base Management System," a two-part article in *Microcomputing*, April 1980 (Screen) and May 1980 (FILEIT).

Pelczarski, M., "A Modular Data Base for the Apple," *Creative Computing*, September 1982, pp. 146–156.

Sanger, J. J., "The Electronic Librarian," *Microcomputing*, November 1979, pp. 44–62.

Seslar, P., "Home Librarian," *Personal Computing*, September 1980, pp. 30–32.

Shapiro, J., "An Operator-Based Data Base Management Program," three-part article in *Microcomputing*, January to March 1980.

Smith, T. A., "Keywords in a Fuzzy Context," *BYTE*, March 1983, pp. 389–415.

Stein, A. H., "Nibble File Cabinet," *Nibble*, June 1984, pp. 17–31.

Swanson, P., "PDQ: A Data Manager for Beginners," *BYTE*, November 1981, pp. 236–262.

Syraic, R. R., "Disk Library Directory," *Personal Computing*, June 1980, pp. 70–74.

Terre, L. A., "FlexCat: A Text Oriented DBM," *80 Micro*, Anniversary Issue, 1983, pp. 264–273.

Translating these program listings into a form usable by your computer is a job that even the nonprogrammer with little or no knowledge of BASIC can undertake. Whereas there are variations from computer to computer, most versions of BASIC share the same grammar, syntax, and command sequences. Although this takes some time and attention to detail, all you need to do is boot up your BASIC program and proceed to enter each numbered line in the listing exactly as shown. As an interactive language, BASIC will tell you immediately whether or not the line you have entered is correct. If it indicates to you that it cannot accept the command line as entered, check the listing and make sure you have entered the command line correctly. If you have not, reenter the command. If you have entered it correctly, then the command in the listing has a different format than the version of BASIC you are using. To find the correct format, refer to the BASIC language manual supplied with your program.

If you are a beginner with little programming experience, a useful alternative is to refer to *The BASIC Handbook,* by David Lien (Compusoft Publishing). This is an encyclopedia of the BASIC computer language that lists over 250 BASIC words and the numerous variations of each used on different computer systems. By referring to this source, it is possible to find the wording for a BASIC command that your system will accept in place of the wording in the listing. Another useful book to have is *The MBASIC HANDBOOK,* by Walter Etlin and Gregory Solberg (Osborne/McGraw-Hill).

If you are interested in learning more about the programming techniques and data structures used to construct both kbase processors and database management programs, the following books, which emphasize the "learn-by-doing" method using BASIC, are recommended: *Microcomputer Disk Techniques,* by Paul Swanson (BYTE/McGraw-Hill), and *DOS Random Access and BASIC File Handling,* vols. I and II, by H. J. Muller (D.S.C. Publishing).

APPENDIX C

List of Software Manufacturers and Vendors

BIBLIOTEK
Scientific Software Products, Inc.
3171 Donald Avenue
Indianapolis, IN 46224
313-299-0467

CARDBOX
Caxton Software
10–14 Bedford Street
Covent Garden, London
WC2E, 9HE United Kingdom
01-379-6502

CARDFILE/NOTEBOOK/
  SYNOPSIS
ProTem Software, Inc.
814 Tolman Drive
Stanford, CA 94305
Distributed by:
Digital Marketing

2363 Boulevard Circle
Walnut Creek, CA 94595
800-826-2222

CATALOG
The Software Store
706 Chippewa Square
Marquette, IN 49855
906-228-7622

CITATION
Eagle Enterprises
2375 Bush Street
San Francisco, CA 94115
415-346-1249

CLIP
Thoughtware, Inc.
P.O. Box 41436
Tucson, AZ 85717
800-821-6010

Datafax
Link Systems
1640 Nineteenth Street
Santa Monica, CA 90404
213-435-1851

DAYFLO
Dayflo, Inc.
Building 400
2500 Michelson Drive
Irvine, CA 92715
714-476-3044

DISK LIBRARY
Instant Software
Wayne Green, Inc.
80 Pine Street
Peterborough, NH 03458
603-924-9471

DISKETTE CATALOG
N.F. Systems Ltd.
P.O. Box 76363
Atlanta, GA 30356
404-252-3302

Documate
Orthocode Corp.
P.O. Box 6191
Albany, CA 94706
415-753-3222

DOCUMAX
Signum Microsystems
120 Mountain Avenue
P.O. Box 621
Bloomfield, CT 06002
800-642-7611

DOCUPOWER!
San Francisco Computing!, Inc.
2519 Greenwich Street

San Francisco, CA 94123
415-567-1634

EAZYFILE/KWICINDX
Miracle Computing
313 Clayton Court
Lawrence, KS 66044
913-843-5863

ELECTRIC BLACKBOARD
Santa Cruz Software Services
711 Quail Hollow Road
Ben Lomond, CA 95005
408-438-2360

EUREKA!
Mendocino Software Company,
    Inc.
P.O. Box 1564
Willits, CA 95490
707-459-9130

Final Word
Mark of the Unicorn, Inc.
222 Third Street
Cambridge, MA 02142
617-576-2760

Find It Quick
Instant Software
Wayne Green, Inc.
80 Pine Street
Peterborough, NH 03458
603-924-9471

Firstdraft/Documentor
PromptDoc, Inc.
833 West Colorado Avenue
Colorado Springs, CO 80905
303-471-9875

FRAMEWORK
Ashton-Tate
10150 West Jefferson Boulevard

Culver City, CA 90230
213-204-5570

FYI 3000
FYI, Inc.
4202 Spicewood Springs Road
Suite 204
Austin, TX 78759
512-346-0133

Idea Processor
Ideaware, Inc.
225 Lafayette Street
New York, NY 10012
212-334-8043

KWICREF/1
Chen Information Systems, Inc.
Suite 205
1499 Bayshore Highway
Burlingame, CA 94010
415-692-4358

LEADING EDGE
Leading Edge Corp.
225 Turnpike Street
Canton, MA 02021
800-343-6833

MASTER CATALOG SYSTEM
  #2
Elliam Associates
24000 Bessemer Street
Woodland, CA 91367
213-348-4278

MASTER DISK/MULTIDISK
  CATALOG III
Sensible Software
6619 Perham Drive
West Bloomfield, MO 48033
313-399-8877

MEMOPLAN
Chang Labs
Suite 200
5300 Stevens Creek Road
San Jose, CA 95129
408-246-8020

MicroLIB
Advanced Micro Techniques
Suite 209
1291 East Hillside Boulevard
Foster City, CA 94404
415-349-9336

MICROSHELL
New Generation Systems, Inc.
2153 Golf Course Drive
Reston, VA 22091
703-476-9143

MICROSOFT WORD/MS-DOS
Microsoft Corp.
10700 Northrup Way
Bellvue, WA 98004
206-828-8080

MicroTOOLS+
Carousel MicroTools, Inc.
609 Kearney Street
El Cerrito, CA
415-528-1300

MultiMate
Softword Systems, Inc.
62 Oakland Avenue North
East Hartford, CT 06108
203-522-2116

PCFILE
TexaSoft, Inc.
Suite 100
3415 Westminster Avenue

Dallas, TX 76205
215-369-0795

Perfect Writer
Perfect Software
702 Harrison Street
Berkeley, CA 94710
415-527-2626

PieWriter
Howard W. Sams and Company
4300 West 62nd Street
Indianapolis, IN 46268
317-298-5725

PROLOG
Prosoft, Inc.
P.O. Box 560
North Hollywood, CA 91603
213-764-3131

QUESTEXT
Information Reduction Research
1538 Main Street
Concord, MA 01742
617-369-5719

Sci-Mate
Institute for Scientific Information
501 Market Street
University City Science Center
Philadelphia, PA 19104
800-523-4092

Search
Micro Alliance Corp.
211 Third Avenue
Pacific Grove, CA 93950
408-375-2820

SELECT/411/Freestyle
Select Information Systems
919 Sir Francis Drake Boulevard

Kentsfield, CA 94904
414-459-4003

Sequitur
Golemics, Inc.
2600 Tenth Street
Berkeley, CA 94710
415-486-8347

SIMPLIFILE
Durant Software
Suite 250
2532 Durant Avenue
Berkeley, CA 94704
415-540-0912

STARMATE
Solution Technology, Inc.
Suite 218
1499 Palmetto Park Road
Boca Raton, FL 33432
305-368-6228

SUPERFILE (FYI 1500)
Software Marketing Associates
4615 West Beecaves Road
Austin, TX 75746
512-327-2882

SYSTEM-ONE
MINDex Infosystems
P.O. Box 5241
Eugene, OR 97405
503-485-5827

ThinkTank
Living Videotext, Inc.
Suite 56
450 San Antonio Road
Palo Alto, CA 94306
415-857-0511

THOR
Fastware, Inc.
200 Freeway Drive East
East Orange, NJ 07018
800-372-2345

UNICA
Knowology, Inc.
P.O. Box 283
Wilsonville, OR 97070

VisiDex/VisiWord
Visicorp, Inc.
2895 Zanker Road
San Jose, CA 95134
408-946-9000

WORD PERFECT
Satellite Software International
288 West Center Street
Orem, UT 84057
801-224-8554

WORD VISION
Bruce and James Publishing
4500 Tuller Road
Dublin, OH 43017
614-766-0110

WordStar/MailMerge/StarIndex
MicroPro International Corp.
33 San Pablo Avenue
San Rafael, CA 84903
415-457-8990

XyWrite II
Xyquest
P. O. Box 372
Bedford, MA 01720
617-275-4439

ZyINDEX
Zylab Corp.
233 East Erie Street
Chicago, IL 60611
312-642-2201

APPENDIX D

Glossary

ALPHANUMERIC CHARACTER: A character (alphabetic letter, numeric digit, or speical symbol) that is entered into the computer with a keyboard.

AND OPERATOR: Used to link keywords and *narrow* the focus of a search request to a kbase program. AND is a Boolean logic operator that operates on a search request by asking the program to locate and retrieve only those records or entries that contain the keywords linked by AND. (Compare OR OPERATOR.)

ASCII FILE: Normal text files that are coded for entry into computer memory according to a standardized 8-bit code used by most personal computers. Each alphanumeric character you enter by the keyboard is translated into a unique seven-letter ASCII code that the computer interprets as standing for that character. ASCII (pronounced askee) stands for American Standard Code for Information Interchange; it was developed originally for teletype communications.

BIT: The basic unit of information stored by a computer. Each bit can be represented by either a 0 (off) or a 1 (on). Bit is a contraction of BInary digiT.

BOOLEAN LOGIC: A special logic used on computers that allows the manipulation and storage of information using simple on/off (0/1) logic. The most commonly used Boolean logic "operators" used in knowledge processing are AND, OR, and NOT.

BYTE: A unit of information composed of bits. A byte is the rough equivalent of a word in English, except that each byte can be only 8 bits long in most personal computers. Depending on the sequence of 0s and 1s, a byte can represent a single numeric or alphabetic character.

CATALOG: A listing of the contents of a diskette. Also called the "directory."

CENTRAL PROCESSING UNIT (CPU):   The central element in any computer, responsible for interpretation and execution of instructions.

COMMAND: A directive given to a program, usually by pressing a key or series of keys, ordering it to perform a specific function.

CONTROL KEY (CNTL, CTRL, ^):   One of the function keys on your computer keyboard. The Control key does not do anything when pressed by itself. It is normally used in conjunction with other keys to direct the program to execute a particular function. This is done by pressing the Control key while simultaneously pressing the alphanumeric key that initiates the desired function.

DATABASE: A collection of discrete items of alphanumeric and tabular data organized into some structure for storage and access. Also a collection of files. (See also KNOWLEDGE BASE).

DEFAULT MODE: The set of operating conditions under which a program operates automatically until modified by the user.

DELIMITER: A special character used by a knowledge-processing program to separate text records in a file, indicating the beginning of one entry and the end of another.

FIELD: The smallest unit of data that can be used to describe an item or fact in a database.

FIELD LENGTH: The size of a field in characters.

FIELD TYPE: The type of information that can be entered into a particular field. For example, in a personnel record, there are different field types for name, age, address, Social Security number, and so on.

FILE: Any collection of information stored on a disk that can be accessed by a common label or name.

FILENAME: The set of characters assigned to identify a particular file or document stored in a computer's memory or disk storage. Filenames are up to 8 characters long on 8-bit computers and up to 16 characters long on 16-bit computers. For example, in FILENAME.EXT, the characters preceding the dot are the filename.

FILE TYPE (EXTENSION):   The set of characters assigned to describe the type of information stored in a file. Limited to three characters in length, the extension follows the filename. In FILENAME.EXT, the last three characters are the extension.

FLOPPY DISK/DISKETTE: The basic mode of storage used for personal computers, floppy disks are made of flexible Mylar plastic (thus the name "floppy") and can be removed from their drives at your discretion. Covered by iron oxide particles, which can be magnetized, they come in two sizes—$5\frac{1}{4}$ and 8 inches in diameter—and in three formats—single-sided single-density (SSSD), single-sided double-density (SSDD), and double-sided double-density (DSDD)—each of which has twice the density of the previous format.

FORMAT: To prepare a file according to specific conditions required by a program. A word-processing file is configured according to specific requirements pertaining to line spacing, page length, and so on. A kbase file is configured to meet specific requirements pertaining to length and delimiting characters.

HARD COPY: A document or text file converted into words on paper. Also called a PRINTOUT.

HARD DISK: An aluminum disk covered by iron oxide that cannot be removed from its drive.

HIERARCHICAL STRUCTURE: A database or data-file structure in which some records or entries are subordinated to others in a tree-like fashion.

INCLUDES OPERATOR: A search request command set up using parentheses. It tells a program to find records, fields, or blocks of text that include a given string of characters, regardless of where they are located.

INDEX: A list of all the keywords by which a screen, block, or set of text is identified and retrieved. Also, a table that a kbase program uses to find the location of a record or text entry.

I/O (INPUT/OUTPUT):   Input is what is sent into your computer by either loading a program or entering it by keyboard. Output is what is received from a program and sent to your display, to a printer, or to another file.

K: Abbreviation for kilo, which in the metric system stands for 1000. However, in the computer industry it usually stands for 1024. Thus 1K bytes is equal to 1024 bytes.

KEYDATE: A date that indexes a screen of information.

KEYWORD: A combination of letters, numbers, or both that indexes a particular text entry in a kbase. Keywords are usually nouns, verbs, and phrases that describe the essence of a text entry.

KILOBYTE: A basic measure of storage capacity for floppy disks, equal to 1024 bytes. (See also MEGABYTE and BYTE.)

KNOWLEDGE BASE (KBASE):   A collection of text records and files organized into some structure for storage and access.

LOAD: To read a file or program from disk into the computer's internal memory. Synonyms include "call up," "boot up," and "open."

MEGABYTE: The basic measure of storage capacity in hard disks, equal to 1,048,576 bytes. (See also KILOBYTE and BYTE.)

MENU: A list of commands or options.

MODE: The command environment within which specific functions or options are carried out, such as the Edit mode or the Search mode.

MULTIPLE-CHARACTER WILDCARD: A special character that can stand for any character or series of characters in a keyword.

NOISE WORD: As opposed to keywords, noise words are common connective words that are common to all text files and do not identify a file in any particular way. Usually noise words include English prepositions, conjunctions, articles, and some common verbs.

NOT OPERATOR: Used in a search request to exclude those files or entries that contain specific keywords. It narrows the search even more than the AND command. A search request that includes a NOT operator directs the program to locate and retrieve text records or files that contain linked keywords *except* for those excluded by the NOT operator.

OPERATING SYSTEM (OS):   The supervisorial program usually inserted into the disk drive before inserting a particular application program. The operating system controls communications between the computer's hardware and the various application programs, keeps track of disk files, and controls information exchange among the various peripherals used within a complete system. Knowledge-processing programs in this book run under six types of operating systems: CP/M, MS-DOS, PC-DOS, Apple DOS, the P-SYSTEM, and UNIX.

OPERATOR: Defines the logical connection between items in a statement. In mathematics, the $\times$, $+$, and $-$ symbols are operators. In kbase and database management programs, AND, OR, and NOT are operators.

OR OPERATOR: Used to link keywords and *broaden* the focus of a search request to a kbase program. OR is a Boolean logic operator that operates on a search request by asking the program to locate and retrieve text records or files that contain keywords linked by OR.

PATHNAME: An additional file identifier used in operating systems such as UNIX that indicates the directory or subdirectories of which the file is a member.

PROGRAM: A collection of ordered commands which collectively instruct the computer to respond in a certain way.

PROMPT: A question or statement issued by the program, indicating that a particular set of choices is available to you.

RAM (random-access memory):   A computer's working storage in integrated circuit form, used for holding data and programs. In order to perform specific functions, a program must be moved from its disk storage area into RAM, where it can be directly accessed by the system's CENTRAL PROCESSING UNIT. Also called read/write memory, dynamic memory, and scratchpad memory.

RANGE OPERATORS: Symbols that a kbase program interprets as meaning "more than," "less than," and "equal to." While there are occasional variations, most programs use the symbols ">," "<," and "=," respectively, to stand for these functions. They let you search for alphanumeric values within a specified range.

READ: The process of retrieving information from a disk. (See also LOAD.)

RECORD: A collection of data fields treated as a unit. A collection of records is a FILE.

RESERVED CHARACTERS: Characters used by the program for special internal functions. They are not to be used in the text entries in a kbase.

RETRIEVAL: After a kbase program completes a search, the results may be retrieved by (1) displaying the files on a screen, (2) printing out a hard copy, or (3) sending the files to a separate output file.

ROM (READ-ONLY MEMORY):   A computer's permanent memory, also stored in the form of integrated circuits. Instructions are stored in the ROM at the time of manufacture which can be read or accessed but not erased or overwritten with new information.

SEARCH REQUEST: The information that tells the program which records you want to find. Such requests can be single words or alphanumeric strings, or multikeyword requests with several keywords or strings linked by Boolean operators such as AND, OR, and NOT. The program matches the search request against the text or against an index containing keywords and their location. Synonyms are "search criteria," "search string," "search pattern selection format," and "selection criteria."

SHORT FORM: A shortened form of a text entry stored in your kbase, usually one or two lines long. Most programs allow you to display the short form rather than the entire entry (the long form) in order to speed up the process of search and retrieval.

SORT: To organize records in a kbase into alphabetical or numerical order.

STORE: To place a screen or block of text on a diskette for later retrieval.

STRING: Any sequence of alphanumeric characters.

UTILITY: A specialized program, usually supplied with your operating system or as an ancillary to an application program, designed to perform a particular narrow function. Whereas a database management program or a knowledge processor can perform a wide range of functions, a utility program performs only one, such as sorting, searching, merging, or file updating.

WILDCARD: A special character substituting for characters in a word.

WRITE: The process of entering characters into your internal memory via the keyboard. This term also describes the process of transferral of text from the internal memory to disk for more permanent storage.

APPENDIX E

Program
Comparison Chart

This program comparison chart has been prepared to simplify the process of choosing the knowledge-processing program most appropriate to your needs and most compatible with your thought processes. Below is a list of the symbols used to describe various features of the programs:

FF	Free-form, general-purpose knowledge processor
I	Indexer
IC	Index card
U	Utility program
D	Disk cataloger
B	Bibliographic citation program
S	Searcher
O	Outline processor
NA	Feature not applicable to this program
•	Feature present
>	More than
<	Less than

FEATURES		SUPERFILE FYI 1500	SUPERFILE FYI 3000	MINDex SYSTEM-ONE	Datafax
		PROGRAM			
Program type		FF, I	FF, I	FF, I	FF
Operating system	CPM	•	•	•	
	MS/PC-DOS	•	•		
	Apple DOS				
	P-SYSTEM			•	•
Drives required (recommended)		1 (2)	2 (2)	2 (2)	2 (2)
Internal memory required		64K bytes	128K bytes	64K bytes	64K/128K bytes
Disk drive type		Hard/Floppy	Hard/Floppy	Hard/Floppy	Hard/Floppy
8-bit or 16-bit		8/16	16	8/16	8/16
Disks per kbase		Unlimited	Unlimited	100	1
Files per kbase		100	100	100	3000 folders
Maximum record size		512K bytes	2M bytes	Unlimited	24 lines/page
Maximum file size		512K bytes	2M bytes	500 records	255 pages/folder
Maximum kbase size		Unlimited	Unlimited	Disk capacity	1M byte
Line length		Unlimited	Unlimited	Unlimited	40/80 characters
Text editor		External	External	External	Internal
Search method	Single word	•	•	•	•
	Multiword	•	•	•	•
Operators	AND/OR	•	•	Search by example	•
	NOT	•	•		•
	Range	(Sort)	(Sort)		(Sort)
	Category			•	
Request length	Single word	64 characters	64 characters	20 characters	28 characters
	Multiword	64 words	128 words	Unlimited	Unlimited
Searches fields in text				•	•
Searches index/table		•	•	•	•
Searches actual text					
Auto-indexes entire text			•		
User-selected keywords		•	•	•	•
Keywords per entry		250	500	Unlimited	60–100/folder
Unique keywords per kbase		3000	65,000	Unlimited	300,000
Keyword Length		64 characters	64 characters	20 characters	28 characters

FEATURES		PROGRAM			
		NOTEBOOK	Sci-Mate	QUESTEXT	DAYFLO
Program type		FF	FF	T, O	FF
Operating System	CPM	•	•	•	
	MS/PC-DOS	•	•	•	•
	Apple DOS		•		
	P-SYSTEM				
Drives required (recommended)		1 (2)	2 (hard)	1 (2)	2 (2)
Internal memory required		64K/128K bytes	64K/128K bytes	60K/96K bytes	256K bytes
Disk drive type		Hard/Floppy	Hard/Floppy	Hard/Floppy	Hard
8-bit or 16-bit		8/16	8/16	8/16	16
Disks per kbase		1	1	1	1
Files per kbase		Disk size	64 user files	Disk size	Disk size
Maximum record size		32K bytes	1894 bytes	1 line	Variable
Maximum file size		Disk size	32,000 records	99 lines	Variable
Maximum kbase size		Disk size	Disk size	32,760 records	2500 records
Line length		57 characters	40/80 characters	65 characters	80 characters
Text editor		Internal	Internal	Internal	Internal
Search Method	Single word	•	•	•	•
	Multiword	•	•	•	•
Operators	AND/OR	•	•		•
	NOT	•	•		•
	Range	•	•		•
	Category			•	
Request Length	Single word	20 characters	255 characters	65 characters	Variable
	Multiword	2 words	255 words	65 characters	Variable
Searches fields in text		•	•	•	•
Searches index/table			•	•	•
Searches actual text		•	•	•	•
Auto-indexes entire text		•			
User-selected keywords		•	•	•	•
Keywords per entry		20 fields	20 fields	NA	100 labels
Unique keywords per kbase		Unlimited	Unlimited	99 major categories 99 subcategories 99 subheads	Variable
Keyword length		20 characters	40/80 characters	65 characters	80 characters

		PROGRAM			
FEATURES		DOCUMAX	DOCUPOWER!	Idea Processor	THOR
Program type		FF, S	FF	FF, IC	T, O
Operating System	CPM	•	•		
	MS/PC-DOS	•	•	•	•
	Apple DOS	•			
	P-SYSTEM				
Drives required (recommended)		1 (2)	1 (2)	2 (2)	2 (2)
Internal memory required		48K bytes	56K/128K bytes	192K bytes	128K bytes
Disk drive type		Hard/Floppy	Hard/Floppy	Hard/Floppy	Hard/Floppy
8-bit or 16-bit		8/16	8/16	16	16
Disks per kbase		1	1	1	1
Files per kbase		1	Disk size	10	Variable
Maximum record size		Unlimited	Variable	8K bytes	40K bytes
Maximum file size		Disk size	Disk size	Variable	8M bytes
Maximum kbase size		Disk size	Disk size	Disk size	8M bytes
Line length		40/80 characters	50 characters	80 characters	80 characters
Text editor		External	External	Internal	Internal
Search Method	Single word	•	•	•	•
	Multiword	•	•	•	•
Operators	AND/OR	•		•	
	NOT	•	Search by comment line	•	
	Range	•		•	
	Category				•
Request Length	Single word	30 characters	NA	14 characters	80 characters
	Multiword	2 words	NA	Unlimited	NA
Searches fields in text			•		•
Searches index/table			•	•	NA
Searches actual text		•	•		NA
Auto-indexes entire text					NA
User-selected keywords			•	•	•
Keywords per entry		All	NA	10	5 categories
Unique keywords per kbase		All	NA	512	NA
Keyword length		NA	50 characters	14 characters	NA

FEATURES		Sequitur	ZyINDEX	VisiDex	CARDFILE
Program type		FF	T, I	IC	IC
Operating System	CPM				•
	MS/PC-DOS	•	•	•	•
	Apple DOS			•	
	P-SYSTEM				
Drives required (recommended)		2 (2)	2 (2)	2 (2)	1 (2)
Internal memory required		96K bytes	192K bytes	48K/96K bytes	48K bytes
Disk drive type		Hard	Hard/Floppy	Hard/Floppy	Floppy
8-bit or 16-bit		16	16	8/16	8/16
Disks per kbase		1	Unlimited	1	1
Files per kbase		750 tables	Unlimited	150 cards	1
Maximum record size		2K bytes	Unlimited	800/1600 characters	1242 characters
Maximum file size		8M bytes	Unlimited	Disk size	14,499 characters
Maximum kbase size		16M bytes	Disk capacity	Disk size	100/320 cards
Line Length		80 characters	Unlimited	40/80 characters	65 characters
Text editor		Internal	External	Internal	External
Search Method	Single word	•	•	•	•
	Multiword	•	•	•	
Operators	AND/OR	•	•		
	NOT	•	•	•	
	Range	•	•	•	
	Category	•			
Request Length	Single word	Variable	16 characters	38 characters	60/80 characters
	Multiword	Variable	160 characters	NA	NA
Searches fields in text		•		•	•
Searches index/table		•	•	•	
Searches actual text		•		•	•
Auto-indexes entire text			•		
User-selected keywords		•		•	•
Keywords per entry		Variable	RAM size	30 per screen	4 fields
Unique keywords per kbase		Variable	NA	1900	2000–6000
Keyword length		Variable	16 characters	38/253 characters	65 characters

FEATURES	CARDBOX	PCFILE	ThinkTank	EAZYFILE
			PROGRAM	
Program type	IC	IC	T, IC, O	T, IC, O
Operating System — CPM	•			
Operating System — MS/PC-DOS		•	•	•
Operating System — Apple DOS			•	
Operating System — P-SYSTEM			•	
Drives required (recommended)	1 (2)	1 (2)	1 (2)	1 (2)
Internal memory required	48K bytes	64K bytes	64K/512K bytes	128K bytes
Disk drive type	Floppy	Hard/Floppy	Hard/Floppy	Hard/Floppy
8-bit or 16-bit	8/16	16	8/16	16
Disks per kbase	1	1	1	1
Files per kbase	1	1	1	Variable
Maximum record size	1404 characters	200 lines	2000–20,000 characters	128 characters
Maximum file size	8M bytes	Disk size	Disk size	1000 records
Maximum kbase size	65K rec./file	Disk size	Disk size	Disk size
Line length	80 characters	65 characters	40/80 characters	40 characters
Text editor	Internal	Internal	Internal	Internal
Search Method — Single word	•	•	•	•
Search Method — Multiword	•	•	NA	•
Operators — /AND/OR	•		NA	NA
Operators — NOT	•		NA	NA
Operators — Range	•		NA	NA
Operators — Category			•	•
Request Length — Single word	65 characters	65 characters	60/80 characters	40 characters
Request Length — Multiword	100 levels	65 characters	60/80 characters	40 characters
Searches fields in text	•	•	•	Searches categories
Searches index/table	•		NA	NA
Searches actual text	•	•	•	NA
Auto-indexes entire text	•		NA	NA
User-selected keywords	•	•	•	•
Keywords per entry	26 fields	8	NA	Variable no. of categories
Unique keywords per kbase	65,000	1600	100 levels	Variable no. of categories
Keyword length		65 characters	65 characters	40 characters

FEATURES		PROGRAM			
		FirstDraft	EUREKA!	MicroLIB	SYNOPSIS
Program type		T, O	D, U	T, D, U	D, U
Operating System	CPM	•	•	•	•
	MS/PC-DOS	•	•	•	•
	Apple DOS				
	P-SYSTEM				
Drives required (recommended)		1 (2)	1 (2)	2 (2)	1 (2)
Internal memory required		64K bytes	<64K bytes	<64K bytes	<64K bytes
Disk drive type		Hard/Floppy	Floppy	Hard/Floppy	Hard/Floppy
8-bit or 16-bit		8/16	8/16	8/16	8/16
Disks per kbase		1	Unlimited	Unlimited	Unlimited
Files per kbase		Variable	Disk size	Disk size	Disk size
Maximum record size		NA	NA	NA	276 characters
Maximum file size		NA	Disk size	Disk size	1000 records
Maximum kbase size		Disk size	255 disks	Disk size	Disk size
Line length		60/80 characters	NA	60/80 characters	30/75 characters
Text editor		Internal	External	External	External
Search Method	Single word	NA	•	•	•
	Multiword	NA	•	•	•
Operators	AND/OR	NA	•		
	NOT	NA	•		
	Range	NA			
	Category	•		•	
Request Length	Single word	NA	50 characters	50 characters	30/40/60/75 characters
	Multiword	NA	4 words	50 characters	6 fields
Searches fields in text		NA	•	•	•
Searches index/table		NA	NA	NA	NA
Searches actual text		NA	NA	NA	•
Auto-indexes entire text		NA	NA	NA	NA
User-selected keywords		•	•	•	•
Keywords per entry		NA	3 fields	1 field	6 fields
Unique keywords per kbase		100 levels	NA	Disk size	Disk size
Keyword length		NA	30/60 characters	50 characters	30/40/60/75 characters

FEATURES		SIMPLIFILE	Search	KWICINDX	KWICREF/1
PROGRAM					
Program type		D, U	S, U	I, U	FF, I
Operating Systems	CPM	•	•		
	MS/PC-DOS		•	•	•
	Apple DOS				
	P-SYSTEM				
Drives required (recommended)		2 (2)	1	2 (2)	2 (2)
Internal memory required		<64K bytes	<64K bytes	<64K bytes	128K bytes
Disk drive type		Floppy	Hard/Floppy	Hard/Floppy	Hard
8-bit or 16-bit		8/16	8/16	16	16
Disks per kbase		Unlimited	NA	NA	1
Files per kbase		Unlimited	NA	NA	32,000
Maximum record size		NA	NA	Line Length	1920 characters
Maximum file size		NA	NA	Disk size	Disk size
Maximum kbase size		Unlimited	NA	80 characters	
Line length		42 characters	NA	80 characters	
Text editor		Internal	Operating system	External	
Search Method	Single word	•	•	NA	•
	Multiword	•	•	NA	•
	AND/OR		•	NA	•
Operators	NOT			NA	•
	Range			NA	
	Category			NA	
Request Length	Single word	42 characters	127 characters	NA	36 characters
	Multiword	42 characters	16 words	NA	Unlimited
Searches fields in text		•	•	NA	
Searches index/table				NA	•
Searches actual text			•	NA	
Auto-indexes entire text				•	•
User-selected keywords		•	•	NA	•
Keywords per entry		1 field	16	NA	NA
Unique keywords per kbase		Disk size	NA	NA	Unlimited
Keyword length		42 characters	Unlimited	NA	36 characters

FEATURES		CITATION	BIBLIOTEK	Find It Quick
			PROGRAM	
Program type		B	B	B
Operating System	CPM	•		
	MS/PC-DOS	•		NA
	Apple DOS		•	
	P-SYSTEM			
Drives required (recommended)		2(2)	1 (2)	1 (2)
Internal memory required		56K/96K bytes	48K bytes	32K bytes
Disk drive type		Hard/Floppy	Floppy	Floppy
8-bit or 16-bit		8/16	8	8
Disks per kbase		1	1	1
Files per kbase		Disk size	Disk size	Disk size
Maximum record size		800 characters	450 characters	90 characters
Maximum file size		Disk size	Disk size	Disk size
Maximum kbase size		Disk size	Disk size	Disk size
Line length		80 characters	Variable	Variable
Text editor		Internal	Internal	Internal
Search Method	Single word	•	•	•
	Multiword	•	•	•
Operators	AND/OR			
	NOT	•		
	Range	•	•	
	Category	•	•	•
Request Length	Single word	20 characters	200 characters	5/30 characters
	Multiword	10 words	200 characters	Unlimited
Searches fields in text		•	•	•
Searches index/table				•
Searches actual text		•	•	•
Auto-indexes entire text				
User-selected keywords		•	•	•
Keywords per entry		6 fields, 6 words	8 words	6 fields, 9 words
Unique keywords per kbase		Disk size	Disk size	280
Keyword length		20 characters	200 characters	5/30 characters

APPENDIX F

A Bibliography
of Sources

In addition to the specific program manuals and my experience with each program, the sources of the material contained in this book include the following. You may find them helpful as additional reading.

Text File/Knowledge Base Management

Bonner, P., "The Powerful New Idea Tools," *Personal Computing,* January 1984, pp. 70–79.

Brent, E. E., Jr., "Writing with a Data-Base Management System," *Byte,* November 1981, pp. 18–22.

Coffey, M., "Keys to Success," *Creative Computing,* September 1983, pp. 33–38.

Heaps, H. S., *Information Retrieval: Computational and Theoretical Aspects,* Academic Press, New York, 1978.

Lancaster, F. W., *Toward Paperless Information Systems,* Academic Press, New York, 1978.

Licklider, J. C. R., *Libraries of the Future,* MIT Press, Cambridge, Massachusetts, 1965.

Rosenthal, S., "Creating Order from Chaos," *PC*, May 15, 1984, pp. 325–328.

Rosenthal, S., "PC Filing: It's in the Cards," *PC*, April 17, 1984, pp. 349–352.

Salton, G., *Automatic Information Organization and Retrieval*, McGraw-Hill, New York, 1968.

Salton, G., and McGill, M. J., *Introduction to Modern Information Retrieval*, McGraw-Hill, New York, 1983.

Sandler, C., "Off the Desk and into the Disk," *PC*, April 1983, pp. 378–381.

Somerson, P., "Five Desktop Managers," *PC*, July 1983, pp. 244–266.

Teskey, F. N., *Principles of Text Processing*, Ellis Horwood Limited and Halsted Press, London, 1982.

Van Rijsenber, C. J., *Information Retrieval*, Butterworths, London, 1975.

Data File/Database Management

Brooner, E. G., *Microcomputer Data-Base Management*, Howard W. Sams and Co., Indianapolis, Indiana, 1982.

Claybrook, B. G., *File Management Techniques*, John Wiley and Sons, New York, 1983.

Hsiao, D. K. (ed.), *Advanced Database Machine Architecture*, Prentice-Hall, Englewood Cliffs, New Jersey, 1983.

Krugglinski, D., *Data Base Management Systems*, Osborne/McGraw-Hill, Berkeley, California, 1983.

Lewis, T., Barnes, G., and Wilson, J., *Database Management Made Easy*, Insoft, Portland, Oregon, 1983.

Martin, J., *Computer Data-Base Organization*, 2nd ed., Prentice-Hall, Englewood Cliffs, New Jersey, 1977.

Martin, J., *Principles of Data-Base Management*, Prentice-Hall, Englewood Cliffs, New Jersey, 1976.

Townsend, C., *CP/M Database Management Systems*, dilithium Press, Beaverton, Oregon, 1983.

Operating Systems

Antonovich, M. P., *User's Guide to the Apple II*, Webster Systems, Cleveland, Ohio, 1982.

Christian, K., *The UNIX Operating System*, John Wiley and Sons, New York, 1983.

Critchfield, M., and Dwyer, T. A., *CP/M and the Personal Computer,* Addison-Wesley Publishing Co., Palo Alto, California, 1983.

Hogan, T., *Osborne CP/M User Guide,* Osborne/McGraw-Hill, Berkeley, California, 1981.

King, R. A., *The IBM PC-DOS Handbook,* Sybex, Berkeley, California, 1983.

Lonmuto, A. N., and Lonmuto, N., *A UNIX Primer,* Prentice-Hall, Englewood Cliffs, New Jersey, 1983.

Overgaard, M., and Stringfellow, S., *Personal Computing with the UCSD P-SYSTEM,* Prentice-Hall, Englewood Cliffs, New Jersey, 1983.

Townsend, C., *How to Get Started with MS-DOS,* dilithium Press, Beaverton, Oregon, 1983.

APPENDIX G

Addendum: Some Recent Introductions

In the time between the final draft of this book and the editing of the page proofs, additional programs of use to writing professionals for knowledge processing have been introduced. Illustrative of the continuing pace of development in this area are the programs discussed below.

Factfinder

Forethought, Inc. (1973 Landings Drive, Mountain View, CA 94043 415-961-4720) markets Factfinder as a free-form text storage and retrieval program configured for use on the Macintosh and Lisa 2/5 and 2/10 personal computers, requiring a minimum of 128K bytes of internal RAM. With this program you store information in a factsheet window, the size of which is limited only by the computer's memory. Text can be entered and edited from the keyboard, cut and pasted from the Macintosh clipboard, or loaded from external MacWrite or MacTerminal text files.

In Factfinder, each kbase consists of associated factsheets collected into stacks, each of which has a maximum size of 1M byte. For all practical purposes, the size of a kbase stack varies with the size of the contained factsheets, the number of keywords, and the storage capacity of the memory disk used. On a 200–300K byte floppy disk, up to 25 factsheets of 2400 words and eight 28-character keywords each can be stored.

To reference and cross reference each factsheet, you enter one or more keywords in an associated keys window either by

1. Typing it in the keys window
2. Typing it into an automatic keywords list for several factsheets
3. Selecting it from the factsheet with the mouse and then marking it as a keyword

Individual factsheets are then accessed by finding the actual keywords or the date the creation or modification of the keywords took place (this is automatically recorded by the program). Search and retrieval is performed using AND, OR, ALL, FROM/TO, and wildcard operators.

411

Designed by Select Information Systems for use with IBM PC systems with hard disk memory, 411 is an autoindexing program similar to ZyINDEX and FYI 3000. In addition, it allows the user to encrypt files with a public key-private key scheme. Designed for use with its SELECT and Freestyle word processing programs, it can also be used with a wide variety of other word processors, as well as spreadsheet and database files. It takes an entire file, scans it for each unique word, and develops a tabular index of those words. When a second document is indexed, its unique words are also added to the list and reference pointers are tacked on to any words already in the index. Indexing is done as a background task, so that users can proceed to other tasks—even using previously indexed text. Noise words (those frequently used words such as "and," "the," and so on) are discarded from the index once it is full, so users do not need to specify a list of noise (omit) words. The program requires about one minute to index a ten-page document on a hard disk. Selected words can be connected with the logical operators AND, OR, NOT. Searches to find keywords and to indicate to the user that they have been found, require about two to ten seconds. The program requires a minimum of 250K bytes of disk space, and usually no more than 400K bytes.

Freestyle

Designed by Select Information Systems for use on IBM PC and compatible systems operating under MS/PC DOS 2.0 or later versions, Freestyle combines the features of a word processor and an outline processor. Taking advantage of the hierarchical file structure of DOS 2.0, this program permits writers to organize their material while working on the final product. For example, it allows you to reorganize whole documents by changing the outline. If, for instance, you decide to move Chapter 3 ahead of Chapter 1, all that's necessary is to select the appropriate heading from the outline, specify its new location, and move it. All of the attached text then moves to the corresponding location in the document. Without Freestyle, the writer would have to use ordinary word processing commands to perform the same operation. It requires a minimum of two disk drives and 192K bytes of RAM.

KAMAS

The tree-structured program, KAMAS (Knowledge And Mind Amplification System), organizes data and allows you to retrieve it quickly with a proprietary access methodology. Designed primarily as a programming tool, source codes can be entered with a built-in text editor and stored in outline form. Designed as an environment for developing and designing applications using outline processing, information retrieval, and word processing, it is available for use on CP/M 2.2 based systems using two disk drives with 160K bytes each and a minimum of 56K bytes of internal RAM. (Compusophic Systems, Dept. 121, 2525 SW 224th Avenue, Aloha, OR 97006 503-649-3765)

With KAMAS you use the outline editing function of the program to store textual information into "topic files" (ranging in size from 8K to 8M bytes each), within which there can be any number of levels containing any number of items. On a floppy disk with about 200K bytes of storage capacity, you can store a kbase topic with up to 1500 items.

Each item in the topic structure is referred to as a *stem*. Taken together, a stem and its descendants are called a *branch*. Each stem in a KAMAS kbase is made up of a title and an optional text leaf. Each title consists of a key with an optional subtitle. Each leaf can contain up to 2420 alphanumeric characters. A subtitle can hold up to 63 characters, a title up to 93 characters, and each key up to 31 characters.

KAMAS can be operated in two modes. In one mode it's similar to ThinkTank, acting like an interactive screen editor that allows you to enter and modify text, titles, and subtitles. It allows you to move back and forth through the structure, similar to the way you scroll through a word processing file. The other mode is menu driven, similar to QUESTEXT. You can also take advantage of KAMAS's capabilities as a programming tool and modify it to suit your own needs.

You search through a KAMAS kbase by category, moving from key to key and branch to branch or by using a "sounds-like" method which matches a particular phrase and word to the text, titles, and subtitles stored in a topic file.

MaxThink

Similar to ThinkTank in that it is a screen-oriented program, Max-Think is an attempt to extend the concept of the outline editor, adding special commands that allow you to use the program for what its developers call "thought processing." (MaxThink, Inc., 230 Crocker Avenue Piedmont, CA 94610 415-428-0104)

Requiring 192K bytes of internal RAM and at least two disk drives, MaxThink is designed for use on IBM PC and 100-percent-compatible systems operating under DOS 2.0. Taking advantage of that operating system's hierarchical file structure, MaxThink provides four methods for organizing the text in your kbase:

1. Free space
2. Sequential text
3. Lists
4. Outlines

First, it provides you with a set of utility commands that operate on single or multiple units of textual information providing the program with its basic add, delete, change, move, store, and retrieve processes. Second, a set of editing commands allows you to manipulate text in a manner similar to a standard word processor. Third, there are the standard outlining commands which provide you with various ways to classify, organize, translate, synthesize, and display your ideas in a structural form. Fourth, the program contains a set of list commands that allow you to group, sort, and reorganize ideas you have arranged into one or more lists. There is also a thought processing language, which, in a manner somewhat similar to KAMAS, allows you to create customized versions of MaxThink for various applications.

SAMNA+

This integrated program by Samna Corp. (2700 N.E. Expressway, Atlanta, GA 30345 404-321-5006) comes as close as possible to the ideal tool for the writing professional, combining word and knowledge processing, a spelling checker, a spreadsheet and list management program, and utilities for mathematical calculations and free-form line drawing. The word processing program features split-screen editing, automatic pagination and footnoting, search and replacement, as well as an electronic fold feature that enables you to "fold" a wide page to compare right and left margins side by side. It also features a zoom mode that allows you to shrink a whole page so it can be viewed in its entirety on the screen. Combined with this is a word base manager that searches through an entire disk in seconds to find every reference to a particular phrase, name, or date. It is designed for use on the IBM PC, XT, and compatibles, the TI Professional, and the DEC Rainbow.

Spotlight

Designed by Software Arts (27 Mica Lane, Wellesley, MA 02181 617-237-400) for use on IBM PC, XT, and Compaq computers operating under DOS 2.0 or higher, Spotlight is a set of "desktop" utilities which can be accessed via a window function while you are editing a file with your word processing program. Of particular use to the writing professional is an index card program which can search and/or alphabetically sort up to 36 separate files, each of which contains 500 cards, each up to eight pages long. Other handy features are:

- An appointment book which allows you to schedule daily and weekly meetings by displaying a monthly calendar and sounding an alarm to remind you of appointments

- A phone book, which allows you to display any name, address, and phone number from 36 lists, each of which can hold up to 500 entries
- A calculator that solves simple arithmetic problems, inserting the answers into the file you are working on

Compatible with most IBM PC programs, Spotlight requires 75K bytes of RAM.

ThinkTank (16 bit)

Building on the success of the 8-bit version of this program for the Apple series of computers, Living Videotext has within the last year introduced 16-bit versions for the IBM PC and Macintosh personal computers.

The transition to these more powerful machines has not been smooth, however. On the 128K byte Macintosh, ThinkTank is, for example, more limited in its capabilities than the original 64K byte version for the Apple series. Where the original allows you to store up to 2048 characters per category or level, the 128K byte Macintosh version allows you to enter categories only, with no text.

On the IBM PC and versions of the Macintosh with 256K/512K bytes, it is possible to store up to 20,000 characters of text under each headline and subhead. In terms of performance, the program is roughly comparable to combination word/outline processors such as Freestyle and the Idea Processor, but with less powerful editing and formatting features.

Surprisingly, Living Videotext does not appear to have taken advantage of the more powerful 16-bit CPUs used in both computers nor their sophisticated tree-structured operating systems.

Index